NEW TESTAMENT MESSAGE

A Biblical-Theological Commentary

Wilfrid Harrington, O.P. and Donald Senior, C.P.
EDITORS

New Testament Message, Volume 4

MARK

Wilfrid Harrington, O.P.

A Michael Glazier Book
THE LITURGICAL PRESS
Collegeville, Minnesota

About the Author:

WILFRID HARRINGTON, O.P., a graduate of the University of St. Thomas, Rome, and Ecole Biblique, Jerusalem, is Professor of Scripture at the Milltown Institute of Theology and Philosophy and the Dominican House of Studies, Dublin. He has lectured in the U.S.A. and Great Britain, Australia, New Zealand, India, and West Indies. Published works include: *Key to the Bible* (3 vols.), *Understanding the Apocalypse, Parables Told by Jesus, The Path of Biblical Theology, Christ and Life, Spirit of the Living God,* and *The New Guide to Reading and Studying the Bible.*

A Michael Glazier Book

published by

THE LITURGICAL PRESS

ISBN 0-8146-5127-5

7   8   9   10   11   12

CONTENTS

EDITORS' PREFACE

New Testament Message is a commentary series designed to bring the best of biblical scholarship to a wide audience. Anyone who is sensitive to the mood of the church today is aware of a deep craving for the Word of God. This interest in reading and praying the scriptures is not confined to a religious elite. The desire to strengthen one's faith and to mature in prayer has brought Christians of all types and all ages to discover the beauty of the biblical message. Our age has also been heir to an avalanche of biblical scholarship. Recent archaeological finds, new manuscript evidence, and the increasing volume of specialized studies on the Bible have made possible a much more profound penetration of the biblical message. But the flood of information and its technical nature keeps much of this scholarship out of the hands of the Christian who is eager to learn but is not a specialist. *New Testament Message* is a response to this need.

The subtitle of the series is significant: "A Biblical-Theological Commentary." Each volume in the series, while drawing on up-to-date scholarship, concentrates on bringing to the fore in understandable terms the specific message of each biblical author. The essay-format (rather than a word-by-word commentary) helps the reader savor the beauty and power of the biblical message and, at the same time, understand the sensitive task of responsible biblical interpretation.

A distinctive feature of the series is the amount of space given to the "neglected" New Testament writings, such as Colossians, James, Jude, the Pastoral Letters, the Letters of Peter and John. These briefer biblical books make a significant but often overlooked contribution to the richness of the New Testament. By assigning larger than normal coverage to these books, the series hopes to give these parts of Scripture the attention they deserve.

Because *New Testament Message* is aimed at the entire English speaking world, it is a collaborative effort of international proportions. The twenty-two contributors represent biblical scholarship in North America, Ireland, Britain and Australia. Each of the contributors is a recognized expert in his or her field, has published widely, and has been chosen because of a proven ability to communicate at a popular level. And, while all of the contributors are Roman Catholic, their work is addressed to the Christian community as a whole. The New Testament is the patrimony of all Christians. It is the hope of all concerned with this series that it will bring a fuller appreciation of God's saving Word to his people.

Wilfrid Harrington, O.P.
Donald Senior, C.P.

INTRODUCTION

IT IS NOT WHOLLY surprising that the gospel of Mark should have remained, for centuries, the neglected gospel. It is notably the shortest of the four and, content-wise, practically all of it may be found in Matthew and Luke. It seemed to have little or nothing to offer. Then, in the nineteenth century, Mark was rediscovered. His rehabilitation was welcome, even if, as we now recognize, it happened for the wrong reason. Mark was taken to be the plain blunt man who had brought to us, unembellished, the earliest traditions about Jesus. Where the other evangelists had given us accounts slanted by theological concern, he had been content to pass on what had come his way. He would let us see the true visage of Jesus of Nazareth. In our century, in the earlier days of form-criticism, Mark was still considered the dunce among the evangelists. And we were thankful for his limited ability because it allowed us to concentrate, without much distraction, on the material he had preserved. We might, it seemed, safely set aside his own poor efforts at being creative.

More recently, this renewed interest in Mark has led to a very different conclusion. He is now regarded as being no less theological than the others. In one respect he is more so in that he emerges as a pioneer, a breaker of new ground. With the emergence of redaction-criticism the distinctively Marcan material had become all-important. We were familiar with the traditional data as something common to all three synoptists. Mark showed his own hand and made his own contribution in his editorial framework.

But is not this sharp division between tradition and redaction rather forced? Surely, we should acknowledge

Mark's contribution also in his selection, adaptation, and presentation of traditional material? It boils down to accepting him as an author who wrote a book. He had written for a purpose and had planned his writing with care. He had, of course, made extensive use of traditional material because he wrote for a community with a firm christian tradition. But he knew what he was about and he exploited his sources with notable freedom and with skill. The end-product is our gospel: a work of art and a document of surprising theological sophistication.

Gospel.

John has told us, with all desirable clarity, the aim of an evangelist. He has no intention of giving us an account of the life and times of Jesus of Nazareth. His selective account of the "signs" of Jesus was written that the christian disciple may go on believing that the historical figure, Jesus, is the Messiah of Jewish expectation, that he is Son of God. He wrote that, through their faith in Jesus, Christians may find life in him (cf. Jn 20:31). The gospels are proclamations of the Good News, not records destined for an archive. If they do seem to concern themselves with what Jesus of Nazareth had done and said, they are aimed at christian communities striving to live the christian way.

Mark, it can be argued, pioneered the gospel form. He had wanted to present the kerygma and had hit on the design of setting it in the framework of a schematized life of Jesus. He had invented the literary form "gospel." Mark was keenly aware that the revelation of salvation takes place in the reality of human existence. It was, then, altogether fitting that God's saving plan should be presented in terms of the human life of Jesus Christ. Conceived and written to this end, the gospel is subtle and complex. It could not be otherwise as the author seeks to express, in terms of a human life, the complex fact of the divine intervention in our world with the tensions that fact involves.

Mark has written for the community of his concern. It is a mixed community, with Christians of Gentile and of

Jewish background. Sustained interest in the Gentile mission and a care to translate Jewish expressions and explain Jewish customs indicate the Gentile element—which would have been predominant. But a care to do justice to the privilege of Israel is a gesture to the feelings of those whose former religion was that of Judaism. The evangelist is intent on knitting his community closer together. Jesus is the bond of union. Their common faith in him should, ideally, make them and keep them one. We must see if we may discover the home of this Marcan community.

Date of the Gospel.

The view that Mark wrote in Rome about the year 65 A.D. had become the prevalent one. But it had not gone unchallenged because the traditional data which point to this provenance and date are of uncertain worth. We are forced back to the text of the gospel: to an anonymous writing of the first christian century. Nothing in the gospel points necessarily, or even at all, to Roman provenance. Latinisms (e.g. quadrans, praetorium) are now seen to be no more than predictable traces of a Roman administrative and military presence. Persecution (cf. 13:9-13) was a fact of wide christian experience, not a prerogative of Roman Christians. The Apocalypse of John, for instance, looks explicitly to the province of Asia. We can be sure that Mark wrote for a determined community and in face of concrete circumstances. We are left to tease out a plausible setting for, and a likely date of, his gospel.

The position taken here is that chapter 13 offers the most promising key—though one must needs read between the lines. It is evident, at least, that the destruction of the Temple is an issue (13:1-2); the Temple was destroyed by the army of Titus in 70 A.D. Our commentary will argue that the Jewish War (66-70 A.D.) is the backdrop to the apocalyptic drama of ch. 13. While it cannot be demonstrated that when Mark wrote the war is over, with Jerusalem and its temple in ruins, one has the impression that ch. 13 was written in the aftermath of this traumatic event. For that matter, it seems that the destruction of the temple raised a problem for Mark's community, one which the evangelist had, resolutely, to face: some had pinned their hope of an imminent parousia on the destruction of the temple, and were disillusioned when the End had not come. We opt for a date soon after 70 A.D. for the gospel of Mark.

Setting.

As for provenance: the intense interest displayed in the fate of Jerusalem and its temple must be taken with great seriousness. Above all, the false prophets and false Christs (13:6, 21-22) must be accounted for. Arguably, the shattering fact and the tragic features of the Jewish War would account for their emergence and the disturbing effects of their activity. At the same time, these factors would suggest a christian community close to the events. It would be natural to think of Palestine. Galilee plays an important role in the gospel, and one could look to there. However, even though Mark is not preoccupied with geographical precision, a native or, at least, a resident in Galilee might be expected to have had a more exact knowledge of Palestinian geography than the evangelist displays. One would propose a christian community somewhere in the Roman province of Syria. It would offer a setting close to the tragic events of 66-70 A.D. The community may even have received christian refugees from the conflict, making it that more immediate.

All of this is impression—one can claim no more for it. The most that can be said is that this stance follows from a serious attempt to listen to the text, from an effort to hear what the evangelist has left unsaid. He wrote for his community. He and they knew very well where they were situated and what were the circumstances and problems of their christian way. He did not have to spell them out. But we, nineteen centuries later, must grasp at straws. Perhaps, some day, we may find ourselves in the happy position of being sure; here and now we must be satisfied to live with uncertainty. The serious aspect is that the rightness of our interpretation of Mark will, necessarily, be affected by the aptness, or not, of our perception.

Purpose.

Happily, there is much in Mark that we can grasp independently of any theory of origin and date. This is particularly true of his christological position and of his understanding of discipleship. These are, in the main, so clear that they may suggest another reason for the neglect of this gospel: it is uncompromisingly uncomfortable. Mark's perspective is certainly clear in one predominant aspect: suffering Messiahship and suffering discipleship. Mark's christian faith is firmly anchored in the risen Lord. But he is keenly conscious of living "between the times": between the resurrection and the consummation. Victory is the destiny of the faithful Christian. But life in the here and now is real and earnest and can be grim. Mark acknowledges that christian existence is paradoxical. He finds it normal that it should be so. Jesus won his victory through suffering and death. There is no other way of christian living nor path to christian victory. Mark has written that his Christians should understand and accept this.

The Plot.

Like most stories, the events and actions of the Marcan story involve conflicts; Jesus is the immediate cause of the conflicts. We may illustrate this factor by glancing, firstly, at the conflicts between Jesus and the authorities, and then at those between Jesus and his disciples.

Jesus versus the Authorities. The authorities involved are the religious and political leaders — and in relation to them Jesus is at a disadvantage. Mark does indeed show Jesus having facile authority over evil spirits — the exorcisms —and over nature — the stilling of the tempest. But Jesus' authority does not extend to lording it over *people.* Yet, what Jesus says and does directly challenges the authorities in Israel. For their part, the authorities see themselves as defending God's Law. They contend that Jesus assumes extensive legal authority for himself, interprets the law in ways they consider illegal, and disregards many religious customs. They respond by making charges against him.

Jesus had been anointed to usher in God's rule (Mk 1:9-11); the issue for him was how to get the authorities to "see" God's authority in his actions and teaching. The narrator carefully created tension and suspense. By the end of the five conflict-stories (2:1-3:6) the sides are clearly established (3:6). The impending clash with the authorities dominates the journey to Jerusalem (8:27-10:52). The climactic confrontation in Jerusalem comes quickly. It is noteworthy that the first accusation against Jesus is the charge of blasphemy: "Why does this man speak thus? It is blasphemy!" (2:7) — so, from the beginning of the story Jesus walks a tightrope. Nevertheless, the reader sees that Jesus is firmly in control. At the trial he himself volunteers the evidence they need. " 'Are you in the Christ, the Son of the Blessed?" And Jesus said 'I am' " (14:61-62). Jesus, not the authorities, determines his fate.

The narrator resolves the conflict between Jesus and the authorities only when they condemn Jesus and put him to death. It is an ironic resolution. The authorities have cooperated in bringing about God's plan. Through the ironic resolution, the story depicts Jesus as the real authority in Israel. They condemn as blasphemy Jesus' claim to be Son of God, but since, in the story world, Jesus' claim is true, *they* are the ones guilty of blasphemy. The irony is, of course, hidden from the authorities, but it is not hidden from the reader. The reader knows that Jesus will be established in power and the authorities condemned (8:28-9:1; 13:24-27, 30-32; 14:62).

Jesus and the Disciples. At stake in the conflict with the disciples is whether Jesus can make them good disciples. The disciples struggle at every point to follow Jesus but are simply overwhelmed by both him and his demands. Jesus' efforts to lead the disciples to understand are matched by their hardness of heart and their fear. Theirs is not that determined opposition to Jesus of the authorities — they are trying to be his followers. Yet, they consistently misunderstand him. In fact, they share the values of the authorities; yet they do follow Jesus to Jerusalem. "The final circumstances of the disciples seem to typify their whole struggle to be faithful followers of Jesus. They simply are not prepared for the unpredictable, overwhelming consequences of following Jesus (14:17-21, 37-42, 43-50, 66-72). Everything overwhelms them; everything happens too quickly. The final depiction of Peter, sobbing after his third denial of Jesus (14:72), is a stark portrayal of how much the disciples want to succeed and how utterly, at the end of the gospel, they fail" (D. Rhoads and D. Michie, *Mark as Story. An Introduction to the Narrative of a Gospel* [Philadelphia: Fortress 1982, p. 93]).

Jesus just cannot lead his chosen disciples to understand him, cannot get them to do what he expects of them. In an effort to bring them to realize how blind and dense they are, he hurls rhetorical questions at them (4:13, 40; 8:17-21, 33; 9:19; 14:37, 41) — and he is met with silence. He tries to prepare them for his impending death and for his absence. He knows that they will fail him in Jerusalem; yet he seeks to urge them to stand by him (14:37, 41-42). The outer conflict reflects an inner conflict within the disciples: they want to be loyal to Jesus, but not at the cost of giving up everything, least of all their lives.

Jesus does not manage to make them faithful disciples. They failed him — and the question stands: will they learn from their failure and, beyond his death, at last, become truly followers of him? When Jesus had warned his disciples of their impending failure (14:26-31), he added a reassuring word: "After I am raised up, I will go before you to Galilee" (14:28). That word is then caught up in the message of the "young man" at the tomb: "Go, tell his disciples, and Peter, that he is going before you to Galilee; there you will see him, as he told you" (16:7). Throughout the gospel "to see" Jesus means to have faith in him. What Mark is saying is that if the community is to "see" Jesus, now the Risen One, it must become involved in the mission to the world that "Galilee" signified. Galilee was the place of mission, the arena where Jesus' exorcisms and healings had broken the bonds of evil.

There, too, the disciples had been called and commissioned to take up Jesus' proclamation of the coming rule of God. "Galilee" is the place of the universal mission, but no disciples are ready to proclaim the Gospel there until they have walked the way to Jerusalem (10:32-34) and encountered the reality of the cross.

The Characters.

Characters are a central element of the story world. *Characterization* refers to the way a narrator brings characters to life in a story. The narrator may do so either as he "tells" the reader directly what characters are like or as he "shows" the characters by having them speak and act and by having others talk about them and speak to them.

Jesus. The narrator of Mark tends to show the characters to the reader. Obviously, Jesus is the dominant character, and his characterization is, not surprisingly, complex. Jesus speaks and acts: what he *says* discloses his understanding of himself and of his mission; what he *does* reveals the extent and nature of his authority from God. In Mark's story, Jesus becomes God's Son at his baptism, for it was then that God declared Jesus to be the Son and anointed him with the Holy Spirit. This was a decisive experience for Jesus. Henceforth, he was convinced that through him "the rule of God has come near". But, if Jesus did have *exousia* — authority — from God that power of his did not have any shade of domination. The hallmark of the use of his authority in relation to people (as distinct from his authority over evil spirits and nature) is consistently, and emphatically, that of *diakonia* ("service").

The death of Jesus was wholly consonant with his understanding of authority. He was the one who had come to serve. And if he *spoke* of renouncing self, being least, and losing one's life, his *doing* of all that lent unanswerable authority to his words. But Mark sees clearly (as Paul, before him, had grasped) that the death of Jesus set the seal of authenticity on every single word and deed of him. Mark makes his point, superbly, by presenting the death of Jesus as a disaster, without any relieving feature at all. "Jesus' death is the supreme moment of illumination in the story. The narrator leads the reader to see in it the ultimate paradox of God's rule, that the anointed one is king not in spite of but precisely because of his loss of life for others. Only when Jesus has "died like this" does the narrator allow a human character in the story to acknowledge Jesus as son of God (15:39); for it is by dying for the good news that Jesus fulfills his role as son of God" (p. 115). Mark does not veil the awesome nature of death. Death is abandonment, isolation and separation. But, paradoxically, the *theologia crucis* of Paul and Mark is a surer ground of hope than a *theologia gloriae* which has little to answer to the harsh questions of reality.

The Little People. Characterization of the authorities and of the disciples (pp. 117-129) is provocative . On the other hand, the characterization of "The Little People" (the minor characters) is eye-opening. One's attention is drawn to something so obvious that it had escaped our attention. The truth is that, in contrast both to opponents and disciples, minor characters in the gospel steadfastly exemplify the values of the rule of God.

The characterization of minor characters in the Gospel of Mark is consistently favourable. In fact, the narrator develops these "little people" as foils to the authorities and disciples and as parallels to Jesus. These minor characters do measure up to Jesus' standards — especially as they exemplify the values of faith, of being least, of willingness to serve. In the first half of the gospel they measure up to Jesus' opening summons: "be converted and put faith in the good news" (e.g. 1:29-31, 40-45; 5:18-20, 21-43; 7:24-30, 31-37; 8:22-27). In the final scenes, in Jerusalem, the minor characters exemplify especially the teaching about being 'servant of all.' Where, earlier, Jesus had served others now, in his time of need, others serve him. The consistent conduct of the "little people" stands in sharp contrast to the negatively consistent conduct of the disciples. In the first half of the story, while there is no direct comparison, the minor characters emerge as models of faith in contrast to the disciples. In the last scenes in Jerusalem the minor characters do fulfill the functions expected of disciples. Here, the "little people" are highlighted (10:46-52; 14:3-9; 15:40-41; 16:1-8). Henceforth, any enlightened reading of Mark's gospel must acknowledge the major contribution of its minor characters.

Christology.

Mark's Christians are followers of Jesus, who believe that he is Christ and Son of God. Yet, they have much to learn. The evangelist sets out to declare who Jesus is, to spell out the nature of his Messiahship. It is easy enough, he realizes, to declare, even with conviction: You are the Messiah. What matters is how one understands that confession. It does not ask too much of one to be a willing disciple of a risen Lord. We, all of us, find triumph and glory congenial. Mark takes an uncompromising stand. Jesus, is, of course, Messiah and Son of God; he is the one who will, without fail, come to gather his elect. But he is, too, the suffering Son of Man, who walked a lone path to his death, who died, as it seemed to him, abandoned even by God. Mark stresses that only one who has come to terms with the cross can understand the resurrection of the Lord. Jesus was one who was glorified because he had accepted the *kenosis*, the self-abasement, of his life and death. That is why Jesus was, for the first time, formally acknowledged by men as Son of God as he hung lifeless on the tree (15:39).

Jesus is the Messiah, of that Mark is sure—but he is a disconcerting Messiah. The question stands, writ large: Who, then, is this? That Jesus would have permitted himself to be taken by his enemies, to be maltreated and mocked by them, and put to death, is something that the contemporaries of Jesus and the readers of Mark could hardly comprehend. Yet, if one has not come to terms with this "scandal" one has not grasped the originality of Jesus, in particular, the Jesus portrayed by Mark. Jesus did not come as judge with sentence and punishment for those who will not receive the gift of forgiveness and salvation he offered to them. He has come as the one who will let himself be crushed by the evil intent of those who resist him and would be rid of him.

In the long run, what is incomprehensible is the passion of the promised Messiah who would establish the kingdom of God, of the Son of God who would reveal the Father. The originality of Jesus flows from the contrast between his heavenly authority and power, and the humiliation of his crucifixion. Mark's "messianic secret" is designed to reconcile two theological affirmations: Jesus, from the first, was indeed Messiah and yet had to receive from the Father, through the abasement of the cross, his title of Messiah. The meaning of his life is that as Son of God sent by the Father, he had come to deliver men from all their enemies, from foes within and foes without. He came to forgive sins not to chastise sinners. He came, but he will not impose. When it comes to the test, rather than force the heart of man, he humbles himself and allows himself to be taken and shamed and put to death.

Discipleship.

Christians may be children of God but they are really such only on condition that they understand what it means and live with its demands. Mark's own understanding of discipleship is the same as Paul's: "if children, then heirs, heirs of God and fellow heirs with Christ, provided we suffer with him in order that we may also be glorified with him" (Rom 8:17). His preoccupation with discipleship follows hard on his concern with Christology. The way of discipleship has been firmly traced by Jesus himself: "If any man would come after me, let him deny himself and take up his cross and follow me" (8:34). For Mark, there is no other way of discipleship than that. Following on the victory of Christ, the Christian is not preserved from all suffering and even death itself, but must walk the same road that Jesus walked (10:30; cf. 8:34-38).

If Mark has presented his Christology in terms of the life of Jesus, he has presented his teaching on discipleship in terms of the disciples of Jesus. They are painted in their fragile humanness. Here, again, is something very close to the realism of Paul. It is not only in Galatians and the letters to the Corinthians that we encounter Christians with more failings than virtue; the "moral" part of each of Paul's letters is addressed to frail and fickle men and women. "The disciples" are a reflex of Mark's community. They are, in a sense, caricatures, as Mark through them stresses the vital importance of coming to know Jesus, and bluntly states his conviction that without the cross there is no hope at all of knowing the Lord. It is this concern that accounts for the unbelievable obtuseness of Peter and the rest. All disciples of the Lord should have the honesty to see themselves in these disciples. They had been called by Jesus and had responded to his invitation. He bore with them, in loving patience. They had failed him, but he had remained true. And Mark closes on a note of quiet confidence as the disciples, on the other side of cross and resurrection, wait for a meeting with the Lord in the "Galilee" of their hope. Not all had failed: the silent, steadfast women had remained faithful to the end (15:40 - 16:8). Perhaps a lesson of Mark, yet to be learned, is that the community of Christ will come of age when the dignity of woman and her place in his church are acknowledged not only in word but in truth.

The Gospel and The Man.
   "Who then is this?" (4:41). The question was wrung from the awestruck disciples of Jesus when, at his word, a great calm had fallen upon the troubled waters and their storm-tossed boat had come to rest. For Mark, that chastened crew might have been the community, the little church for whom he wrote. He wrote for people such as they who needed to know Jesus, who wanted to understand who he really was. He wrote for Christians who doubted and were fearful: "Teacher, do you not care if we perish?" (v.38). He wrote for Christians who did not relish the idea of being disciples of a suffering Messiah. He wrote for Christians very like ourselves. His gospel is a tract for our times.
   We may ask, what of Mark? His gospel shows him to be a writer of great natural talent, a man with an eye for telling

detail, a man who could effectively structure his material. Mark emerges, too, as a theologian of stature. Much has been written about Pauline influence on Mark. Whatever of that, the Christ of Mark is a Christ whom Paul could recognize and acknowledge and the gospel of Mark is one which Paul would not have disdained to call his own. Mark, even though his theory did not reach so far, had grasped the reality of the incarnation. His gospel is "the gospel of Jesus Christ, the Son of God" and closes with the resounding declaration: "Truly, this man was the Son of God." And yet his Jesus is a man who was indignant and angry, who took children into his arms, a man who suffered and died. This Son of Man who "came not to be served but to serve, and to give his life as a ransom for many" (10:45) is the Christ whom Paul preached: "When I came to you brethren, I did not come proclaiming to you the testimony of God in lofty words or wisdom. For I decided to know nothing among you except Jesus Christ and him crucified" (1 Cor 2:1-2). Paul the apostle, the first great christian theologian, had come to terms with the scandal of the cross. Mark the evangelist is, perhaps, the next notable christian theologian in line.

PLAN OF THE GOSPEL

PART I. THE MYSTERY OF THE MESSIAH:
Revelation of Jesus' Person. 1:14 - 8:30.

Three sections, each *beginning* with a summary
of the activity of Jesus and a narrative concerning
the disciples, and *concluding* with the adoption
of an attitude in regard to Jesus.

A. Jesus Welcomed and Challenged. 1:14-3:6
(1:14-15, 16-20; 3:6)
B. He Came to His Own. 3:7-6:6a (3:7-12, 13-16;
6:1-6a).
C. Discipleship and Mission. 6:6b-8:30 (6:6b,
7-31; 8:27-30).

Conclusion and Transition: Who is Jesus?
8:27-33.

PART II. THE MYSTERY OF THE SON OF MAN:
Revelation of Jesus' Suffering. 8:31 - 16:8.

A. The Way of the Son of Man. 8:31 - 10:52.
Signposted by three announcements of the
fate of the Son of Man leading to three in-
structions on the way of discipleship.

B. Jesus in Jerusalem. 11:1 - 13:37.

C. Passion and Resurrection. 14:1 - 16:8.

The Endings of the Marcan Gospel.

1

THE BEGINNING. 1:1-13.

ST. MARK OPENS his gospel with a passage which serves as an introduction to the whole work. He states the theme of the gospel in 1:1, and then he introduces the traditional prelude to the Good News: "beginning from the baptism of John" (Acts 1:22). The baptism of John and the temptation lead to the start of the Galilean ministry.

THE TITLE.
1:1.

> **1** The beginning of the gospel of Jesus Christ, the Son of God.

The opening verse is intended as a title for the gospel; it defines the whole work as "the gospel of Jesus Christ." It also indicates that the gospel—the Good News—which centered on the person of Jesus Christ, had begun with the preaching of John.

"The gospel" occurs seven times in Mark (1:1; 1:14; 1:15; 8:35; 10:29; 13:10; 14:9). Apart from 1:1 ("the gospel of Jesus Christ") and 1:14 ("the gospel of God") the absolute "the gospel" (*to euaggelion*) is characteristic of Mark's style. Again apart from 1:1 and 1:14, the term, though belonging to the missionary language of the early church, is found only on the lips of Jesus. The gospel in the Marcan sense is not, as in Matthew, "the gospel of the kingdom" but, in the post-Easter situation, is much more closely linked to the person of Jesus Christ—this full personal name occurs here only in Mark. Nor is it, as in Luke, "preaching

2

the Lord Jesus" (Acts 11:20), or the "word of the Lord" (15:35), or simply, "the word"; rather it is the gospel of the crucified and risen Lord, as this is presented throughout the work of Mark. The gospel can be equated with Jesus himself (8:35; 10:29). That is why one can give one's life for the gospel (8:35). For Mark the gospel is somehow the presence and the saving power of Jesus himself.

The superscription contains two of Mark's significant christological titles: Christ (Messiah), and Son of God—the latter, though omitted by some manuscripts, should be regarded as original. The beginning and abiding source of this gospel lies in the historical appearance of Jesus who, in the perspective of the Easter faith of the Church, was recognizable as the Son of God.

JOHN THE BAPTIZER.
1:2-8 (Lk 3:1-18; Mt 3:1-12).

²As it is written in Isaiah the prophet,
"Behold, I send my messenger before thy face,
who shall prepare thy way;
³the voice of one crying in the wilderness:
Prepare the way of the Lord,
make his paths straight—"
⁴John the baptizer appeared in the wilderness, preaching a baptism of repentance for the forgiveness of sins. ⁵And there went out to him all the country of Judea, and all the people of Jerusalem; and they were baptized by him in the river Jordan, confessing their sins. ⁶Now John was clothed with camel's hair, and had a leather girdle around his waist, and ate locusts and wild honey. ⁷And he preached, saying, "After me comes he who is mightier than I, the thong of whose sandals I am not worthy to stoop down and untie. ⁸I have baptized you with water; but he will baptize you with the Holy Spirit."

After the thematic title, the opening of Mark's gospel is dramatic. John the Baptizer appears on the scene and solemnly proclaims the coming of the greater than he who will pour out the gift of the Spirit. The arrival of John himself had not been unprepared: he is the messenger (Mal 3:1) and the wilderness prophet (Is 40:3) announced in the scriptures. The combination of scripture texts, here (vv.2-3) under the rubric "Isaiah the prophet," is characteristic of Mark. The "messenger" of Mal 3:1 is identified as Elijah in Mal 4:5; he who would come again to purify Israel before the day of Yahweh (*Kyrios*). In the light of a christian faith which confessed Jesus as Lord (*Kyrios*), John came to be regarded as that new Elijah. The good news which concerns Jesus Christ begins with the wilderness prophet John, clothed like Elijah (2 Kgs 1:8) and subsisting on wilderness fare (v.6). John is the sign that in the wilderness God is about to renew his covenant with Israel (Hos 2:14-23; Jer 2:1-3).

This mission explains his clarion call to repentance or *metanoia*, a coming to one's senses resulting in a change of conduct, a radical conversion—followed by an outward expression in baptism. The response of "all" Judea and Jerusalem (v.5) serves to underline the fact that the divine call to repentance was addressed to the whole of Israel. John's call to repentance and his baptism should be seen against the background of a prophetic tradition which looked to the wilderness for the unveiling of God's final salvation.

John who had proclaimed the call to repentance now proclaims the coming of the greater than he who will baptize the people with the Holy Spirit (1:7-8). His role of forerunner was already subtly intimated in v.3 where the quotation from Is 40:3 is changed to read "his paths" (instead of "the paths of our God"): "the Lord" is now Jesus whose way John prepares. He thinks himself not fit to be the slave of the mightier one. In contrast to the other synoptists who give a summary of the ethical preaching of the Baptist (Mt 3:7-10; Lk 3:7-14) Mark focuses on him as the pointer to the Coming One. In v.8 the contrast is emphatic: "*I* . . . but *he* . . ." In the Old Testament God had promised to pour out his Spirit in the time of salvation (Joel 2:28-29; Is 44:3; Ezek 36:26-27; Zech 12:10; 13:1). Baptism "with the Holy

Spirit" is this outpouring of the Spirit. The idea was prevalent, too in the Qumran community. In the parallel texts
of Mt 3:11 and Lk 3:16 this baptism is described as being
"with the Holy Spirit *and with fire*." "Baptism with fire"
is a baptism of judgment (Amos 7:4; Is 31:9; Mal 3:2; 1 Cor
3:13; 2 Thess 1:7-8); the idea of judgment is uppermost in
the winnowing and chaff-burning context of Mt 3:12 and
Lk 3:17. It is likely that the Baptist spoke only of baptism
with fire. We must suppose that in the course of christian
preaching a more christian-sounding turn came to be given
to the Baptist's words. A threat of imminent judgment has
been transformed into a prophecy of the outpouring of
the Spirit, the work of the risen Lord. In Mark, neither
John nor Jesus preach judgment.

THE BAPTISM AND TEMPTATION OF JESUS.
1:9-13 (Lk 3:21 - 4:13; Mt 3:13 - 4:11).

> [9]In those days Jesus came from Nazareth of Galilee
> and was baptized by John in the Jordan. [10]And when
> he came up out of the water, immediately he saw the
> heavens opened and the Spirit descending upon him like
> a dove; [11]and a voice came from heaven, "Thou art my
> beloved Son; with thee I am well pleased."
> [12]The Spirit immediately drove him out into the wilder-
> ness. [13]And he was in the wilderness forty days, tempted
> by Satan; and he was with the wild beasts; and the angels
> ministered to him.

The Forerunner has made his solemn proclamation; we
await the appearance of the Coming One. And straightway
Jesus comes from Nazareth of Galilee to be baptized by
John. The description of the baptism is matter-of-fact.
There is no trace of the embarrassment shown in Matthew's
text (3:14-15): Mark ignores the difficulty raised by the fact
of Jesus submitting to John's baptism "for the forgiveness
of sins." In Mark's eyes, Jesus is not only the true Israelite
whose repentance is perfect; he is the Son of God receiving

the sign of repentance on behalf of the people of God. Here the contrast between the "all" of v.5 ("all the country of Judea, and all the people of Jerusalem") and the "one" of v.9 becomes acute. In Mark's Gospel Judea and Jerusalem are implacably hostile in contrast to Galilee, the land of Jesus. The "all" did not really respond to the Baptist's summons; only this Nazarene offered himself in true submission. Only in his case was the "coming up" from the water answered by a "coming down" from heaven.

According to Mark, at the baptism Jesus alone saw and heard the heavenly happenings (1:10-11). This transaction between Father and Son is a secret beyond human experience; and yet it is revelation, for the reader now knows who Jesus is. "The Spirit" is the power of God coming upon Jesus, the Son, a consecration for his messianic mission: "how God anointed Jesus of Nazareth with the Holy Spirit and with power" (Acts 10:38). The phrase, "like a dove," is found in all three synoptists; its symbolism, likely, has reference to the mission of Jesus, although its precise meaning is unknown to us.

The title "only Son" (for that is what "beloved Son" means) so solemnly attested (v.11, in terms echoing Ps 2:7) transcends messiahship and points to a unique relationship to God; it expresses the faith of the early church and marks a stage in christological thinking. The heavenly voice is for the christian reader, telling him the truth about Jesus. The baptism story, as we find it in Mark, was meant to assert that Jesus was constituted and declared Son of God at the time of his baptism by John. In this he differs from Matthew and Luke who with their infancy gospels had pushed the moment of Sonship back to the conception of Jesus; for them the baptism marks the beginning of the Son's messianic mission. Jesus is the "Servant" in whom God is pleased and whom he has appointed to deliver his people. We should keep in mind that Mark's christological thought has not reached the concept of pre-existence and incarnation, and in this respect he joins hands with the other synoptists. Yet Jesus is for him formally Son of God and was so throughout his messianic career. Mark's christology is not fully rounded off but it is a true christology, representing an intermediate stage in the growth of christological thought.

The title "Son of God" is found eight times in Mark (1:1; 1:11; 1:24; 3:11; 5:7; 9:7; 14:61; 15:39). It is used sparingly and, in nearly every case, significantly. We find a confessional use of it in the superscription of the gospel (1:1), the challenging question of the priest (14:61) and the confession of the centurion at the cross (15:39). It is found in testimonies to Jesus: by the Father at baptism and transfiguration (1:11; 9:7) and by unclean spirits in the redactional summary, 3:11. That this last is to be taken in the full christian sense is shown by the imposition of secrecy (3:12). On the other hand, the remaining two usages occur as part of the account of an exorcism (1:24; 5:7); they are no more than a standard recognition of an exorcist by the patient. Son of God is obviously of major importance for Mark and he has deployed it with care and skill. In every case (1:24; 5:7 aside) it is a signal to the reader, a reminder of who this Jesus is.

Son of God.

Mark, the story-teller, takes care to identify his own evaluative point of view — that is, how he really "thinks" about Jesus — with that of the protagonist of his story, namely Jesus himself. Consequently, there is only one correct way in which to view things: the way of Jesus, which is Mark's own way. The evangelist takes it a step further and makes certain that his evaluative point of view and that of Jesus are in accord with the evaluative point of view of God. It follows that the conception of Jesus which is normative in Mark's story is God's conception. If this is so, then the title which *God* bestows on Jesus is of paramount importance.

The heading of the gospel — "The beginning of the gospel of Jesus Christ, the Son of God" (1:1) — informs the reader of Mark's own evaluative point of view of Jesus' identity. In the baptismal scene the heavenly voice (the voice of God) declares of Jesus: "Thou art my beloved Son" (1:11). As Jesus is about to embark on his public ministry God solemnly affirms both his status and his call. Similarly, at the Transfiguration, God declares (this time for the benefit of the three disciples): "This is my beloved Son" (9:7). *Only* at baptism and transfiguration does God appear as "actor" in the story. And not alone does God, each time, declare that Jesus is "Son": the baptism declaration confirms the truth of Peter's confession of Jesus as the "Messiah" (8:29). Finally, at the climactic moment of the death of Jesus the title is *Son of God:* "Truly, this man was the Son of God" (15:39). This centurion is the first human being in Mark's story truly to penetrate the secret of Jesus' identity, because he is the one who had to come to terms with the cross.

As for the *meaning* of "Son of God," the voice from heaven of 1:11 is a composite quotation from Ps 2:7; Is 42:1; Gen 22:2. In Is 42:1 the servant in whom God delights is one "chosen" for ministry; in Gen 22:2 Abraham's beloved son is his "only" son. Most importantly, in Ps 2, "My son are you" is declared by Yahweh of the Davidic king. Consequently, God solemnly affirms that "Jesus, the Anointed One (Messiah King) from the line of David, is the only or unique Son whom he has chosen for eschatological ministry" (J.D. Kingsbury, *The Christology of Mark's Gospel* [Philadelphia: Fortress 1983, p. 66]). Jesus is the Davidic Messiah-King, the Son of God.

With the emergence of the beloved Son a new era has begun, the era of eschatological hope. An essential feature of this hope is the overthrow of Satan. This Mark conveys by combining the temptation narrative (vv.12-13) with the baptism narrative (vv.9-11). He has managed, too, a striking contrast in his presentation of the Forerunner and Coming One. John is a man among crowds, preaching and baptizing. With the appearance of Jesus we enter another world: the heavens opened, the Spirit descending, a divine Voice, the Son of God, the power of the Spirit, Satan tempting, and ministering angels. The baptism of Jesus by John, a happening at a given place and time, is also the initial encounter between the Spirit-filled Son of God and the ruler of this present age (cf. Jn 14:30). Anointed with the Spirit for his task and confirmed in his divine Sonship, Jesus faces a trial of strength. The Spirit "drove"—a strong word— Jesus into the wilderness. In the context of the temptation, a struggle with evil, the wilderness is the traditional haunt of evil spirits (symbolized by "wild beasts"); and there Jesus encounters Satan, the prince of evil, the enemy of God.

Jesus was tempted; the Greek word carries all the nuances of temptation, trial, tribulation, test. For Jesus, temptation did not end here (cf. 14:32-42); and the implied victory over Satan, reflected in his subsequent exorcisms, will have to be won all over again on the cross. "Forty days" recalls Moses (Ex 34:28) and the forty years of testing in the wilderness. It reminds us, too, of Elijah, who also received the ministration of angels (1 Kgs 19:5-8). Here we are doubtless to understand that the ministering angels supplied Jesus with food; Mark has no reference at all to a fast of Jesus. At this first struggle Jesus is not God-forsaken as he will be at his last (15:34).

Part I
The Mystery of the Messiah:
Revelation of Jesus' Person.
1:14 - 8:30.

A. JESUS WELCOMED AND CHALLENGED.
1:14-3:6

THE MINISTRY BEGINS:
OPENING SUMMARY STATEMENT.
1:14-15 (Lk 4:14-15; Mt 4:12-17).

> [14]Now after John was arrested, Jesus came into Galilee, preaching the gospel of God, [15]and saying, "The time is fulfilled, and the kingdom of God is at hand; repent, and believe in the gospel."

NOW THAT JESUS has been acknowledged as God's Son and has thrown himself into a totally committed struggle against evil, he can begin to preach the Good News. In a single sentence that smacks of his theology, Mark sketches that beginning and gives a summary of that initial preaching. His very first words are ominous: "after John was delivered up." The fate of the Baptist was to be delivered up to his enemies in accordance with the divine will (6:17-29). The alert reader, conscious that Jesus suffered a like fate, will perceive in John a type of the suffering Messiah. The long shadow of the cross reaches to the start, and Mark will never let us lose sight of that cross.

Next he introduces Galilee—much more than a place-name. The occurrence of the name throughout the gospel is distinctive. It occurs almost always in passages peculiar

11

to Mark (1:9,14,16,28,39; 3:7; 7:31; 9:30; 14:41). A sharp contrast is set up and maintained between Galilee, land of preaching, of miracles, and of the consummation (16:7) and Jerusalem, city of the Jewish authorities where Jesus will suffer his passion. In the evangelist's presentation Jesus finds acceptance and meets with success in Galilee. Then his way descends to death in Jerusalem only to open again to eschatological hope in Galilee.

Jesus came preaching "the gospel of God," the good news from God. It is the christian message of salvation (cf. 1 Thess 3:2,8-9; 2 Cor 11:7; Rom 1:1; 15:6; 1 Pet 4:17). And the summary of that preaching uses early christian theological language. The appointed time is fulfilled; compare Gal 4:4— "when the time had fully come." God's kingly rule had drawn near; indeed it has arrived. Jesus is God's agent who inaugurates the new age in the present: as Son of Man he will bring it to consummation in the future (8:38; 9:1; 13:26-27; 14:62). Like the Forerunner, Jesus calls for a thoroughgoing conversion; but, more urgently, he calls on men to embrace the Good News. While the sentence, "The reign of God has come; repent and believe the Good News" is an admirable summary of the message of Jesus, Mark himself undoubtedly understood the words "believe the gospel" in the christian sense of faith in the good news of salvation through Jesus Christ. And this is how his reader must take it.

Kingdom of God.

"Kingdom of God" (more precisely the kingly rule or kingly activity of God) in the message of Jesus, operates as a symbol: it is a sign representing something else. It is a symbol which is based on Israel's consciousness of itself as the people of God and on its conviction of a God active in history on behalf of his people (cf. Ex 15:18 and the Kingship of Yahweh psalms: Pss 47; 93; 96; 97; 98; 99). By the time of Jesus "kingdom of God" had come to represent particularly the expectation of a final eschatological act of God. It is a type of symbol having a set of meanings that can neither be exhausted nor adequately expressed by any one concretized meaning. It is susceptible of a variety of interpretations and representations, for instance in the exuberance of apocalyptic imagery.

In the Jewish world of Jesus' day there was intense yearning for the "kingdom of God" — a kingdom that was diversely understood by different groups. In general one might say that the vision which fuelled expectation was of Israel as a "kingdom of priests and a holy nation" (Ex 19:6). And the conviction was that God's intervention on behalf of his people could be prepared for and hastened by their efforts to become the kingly and priestly people of God. In the main it was believed that the desired result could be achieved by faithful observance of Torah and through the Temple cult. The various groups within Judaism each had its own manner of hastening the coming of the kingdom. Thus, the Pharisees relied mainly on meticulous observance of Torah; the Essenes of Qumran, though they had distanced themselves from the official priesthood, (in their book an illegitimate priesthood) saw themselves as the priestly elect of the nation; the Zealots would defend the Law and tradition with the sword.

In the midst of this diverse concern for the renewal of the people of Israel as God's holy elect stood Jesus who shared that concern. But he would not define the holiness of God's people in cultic terms. He redefined it in terms of wholeness. And where all other groups were, in their various ways, exclusive, the Jesus movement was inclusive. His challenge and his invitation, were to *all*.

What Jesus claimed was that this decisive intervention of God was happening in his ministry: God is acting in and through the ministry of Jesus and his disciples. The Kingdom is here and now present in history in that the power of evil spirits is broken, sins are forgiven, sinners are gathered into Jesus' friendship. These events are present to human experience, and they are so whether men are aware of them or not. The kingdom comes as a present offer, in actual gift, through the proclamation of the gospel. But it only fully arrives on condition of the positive response of the hearer. In Jesus himself, wholly responsive as he was to the will and purpose of his Father, the kingdom was already fully present. It was offered to all who heard his message. To those who responded positively the kingdom became also present, a matter of personal experience.

If Jesus could declare that the kingdom was present in him, he did also speak of it as an event awaited in the future. It is characterized by growth and by conflict; it must be entered or may be received (4:26-30; 3:24; 13:8; 9:47; 10:23-25; 12:34). Jesus looked to a consummation of that which had begun and which was a present reality. But nowhere does he specify the exact nature of that consummation. For us, too, the state of tension between present and future remains.

THE CALL OF THE FIRST DISCIPLES.
1:16-20. (Lk 5:1-11; Mt 4:18-22).

> [16]And passing along by the Sea of Galilee, he saw Simon and Andrew the brother of Simon casting a net in the sea; for they were fishermen. [17]And Jesus said to them, "Follow me and I will make you become fishers of men." [18]And immediately they left their nets and followed him. [19]And going on a little farther, he saw James the son of Zebedee and John his brother, who were in their boat mending the nets. [20]And immediately he called them; and they left their father Zebedee in the boat with the hired servants, and followed him.

This passage, containing two parallel episodes, was shaped by Mark to bring out the nature of Jesus' call and of the christian response, to show what "following Jesus" means. The evangelist has placed it here to prepare the way for the role of these disciples in 1:21-39. Both callings are modeled on the call of Elisha by Elijah (1 Kgs 19:19-21); the prophet's call involved for Elisha a break with his family and his occupation.

Set by the lake, the ministry in Galilee has begun. Simon

(Peter) is named frequently in the gospel; all we learn of Andrew (1:29; 3:18; 13:3) is that he was Peter's brother and lived with him at Capernaum; that he became one of the twelve and was one of the four who heard the apocalyptic discourse. The brothers James and John are often named together throughout the gospel. The verb *akolouthein*, "to follow," very frequent in Mark, is a technical term for discipleship; here, in vv. 17,20 it is reinforced by the addition of *opisō*, "after." These fishermen will be transformed into fishers of men, called to gather together the community of the faithful. "I will make you become": the apostolate lies in the future; the immediate call is to discipleship. While the response of each pair of brothers is immediate, the emphasis in each of the two callings is different: the first story stresses the prompt response of the disciples while the other stresses the completeness of their renunciation.

Does Jesus now begin to emerge as a rabbi? He is going to be addressed as "Rabbi" by his followers (4:38; 10:35; 13:1), by Pharisees (12:14), by Sadducees (12:18) and by a scribe (12:32). Outwardly, Jesus and his disciples have something of the appearance of a rabbinic group of master and disciples—but it is only appearance. The Jewish disciple sought out his master, attached himself to him for the purpose of studying the Law, and aspired to become a rabbi in his turn. But Jesus took the initiative and summoned his disciples, not to study the Torah or Jewish Law but to follow him and engage in his work. And Jesus' disciple will remain a disciple (cf. Mt 23:8-11).

The narratives illustrate the call to discipleship in the fullest sense. We are shown that the sovereign call of Jesus evokes the response of those called, a free response as we learn in the episode of the one who could not bring himself to follow (10:17-22). They leave all, nets, boat and father, to follow Jesus without hesitation. The decisive factor is the person of Jesus himself. In order to become a disciple of Jesus it is not necessary to be an exceptional person; what counts is not intellectual or moral aptitude but a call in which Jesus takes the initiative. It is the mighty, immediate impression of Jesus on Peter and his companions, reinforced by his personal word of call, which brought them into his following and made them his disciples. Mark is not intent on describing a scene from the ministry of Jesus. Rather, he is more concerned with the theological dimension of a typical call to discipleship.

A DAY IN THE LIFE OF JESUS—AT CAPERNAUM. 1:21-34 (Lk 4:31-41).

This section, composed of four closely-knit episodes, is intended to give a typical picture of the early ministry. The episodes are: a demonstration of the authority of Jesus in terms of teaching and of exorcism (1:21-28); the healing of Peter's mother-in-law (1:29-31); healings at evening (1:32-34).

DEMONSTRATION OF THE AUTHORITY OF JESUS. 1:21-28 (Lk 4:31-37; Mt 7:28-29).

> [21]And they went into Capernaum; and immediately on the sabbath he entered the synagogue and taught. [22]And they were astonished at his teaching, for he taught them as one who had authority, and not as the scribes. [23]And immediately there was in their synagogue a man with an unclean spirit; [24]and he cried out, "What have you to do with us, Jesus of Nazareth? Have you come to destroy us? I know who you are, the Holy One of God." [25]But Jesus rebuked him, saying, "Be silent, and come out of him!" [26]And the unclean spirit, convulsing him and crying with a loud voice, came out of him. [27]And they were all amazed, so that they questioned among themselves, saying, "What is this? A new teaching! With authority he commands even the unclean spirits, and they obey him." [28]And at once his fame spread everywhere throughout all the surrounding region of Galilee.

The episode in the synagogue of Capernaum is two-faceted: a teaching of Jesus which evokes the admiration of his hearers, and the expulsion of an unclean spirit which awakens a reverential fear in the beholders. For Mark and his readers, Jesus is God's own Son. His divine authority must be manifest. And indeed that authority, evident in word and deed, is shown to have been recognized by his hearers from the beginning—although they did not grasp the full measure of it. In 3:22-30 exorcisms are interpreted in terms of the struggle between the Spirit and Satan begun in the temptation (1:12-13). Each specific exorcism is a particular instance of the unrelenting hostility between Jesus and the spirits of evil, a struggle continued in the life of every Christian.

The opening verses (1:21-22) serve as a transition from the preparatory events to the full flow of the public career of Jesus. Capernaum, one of the few place-names in the first half of the gospel, is Tell Hum on the northwest shore of the lake of Galilee. The ruins of a second century A.D. synagogue probably mark the site of an earlier synagogue of Jesus' day. The synagogue service consisted of prayers and readings (with commentary) from the Law and the Prophets. The readers were well-instructed members of the assembly or visitors known to be expert in Scripture. It was natural, then, that Jesus should have been invited to preach the homily. Cf. Lk 4:16-21. He "taught": though he gives few of his sayings, Mark lays emphasis throughout on the teaching ministry of Jesus (cf. 2:13; 4:1; 6:2,6,34, etc.). Astonishment, a favorite word of Mark (cf. 1:22; 6:2; 7:37; 10:26; 11:18), indicates the amazement occasioned by a supernatural aspect of Jesus. In this case what astonishes is the note of assurance and authority in his teaching. He speaks with prophetic authority in a manner very different from the traditionalism of the scribes. The spirit of the gospel stands out firmly against the spirit of legalism.

For Mark an "unclean" spirit is an evil spirit, a demon; he uses the terms "unclean spirit" and "demon" synonymously and with equal frequency. At the time illness, and particularly mental illness, was generally attributed to the influence of or to possession by demonic spirits. The concept contains the truth that illness is something which belongs to a hostile world. "He cried out" (the Greek uses a strong word meaning "to cry aloud," "to shout")—the demoniac shouts brazenly at Jesus. "Have you come to destroy us?" is better understood as a defiant accusation: "You have come (into the world) to destroy us!" "I know who you are" is an attempt to gain magic power over Jesus by uttering his secret name: the "Holy One of God." Recognition of Jesus as God's agent is common among the demons (3:11). This demon acknowledges, besides, that Jesus' mission is bent on destroying the demonic power-structure. Ironically, it is an "unclean spirit" who draws attention to who Jesus is and to the ultimate purpose of his coming.

Jesus "rebuked" or "strictly charged" (*epitimaō*) the spirit: in the New Testament the word means a formal command which must be obeyed. Hostility is mutual: a defiant shout (v.24) is answered by a stern command. "Be silent," literally, "be muzzled" (the verb is used again in addressing the storm, 4:39): the arrogant demon is being told to "shut up." Jesus' word of command (and a word is enough) produces convulsions and shouting. This is not only a manifestation of spiteful anger: the exorcism stories show a contrast (implicit here) between the demons' violence and hurtfulness towards the person posessed and the gentleness of Jesus and his communion with the liberated person (cf. 9:26-27; 5:2-5,15).

The extreme astonishment (v.27) of those present was occasioned by the authoritative teaching and the effortless exorcism. "With authority" is best taken along with "a new teaching" to mean "a new teaching with authority behind it." This is only the beginning, and yet the fame of Jesus has spread—significantly, throughout the whole of "Galilee." This summary statement anticipates 1:39 and the first phase of the mission. Expressions of astonishment at an action of, or before the person of, Jesus are frequent throughout Mark (cf. 2:12; 3:10; 4:41; 5:15,20,33,36,42; 6:2,51, etc.). It is the evangelist's way of drawing the attention of the reader to a manifestation of Jesus' true nature. The crowds are astonished because they do not understand what is really taking place and who it is that stands before them. The christian reader must not miss the full message of the text.

THE HEALING OF PETER'S MOTHER-IN-LAW. 1:29-31 (Lk 4:38-39; Mt 8:14-15).

> ²⁹And immediately he left the synagogue, and entered the house of Simon and Andrew, with James and John. ³⁰Now Simon's mother-in-law lay sick with a fever, and immediately they told him of her. ³¹And he came and took her by the hand and lifted her up, and the fever left her; and she served them.

The previous narrative had shown that Jesus could cast out demons; now he is shown to have power over sickness. There is a close connection between the two. Jews tended to think of illness as due to demonic action (cf. Lk 13:11-16). And we find that in Luke's parallel passage (Lk 4:39) Jesus "rebuked" the fever, the same strong term that we have met above in 1:25: Jesus exorcised the spirit of fever. It would seem that the same idea is implicit here in v.31 where the phrase "the fever left her" might be understood as "the demon of fever went away." Like the exorcisms, the miracles of healing are signs of salvation.

The early christian community was not interested in the miracles of Jesus merely as brute facts. It seems to have regarded them in a twofold light: as a manifestation of the power of God active in Jesus, a proclamation of the fullness of time (cf. 1:15), and as signs of the redemption which Jesus had wrought, as prophetic signs. Here, the power of Jesus over fever, which yielded to his imperious gesture, proclaims that the reign of God is a present reality (cf. Acts 2:22). It seems, moreover, that the phrase "he raised her up" (the Greek verb *egeirō*, "to lift up" also means "to raise from the dead," cf. 14:28; 12:26), had a special symbolic meaning in a catechetical milieu: Jesus is the Savior who by the deeds of his earthly life has prefigured the realities of the divine life now communicated to believers. Understood in this way, the story is the symbolic portrayal of the believer: one who had been prostrate beneath the power of sin but now, raised up by the Lord, is called upon to serve him (v.31).

HEALINGS AT EVENING.
1:32-34 (Lk 4:40-41; Mt 8:16-17).

> ³²That evening, at sundown, they brought to him all who were sick or possessed with demons. ³³And the whole city was gathered together about the door. ³⁴And he healed many who were sick with various diseases, and cast out many demons; and he would not permit the demons to speak, because they knew him.

We have been shown a typical exorcism and a typical healing. Now, at the close of this specimen day, "all" the sick and possessed of the town are brought to Jesus. This summarizing passage describes Jesus' mission in terms of his healings and exorcisms. It also marks a transition to the further spread of his work of teaching and healing (1:35-39). In 1:25 silence imposed on the unclean spirit was part of the detail of an exorcism story. It is not the same here in v.34. The demons understood, as the crowds and the disciples do not, that Jesus is the envoy of God. It is precisely "because they knew him" that they are bidden to keep silence. Here begins the "messianic secret," pointing forward to the more explicit statement (3:11-12) in the next summary (3:7-12). The "secret" has to do with the true messianic status of Jesus. Mark would have readily accepted that the demons knew Jesus to be Son of God. But he is sure that what Son of God really means can only be understood when Jesus had shown, through suffering and death, what it means. That is why Jesus cannot be proclaimed "until the Son of man should have risen from the dead" (cf. 9:9).

I WAS SENT FOR THIS PURPOSE.
1:35-39 (Lk 4:42-44).

> ³⁵And in the morning, a great while before day, he rose and went out to a lonely place, and there he prayed. ³⁶And Simon and those who were with him followed him, ³⁷and they found him and said to him, "Every one is searching for you." ³⁸And he said to them, "Let us go on to the next towns, that I may preach there also; for that is why I came out." ³⁹And he went throughout all Galilee, preaching in their synagogues and casting out demons.

Reference to the prayer of Jesus may give us a proper understanding of the episode. Mark mentions Jesus' prayer on two further occasions: after the multiplication of loaves (6:46) and in Gethsemane (14:35,39). Each time the true nature of Jesus' messiahship is in question and he has to contend with the incomprehension of his disciples (6:52; 14:40). So, here, the disciples have "hunted him out" (v.36) because they felt that he, the wonder-worker, was missing a great opportunity. This is not the attitude of true disciples; this is not the following of Jesus to which they had been called. They are no more than representatives of the curious crowd who are "searching" for him. The verb *zētein,* to search for or seek out, is used throughout either in the hostile sense of Jesus' enemies seeking to arrest and kill him (11:18; 12:12; 14:1,11,55) or, as here, in the sense of attempting to turn him from his true mission (cf. 3:32). Luke specifies that the people "would have kept him from leaving them" (Lk 4:42). But Jesus is not going to be turned from his purpose of proclaiming the kingdom (1:14). "That is why I came out" (v.38). (This may be an allusion to the phrase, "he went out" in v.35.) Jesus explains to his disciples that he must not linger to satisfy the curiosity of the people of Capernaum. However, Mark's *gar,* "for this purpose," directs the reader to an association or allusion that is not evident from the immediate context. Luke had correctly caught the Marcan nuance when he wrote: "for I was sent for this purpose" (Lk 4:43), that is, sent into the world by the Father. A closing statement (v.39) shows the carrying out of the program sketched in v.38. It is a transitional statement which summarizes 1:32-34 and anticipates 3:7-12. Again there is the firm reference to Galilee as the privileged place of the mission of Jesus.

YOU CAN MAKE ME CLEAN.
1:40-45 (Lk 5:12-16; Mt 8:1-4).

This passage sits lightly in its Marcan context; yet we may discern a reason for the evangelist's insertion of it at this point. It would seem that the Jewish attitude to leprosy (a term which in the Bible covers a variety of diseases, Lev 13) is important here: it is the ultimate uncleanness which cuts the afflicted one off from the community as being a source of ritual defilement to others. Significantly, in the New Testament the removal of leprosy is never described as healing but always as "cleansing." The Law was helpless in regard to leprosy; it could only defend the community against the leper. But what the law could not achieve Jesus rightly accomplishes. One thinks of Rom 8:3 "For God has done what the law, weakened by the flesh, could not do: sending his own Son in the likeness of sinful flesh and as a sin offering he condemned sin in the flesh."

The evangelist will have placed the passage here, after his summary account of Jesus' ministry, because of the strong light it throws on the salvation now accessible to all people. It is also notable that the conflict-stories (2:1-3:6) which follow immediately contain charges against Jesus as a violator of the Law. The present story shows that Jesus respected the Law: he commanded the healed leper to carry out the requirements of the Law (v.44). Mark could have felt that the story at this point would establish the falsehood of the subsequent charges.

> 40And a leper came to him beseeching him, and kneeling said to him, "If you will, you can make me

clean." ⁴¹Moved with pity, he stretched out his hand and touched him, and said to him, "I will; be clean." ⁴²And immediately the leprosy left him, and he was made clean. ⁴³And he sternly charged him, and sent him away at once, ⁴⁴and said to him, "See that you say nothing to any one; but go, show yourself to the priest, and offer for your cleansing what Moses commanded, for a proof to the people." ⁴⁵But he went out and began to talk freely about it, and to spread the news, so that Jesus could no longer openly enter a town, but was out in the country; and people came to him from every quarter.

According to our translation here (v.41) Jesus was "moved with pity" at the petition of the wretched man, and this indeed is the reading of the great majority of manuscripts. But there can be little doubt that "moved with anger," not nearly so widely attested, is the original reading. It is easy to understand why scribes would have changed it to "moved with pity;" it is incredible that they should have done the reverse. It is significant that "moved with pity" is not found in the parallel texts of Matthew and Luke. The anger of Jesus is his reaction to the disease which brings him face to face with the powers of evil. Jesus did not hesitate to touch the leper, a seemingly unthinkable action, and his powerful word of command was at once efficacious. "Left"—the same word as in v.31— perhaps here, too, with the idea that the demon of leprosy departed. This is borne out by the use of the verb "he sternly charged" (v.43), a rendering of a technical semitic term for exorcising demons. The story as used by Mark had become somewhat jumbled. Originally it was the demon, and not the man as it now appears, who was "driven out" (v.43).

The procedure to be followed after cleansing is that prescribed in Lev 14:2-32. Where there was no conflict with the spirit of his own teaching Jesus recognized the validity of the Law. "For a proof to the people" is interpretative; the Greek simply has "to them" and so is ambiguous. The RSV translation suggests that the priest would have given the man a certificate confirming his cure and thus enabled him to resume social life. However, the same phrase occurs in 6:11 where it certainly means "for a testimony *against* them." Taken in the same way here it could mean that this miraculous purification will be a challenge to the priests (who are unvariably hostile in Mark). Already there is a suggestion of the controversy atmosphere that will dominate the following section.

The former leper began to tell his tale to everyone he met. Yes, but what of the words used? "To talk" is *keryssein* meaning "to proclaim" (5:20; 7:36) and "news" is *logos,* "the word." These terms have unmistakable christian overtones which Mark's readers would not have missed. A Christian is one "cleansed" by Christ in baptism, one who then ought to "preach" and "spread abroad the Good News." The story concludes with the observation that as a result of the incident Jesus could no longer enter a town publicly without being mobbed; he stayed outside in quiet country places (cf. 1:35). The people flocked to him from all sides: an excellent Marcan climax to his account of the opening stage of the ministry of Jesus (cf. 1:28,33,37).

THE CONFLICT STORIES. 2:1-3:6.

Up until now Jesus had been carrying out his mission in Galilee, teaching, healing, casting out demons. At this point comes his first explicit confrontation with official Judaism. It is documented in a series of five controversies: on forgiveness of sins (2:1-12), on eating with tax-collectors and sinners (2:13-17), on fasting (2:18-22), on grainfields and the sabbath (2:23-28), and concerning healing on the sabbath (3:1-6). These conflicts are arranged in progressive order. At the cure of the paralytic the opposition to Jesus was latent: the scribes "questioned in their hearts" (2:6-7). During the meal in the house of Levi they addressed the disciples, aiming through them at Jesus (2:16) while with regard to fasting they questioned Jesus about an omission of his disciples (2:18). In the matter of the grainfields, the charge against the disciples is direct violation of the Law

(2:24). In the final episode the adversaries spy on Jesus (3:2) and then meet together to plot his destruction.

These five conflicts are associated in Lk 5:17-6:11. The first three only are present in the same context of Matthew (Mt 9:1-17), while the other two come later, in a different context (Mt 12:1-14). We suggest that the grouping of the five controversies is the work of Mark. And he has done so with skill, arranging the five units in a chiastic pattern: A-B-C-D-C'-B'-A'.

A. 2:1-9—cure by Jesus—silence of the adversaries— "Questioning in their *hearts*";
  B. 2:10-12—declaration on the Son of man;
    C. 2:13-17—action of Jesus—reaction of opponents to the disciples;
      D. 2:18-22—sayings of Jesus on *Bridegroom* and *Newness;*
    C'. 2:23-26—action of the disciples—reaction of the opponents to Jesus;
  B'. 2:27-28—declaration on the Son of man;
A'. 3:1-6—cure by Jesus—silence of the adversaries— "hardness of *heart.*"

The plan clearly shows the articulation of the ensemble ABC and C'B'A' around the point D. We must take account of the thematic unity of the two groupings and respect the role of the central text 2:18-22.

One purpose of the composition of this section was to illustrate and explain the opposition to Jesus, the hostility that led to his death. We are shown that the opposition came not from the people but from the religious authorities who were determined to preserve the established religious order. They saw in Jesus a threat to their notion and practice of religion. Because they were unable to understand him they ended by determining to destroy him. And this situation of the ministry of Jesus has a bearing too on the hostile attitude of official Judaism to Mark's christian community (cf. 13:9).

At the same time, the section sets the teaching of Jesus in relief: the section is not only apologetic but is markedly catechetical as well. The fact is that each of the separate units which make up the complex is not only a conflict story, a debate with adversaries, but a pronouncement story, leading to a declaration or pronouncement of Jesus. We can see that the saving message of each is to be found in a saying of the Lord—the stories are so many illustrations of that "new teaching with authority behind it" (1:27). If we set out the five climactic sayings one after another we can readily perceive how valuable they are for an understanding of the christian gospel:

> The Son of man has authority on earth to forgive sins (2:10).

> I came, not to call the righteous but sinners (2:17).

> Can the wedding guests fast while the Bridegroom is with them? (2:19).

> The Son of man is Lord even of the sabbath (2:28).

> Is it lawful on the sabbath to do good or to do harm, to save life or to kill? (3:4).

These sayings—all of them in part or in whole christian formulations—have a vital bearing on the content of the gospel message and on the early church's understanding of its Lord.

> 2   And when he returned to Capernaum after some days, it was reported that he was at home. 2And many were gathered together, so that there was no longer room for them, not even about the door; and he was preaching the word to them. 3And they came, bringing to him a paralytic carried by four men. 4And when they could not get near him because of the crowd, they removed the roof above him; and when they had made an opening, they let down the pallet on which the paralytic lay. 5And when Jesus saw their faith, he said to the paralytic, "My son, your sins are forgiven." 6Now some of the scribes were

sitting there, questioning in their hearts, [7]"Why does this man speak thus? It is blasphemy! Who can forgive sins but God alone?" [8]And immediately Jesus, perceiving in his spirit that they thus questioned within themselves, said to them, "Why do you question thus in your hearts? [9]Which is easier, to say to the paralytic, 'Your sins are forgiven,' or to say, 'Rise, take up your pallet and walk'? [10]But that you may know that the Son of man has authority on earth to forgive sins"—he said to the paralytic—[11] "I say to you, rise, take up your pallet and go home." [12]And he rose, and immediately took up the pallet and went out before them all; so that they were all amazed and glorified God, saying, "We never saw anything like this!"

[13]He went out again beside the sea; and all the crowd gathered about him, and he taught them. [14]And as he passed on, he saw Levi the son of Alphaeus sitting at the tax office, and he said to him, "Follow me." And he rose and followed him.

[15]And as he sat at table in his house, many tax collectors and sinners were sitting with Jesus and his disciples; for there were many who followed him. [16]And the scribes of the Pharisees, when they saw that he was eating with sinners and tax collectors, said to his disciples, "Why does he eat with tax collectors and sinners?" [17]And when Jesus heard it, he said to them, "Those who are well have no need of a physician, but those who are sick; I came not to call the righteous, but sinners."

[18]Now John's disciples and the Pharisees were fasting; and people came and said to him, "Why do John's disciples and the disciples of the Pharisees fast, but your disciples do not fast?" [19]And Jesus said to them, "Can the wedding guests fast while the bridegroom is with them? As long as they have the bridegroom with them, they cannot fast. [20]The days will come, when the bridegroom is taken away from them, and then they will fast in that day. [21]No one sews a piece of unshrunk cloth on an old garment; if he does, the patch tears away from it, the new from the old, and a worse tear is made. [22]And no one puts new wine into old wineskins; if he does, the wine

will burst the skins, and the wine is lost, and so are the skins; but new wine is for fresh skins."

[23]One sabbath he was going through the grainfields; and as they made their way his disciples began to pluck ears of grain. [24]And the Pharisees said to him, "Look, why are they doing what is not lawful on the sabbath?" [25]And he said to them, "Have you never read what David did, when he was in need and was hungry, he and those who were with him: [26]how he entered the house of God, when Abiathar was high priest, and ate the bread of the Presence, which it is not lawful for any but the priests to eat, and also gave it to those who were with him?"

[27]And he said to them. "The sabbath was made for man, not man for the sabbath; [28]so the Son of man is lord even of the sabbath."

3   Again he entered the synagogue, and a man was there who had a withered hand. [2]And they watched him, to see whether he would heal him on the sabbath, so that they might accuse him. [3]And he said to the man who had the withered hand, "Come here." [4]And he said to them, "Is it lawful on the sabbath to do good or to do harm, to save life or to kill?" But they were silent. [5]And he looked around at them with anger, grieved at their hardness of heart, and said to the man, "Stretch out your hand." He stretched it out, and his hand was restored. [6]The Pharisees went out, and immediately held counsel with the Herodians against him, how to destroy him.

THE PARALYTIC AND FORGIVENESS.
2:1-12 (Lk 5:17-26; Mt 9:1-8).

Several indications point to the composite character of this passage. On the whole, it seems reasonable to regard vv. 1-5a,11-12 as a coherent miracle story, corresponding to the classical scheme of the healing of a paralytic, as in Jn 5:5-9 and Acts 9:32-35. Here, however, the story is augmented by a passage on the remission of sins (vv. 5b-10). Mark has converted a miracle story into a controversy story. The evangelist is telling us that the cure of the paralytic was intended to manifest the sin-forgiving power of the

Son of man. In the early kerygma the remission of sins was regarded as intrinsic to the experience of being a Christian. Thus Acts 10:43 states, "To him (Jesus) all the prophets bear witness that every one who believes in him receives forgiveness of sins through his name." In the light of this and similar texts it is evident that the early Christians proclaimed the forgiveness of sins as a present fact. This meant a head-on clash with Jewish belief which considered forgiveness a future benefit to be hoped for.

The evangelist has carefully directed us to the key point of this passage. He has done so by his insertion technique: the bracketing of an item of special interest by near identical frame-verses. The phrases "questioning in their hearts" (v.6) and "they questioned within themselves" (literally, "in their hearts," v.8b) focus attention on forgiveness of sins; while the phrases "rise and take up your pallet" (v.9b) and "rise, take up your pallet" (v.11a) emphasize the Son of man's authority to forgive sins on earth.

The Jewish problem is highlighted in v.7—"Who can forgive sins but God alone?" It is axiomatic in the Old Testament and Judaism that forgiveness of sins is a prerogative of God (cf. Ex 34:6-7; 2 Sam 12:13; Is 43:25; 44:2; Pss 51; 103:3), a prerogative exercised in heaven. Yet Jesus, in his own name, has made an authoritative declaration of forgiveness of sins (v.5) and has done it here and now on earth. No wonder the scribes (appearing in Mark for the first time) are aghast. And their logic is apparently unimpeachable: Jesus' arrogation to himself of a divine prerogative is tantamount to blasphemy. The accusation of blasphemy at the trial scene is foreshadowed (14:60-64). Their error is that they take him for an ordinary man and fail to recognise that he is God's messianic agent and that with him the kingdom of God—the era of God's forgiveness—has begun. He already has manifested forgiveness of sin in his loving and merciful attitude to and works on behalf of humanity. God's forgiveness of sins happens, through Jesus, here on earth.

The very presence of the forgiveness of sins issue in the gospel is an indication that it was a live issue for Mark's community. Their assertion of forgiveness of sins on earth was blasphemy to their Jewish adversaries. Their defence is their claim of a share in the authority (*exousia*) of the eschatological Son of man (v.10). For Mark, the full revelation of the Son of man is in his suffering, death and resurrection and so is accessible only to believers. When, however, those who believe in Jesus seek to live and act in the Spirit of Jesus, they participate in his power to forgive sins. The story is thus a vindication of the church's claim to declare the forgiveness of sins in the name of Jesus (cf. Jn 20:23), a forgiveness achieved in baptism. This claim inevitably brought Christians into conflict with Judaism.

The healing words of Jesus (v.11) are spoken as a command. The strong amazement of those present greets the miracle (v.12; cf. 1:27); their exclamation is strikingly true to life. It is significant that their amazement bears on the miracle, not the forgiveness of sins. Verses 11-12 do form an excellent conclusion to the miracle story of vv. 1-5a.

Son of Man.

The title Son of man (*ho huios tou anthropou*) is an over-literal translation of the Aramaic *bar enāshā* meaning "the man" or "a man." In rabbinic circles the expression "son of man" was used by a speaker to refer to himself when not wishing to push himself forward. The meaning of the phrase remains "man" but the context makes clear that the speaker is referring to himself. Jesus, too, used the idiom in this way as a circumlocution for "I." As for instance, in Mt 8:20, "Foxes have dens, and the birds of the air nests; but the son of man has nowhere to lay his head"; and Mk 10:45, "For the son of man came also not to be served but to serve." In both cases Jesus is referring to himself. Jesus, then, used the expression "son of man" to refer to himself; its appropriate sense is taken from the contexts in which it is found. While the pervasive underlying sense is Jesus' claim to authority, it does not seem that he was looking to the singular use of "son of man" in Dan 7:13-14.

The interpretation of the seer's vision given in Dan 7:18-

27 identifies the "son of man" of Dan 7:13 as "the saints of the Most High," the faithful persecuted people of the Maccabean crisis. In a later period the Danielic "son of man" was understood in individualistic terms and, in apocalyptic literature, became a title for the future redeemer. Then, in the course of christological development, the title, taken in this individual sense, played its part in the effort to explain who and what Jesus was. While only in 13:26 and 14:62 is there explicit reference in Mark to Daniel's son-of-man vision, the term Son of man, throughout Mark, always carries a messianic or eschatological meaning. Jesus had used "son of man" as a circumlocution. The early Church, in its christological endeavour, grasped eagerly at an expression with such a rewarding potential. But it seems that Jesus did not think of himself as the Son of man of Daniel, nor as the Servant of the Lord of Second Isaiah. He regarded himself rather as the Son standing in unique relationship to the Father. That said all there was to say about him.

While "Son of man" carries emphatically christological overtones in our gospels, it is becoming increasingly accepted that Jesus did not speak of himself as Son of man in any theological sense. Among the arguments in favor of this view the most compelling might well be that Jesus did not need to explain to himself who he was. He was *Son*, and that is all there was to it. Nor did he seek to spell out for his disciples, not even the twelve, who he was. They would come to know him from his presence, his deeds, his words. He gave himself no titles nor claimed any.

"Son of man" appears fourteen times in Mark and, apart from 2:10,28, always in the second half of the gospel after Caesarea Philippi. The evangelist has employed the title in creative fashion to present his own christology. It occurs with different emphases, notably of present authority, (2:10,28), necessary suffering (8:31; 9:12,31; 10:33-34,41), and future glory (8:38; 13:26; 14:62). Besides, 14:21 (twice) and 14:41 speak of betrayal ("delivered up") and 9:9 is future from the standpoint of the narrative.

TABLE-FELLOWSHIP WITH OUTCASTS.
2:13-17 (Lk 5:29-32; Mt 9:9-13).

This passage, too, is composite. First there is the short transitional summary with its characteristic emphasis on the teaching of Jesus (v.13). Then the call of Levi (v.14), parallel to the call of the first disciples (1:16-20), serves as an introduction to the pronouncement story (vv.15-17). The whole passage illustrates Jesus' attitude towards outcasts and strikingly brings to the fore the amply attested fact that Jesus' concern for outcasts was a scandal to the religious authorities. We know that table-fellowship (between Christians of Jewish and of Gentile backgrounds) was something of a problem in the primitive church (cf. Acts 11:3; Gal 2:12); and it would have been crucial in the matter of eucharistic table-fellowship. It may well be that this interest accounts for the formation and preservation of the original story.

For the evangelist, however, the episode is closely associated with the preceding cure of the paralytic. There the center of interest was the authority of the Son of man to forgive sins; here it is the presence of the "Physician" able to "cure" the sick who are sinners. The fact that Jesus associates with sinners is a sign not only of the remission of sins but of the presence of the one who can remit sin. In the Old Testament Yahweh alone is the Physician, the Healer (cf. Hos 14:4; Jer 3:22; 17:4; 30:17; Sir 38:1-15), and healing is a sign of the messianic age (cf. Is 61:1; Mt 10:1,8). Against this background, Jesus' reference to himself as "physician" implies more than a proverbial justification of his conduct: if he eats with sinners it is because the sick have need of *the* Physician. For those who can see, his action is a declaration that the messianic age has dawned: the Physician has come.

The saying of v.17 infers that messianic forgiveness is the basis of table-fellowship. And the fact was, as the early Christians were well aware, that the saving call of Jesus had been to sinners. It was for this that Jesus had come into the world: to summon such as they to the messianic banquet. This was the comforting assurance addressed to all who have ever heard the call of Jesus (cf. 1 Jn 1:8-10). The early

Christians knew that the Church was made up of sinners; it is the nature of the whole Church always.

ON FASTING AND NEWNESS.
2:18-22 (Lk 5:33-38; Mt 9:14-17).

This passage is the center of the chiastic structure referred to above (D) and is therefore the focus of the whole passage 2:1 - 3:6. It is made up of a pronouncement story (2:18-20) to which two sayings, on patches and wineskins, have been added (2:21-22). The main story manifests, once again, the presence of the messianic age: the fact that the disciples of Jesus do not fast brings home to those who can understand that the Bridegroom is with them. But those who do not recognize the signs of the times (cf. Mt 16:2-3) are scandalized by such conduct. The two appended sayings (vv. 21-22) are designed to make clear that the new movement which Jesus inaugurated cannot be confined within the limits of the old religion. The question is raised: whether the messianic Bridegroom has come? Whether the new reign is really present? And the further question would arise whether fasting could have any place in the New Age.

The opening verse (18) is an explanatory note; the story would have begun, "And people came and said to him." The disciples of John, here introduced for the first time as a clearly defined group (cf. 6:29), naturally shared the asceticism of their master (Mt 11:18). The phrase, "the disciples of the Pharisees," occurs nowhere else; Pharisees did not have disciples. There can be little doubt that the original contrast was between the practice of the disciples of John and that of the disciples of Jesus, similar to the contrast between John and Jesus in Mt 11:18-19. [Groupings of disciples of the Baptist co-existed with christian communities (cf. Acts 19:1-7).] But, disciples of Jesus can no longer adhere to the Baptist's vision of things. John is relegated to the sphere of the "old garment" and the "old wineskins" (vv. 21-22). One is reminded of Jesus' verdict in Mt 11:11: ". . . he who is least in the kingdom of heaven is greater than he." The introduction of "the Pharisees" and "the disciples of the Pharisees" brings the narrative into the group of conflict stories which serve to illustrate the breach between Jesus and the Jewish religious authorities.

In v.19 "wedding guests" (literally, "the sons of the bride-chamber") is a hebraism, meaning either the groomsmen or the wedding guests. Though the second half of the verse is omitted by several manuscripts and is not found in the parallel texts of Luke and Matthew, it is most likely authentic; such explanatory addition is in the style of Mark. While the image of the wedding-feast was used to express the joy of the messianic age, neither in the Old Testament nor in later Jewish literature was the Messiah represented as the bridegroom. On the other hand, Yahweh is presented as the husband of his covenant people (cf. Hos 2:19; Is 54:3-6; 62:5; Jer 2:2; Ezek 16). Jesus' implied claim to be the bridegroom places him somehow on a par with Yahweh. And, in view of the contrast between joy and sorrow, "fasting" is best taken in the metaphorical senses of experiencing sorrow.

The bridegroom is manifestly Jesus and his being "taken away" (v.20) is a veiled reference to his impending death. It is an echo of Is 53:8—"by oppression and judgment he was taken away." "The days will come" is a phrase introducing an oracle of woe (cf. Lk 17:22; 21:6). Like the disciples of John (cf. 6:29) the disciples of Jesus, too, will have their time of mourning (cf. Jn 16:20). The qualification "and then they will fast in that day" would suggest that fasting had become a practice in the Marcan community, apparently in view of the absence of the Lord (before the parousia).

Though the parabolic sayings (2:21-22) certainly had an independent existence, it is clear that in their Marcan context they illustrate a contrast between the old spirit and the new. Both sayings are constructed in the same manner: first, a negative principle, and then a warning of what must happen if it is not observed. A patch of unshrunk cloth will shrink at the first wash and tear apart the weakened fabric of the old garment. Old wineskins become thin and brittle; the new fermenting wine would burst the skins and both wine and skins would be lost. The parables illustrate a contrast between the old spirit and the new and are similar to the teaching of Paul on the incompatibility of the new spirit of Christianity with the spirit of Judaism. The new spirit is not a piece added to the old nor a new element poured into the old: it is rather a vivifying force which transforms the abiding teachings of the old revelation. This is what Jesus outlines in the Sermon on the Mount of Matthew: the Gospel which Paul develops in his turn.

THROUGH THE GRAINFIELDS ON THE SABBATH. 2:23-28 (Lk 6:1-5; Mt 2:1-8).

Like most of these conflict stories this one is complex. It is made up of a pronouncement story (vv.23-26) to which the sayings of vv. 27-28 have been appended. In Luke and Matthew, too, the passage appears as a sabbath controversy, but its original sense seems to have been other. The argument which Jesus brings up against the Pharisees (vv.25-26) does not regard the problem of the sabbath; what was forbidden to David was taking and eating bread of the Presence—the sabbath does not enter in at all. The original narrative would have had the following meaning: while crossing a grainfield Jesus' disciples plucked some ears of grain to eat. The reproach made to them is in line with Dt 23:25, "When you go into your neighbor's standing grain, you may pluck the ears with your hand, but you shall not put a sickle to your neighbor's grain." The disciples evidently objected that this text did explicitly allow the plucking of grain in such circumstances; it was rigorist Jewish tradition which restricted this permission. And they remarked that the example of David also presupposed a wider interpretation: in case of need law had to yield to human concern. Even now, when it has been placed in a sabbath setting, the discussion has no obvious relation to work. Plucking of ears of grain and rubbing them in the hands was, technically, "reaping" and forbidden on the sabbath. In Mark (unlike Matthew and Luke) the essential factor remains the comparison between David and Jesus. The interest is christological: Jesus, as God's anointed one, has the same freedom as David in respect of the law. Mark names Abiathar as high priest. This is incorrect; the high priest in question was Abiathar's father, Ahimelech (1 Sam 21:1). The fact of the matter seems to be that, while the biblical background is 1 Sam 21:1-6, the immediate source is a haggadic development of the passage. And it may well be that, in a free version of the Old Testament story, Abiathar, the priest and associate of David, had replaced the lesser known Ahimelech.

The counter question in 2:25-26 would have ended the argument; the vv. 27-28 have been added. The Marcan link-formula, "And he said to them," is an indication of that. The wisdom saying of v.27, which has a rather close rabbinical parallel, "The sabbath is delivered unto you, and ye are not delivered to the sabbath" (*Mekilta* on Ex 31:14), now rounds off the story. The meaning of the saying is that God ordained the sabbath for man's sake; it is a reaction against a false evaluation of the sabbath whereby man becomes a slave to sabbath observance. Mark's christological point is made in v.28 (cf. 2:10): in the light of 2:23-27 ("so then") the Son of man is lord of the sabbath. The matter is of importance because sabbath observance was a lively issue in the early Church (cf. Lk 14:10-17; Jn 5:1-19; 9:1-11). At an early stage, Christians began to keep not the Jewish sabbath but the day of the Resurrection, "the Lord's day" (Rev 1:10); this, of course, brought them into conflict with Judaism. They maintained that their Lord had set the sabbath free; and their distinctive observance was traced back to his authority.

TO SAVE LIFE OR TO KILL.
3:1-6 (Lk 6:6-11; Mt 12:9-14).

The fifth conflict story is the climax of the series. Here Jesus himself is more aggressive and the plot against him (v.6) points to the inevitable end of this persistent hostility. But the issue is, too, of immediate interest to Mark's community. If Christians had chosen to observe the Lord's Day rather than the Jewish sabbath, they had thereby opted for some form of sabbath observance. The question then remained as to how far to push that observance and in what spirit. The challenge of Jesus (v.4) and his deed of mercy will have given them their principle and their pattern.

The man's affliction (v.1) seems to have been some form of paralysis. The hostility of the adversaries of Jesus, the Pharisees (v.6), is obvious; they watch him closely, just waiting for a chance to accuse him of a breach of the sabbath law. The rabbinical principle was that relief might be given to a sufferer on the sabbath only when life was in danger. In the present case there is no danger to life. It is a clear test whether Jesus will observe the rabbinic ruling or not. Jesus takes up the unspoken challenge. Just as in 2:8 he is credited with the capacity to read men's thoughts. He calls the man out into the open so that what he is about to do may be seen by all (v.3). The phrase "and he said to the man," (repeated in v.5, "he said to the man") serves to spotlight the question of Jesus and his reaction to the silence that greeted it.

In the parallel passage, at this point, Matthew adduces Jewish practice and concludes with an *a fortiori*: a sheep can be rescued from a pit on the sabbath, of how much more value is a man than a sheep. Consequently, it is permissible to do a good deed on the sabbath (Mt 12:9-12). Mark's source may have been just as specifically Jewish; but he has formulated the argument in a more generalized form and has given it a universal bearing. Jewish preoccupation was the upholding of the sabbath observance; for Pharisees a vital question was to define "work" and so to determine what was forbidden on the sabbath. Jesus lifts the matter on to the moral level. To heal a man is to "do good;" to leave him in his infirmity is to "do evil." In forbidding healing on the sabbath the rabbis would equivalently admit that, on this day, moral values are reversed: it is forbidden to "do good" and prescribed to "do evil!" The real issue is no longer what one is permitted to do; it is the obligation of doing good at all times and in all circumstances. Jesus asks, "On the sabbath day should one rather do good than evil, rather save a life than kill?" How sad it is that the spirit of legalism has so often and so firmly asserted itself in the christian church. We had been eager to observe rules, as well as to impose them, anxious to measure our Christianity by the punctiliousness of our "observance."

"But they were silent"—the context shows that Jesus interpreted their stubborn silence as proof of their malice and spiritual blindness. Mark frequently mentions the searching look or glance of Jesus (3:34; 5:32; 9:8; 10:23; 11:11); here (v.5) with judgmental overtones. "With anger" and "grieved," Mark stresses the human emotions of Jesus (cf. 1:41,43; 7:304; 8:12; 10:14,21) a factor discreetly left aside by the other synoptic gospels. In the parallel to our verse Luke has: "And he looked around on them all" (Lk 6:10). Jesus is sad and indignant at the obtuseness of men whose subborn attachment to the minutiae of the Law blinds them to proper moral values. "Hardness of heart" (cf. 6:52; 8:17; Rom 11:25; Ep 4:18) is blindness of heart, insensitivity to spiritual truth. In a rounding off of the story, Jesus bade the man stretch out his paralysed hand which was healed forthwith.

Only now (v.6) do we learn that the "they" of the story are the Pharisees. They had lost no time in plotting revenge. The "Herodians," named again in 12:13, were influential men who supported Herod Antipas. The odd association of Pharisees and Herodians may be explained by the link between the Baptist and Jesus. The typical opponents of Jesus (Pharisees) join with the supporters of the man who had John executed (Herod Antipas) to have Jesus put to death. Now we know that the hostility of the religious authorities can have no other issue; and death looms as a dark cloud over the future course of Jesus' ministry.

B. HE CAME TO HIS OWN.

3:7 - 6:6a

CROWDS BY THE LAKESIDE—A SUMMARY.
3:7-12 (Lk 6:17-19; Mt 12:15-21).

> [7]Jesus withdrew with his disciples to the sea, and a great multitude from Galilee followed; also from Judea [8]and Jerusalem and Idumea and from beyond the Jordan and from about Tyre and Sidon a great multitude, hearing all that he did, came to him. [9]And he told his disciples to have a boat ready for him because of the crowd, lest they should crush him; [10]for he had healed many, so that all who had diseases pressed upon him to touch him. [11]And whenever the unclean spirits beheld him, they fell down before him and cried out, "You are the Son of God." [12]And he strictly ordered them not to make him known.

TOGETHER WITH THE CALL of the twelve (3:13-19a) this passage shows like a ray of light breaking between dark clouds of hostility (2:1 - 3:6 and 3:19b-35). Coming after the conflict stories, which underlined the prejudice of the scribes and Pharisees and their rejection of Jesus, the passage 3:7-12 points again to the enthusiasm of the people and to the perception of the evil spirits who discerned what the religious authorities failed to see.

Jesus withdrew from towns and synagogues to carry on his ministry by the lakeside (cf. 1:45). Mark, it would appear, views the withdrawal as a turning from the old Israel

to the shaping of the new Israel (3:13-19a). A great multitude came to Jesus not only from friendly Galilee but from
much further afield. While Judea, Idumea, and Perea point
to broadly Jewish territory, the country about Tyre and
Sidon is the wider "Galilee of the nations." Mark is at pains
to stress not only that the Jewish people crowded to Jesus
from every corner of the land but that Jesus was evoking
a response of faith from among gentiles. The theological
rather than geographical interest of the evangelist here is
indicated by the bracket-phrase "a great multitude" (vv.7,8).

The enthusiasm of the crowd threatened to get out of
hand, so Jesus arranged to have a boat placed nearby at his
disposal. The touch is graphic, in the Marcan style. In the
first half of the gospel the lakeside is the constant place of
meeting with the crowds (cf. 2:13; 3:7; 4:1; 5:21; 6:34). Because Jesus healed all who came to him (as in 1:34 "many"
does not imply that some were not healed but simply means
"all") he was thronged by those eager to touch him (cf.
5:27-34; 6:56). Luke explains that "power came forth from
him and healed all" (Lk 6:19; cf. Mk 5:30). The reaction of
the unclean spirits is what we have come to expect—they
know, too well, whom it is they face. "You are the Son of
God": the confession of the unclean spirit is given a christian turn, for the title is an important feature of the evangelist's Christology. The stern imposition of silence (v.12)
leaves no doubt that this is not, as in 1:24 and 5:7, merely
a detail of exorcism procedure. Here it is clearly asserted
that demons perceived what neither people nor disciples
discerned, the true nature of Jesus. Even the unclean spirits
have become guides to the reader!

THE APPOINTMENT OF THE TWELVE.
3:13-19a (Lk 6:12-16; Mt 10:3-4; cf. Acts 1:13).

> [13]And he went up into the hills, and called to him
> those whom he desired; and they came to him. [14]And he
> appointed twelve, to be with him, and to be sent out to
> preach [15]and have authority to cast out demons: [16]Simon
> whom he surnamed Peter; [17]James the son of Zebedee

and John the brother of James, whom he surnamed Boanerges, that is, sons of thunder; [18]Andrew, and Philip, and Bartholomew, and Matthew, and Thomas, and James the son of Alphaeus, and Thaddaeus, and Simon the Cananaean, [19]and Judas Iscariot, who betrayed him.

This is a solemn moment. Luke has thoroughly grasped the significance of it and has emphasized the importance of the choice of the twelve by specifying a night-long prayer of Jesus (Lk 6:12). For Mark "the mountain" is the setting for a sovereign act of Jesus. From among the enthusiastic crowd he proceeds to make a choice of those who are "to follow" him. And out of these again he appoints twelve—the foundation stones of the new Israel (cf. Rev 21:14).

In v.16 the phrase, "And he appointed the twelve," though not found in many manuscripts, (and omitted in the RSV) is sufficiently well attested and should be read at the beginning of the verse. It is a conscious repetition of the phrase "and he appointed twelve" in v.14. Together they frame a Marcan insertion and draw our attention to the intervening vv.14-15 as the focus of his concern. The number twelve has reference to the twelve tribes of Israel (cf. Mt 19:28; Lk 22:30); by this solemn act of appointment Jesus has founded the new Israel. Though many manuscripts read "whom also he named apostles" (after "he appointed twelve," v.14) it is better omitted as being an assimilation to Lk 6:13. From this moment onwards, Jesus turns his attention to the little group.

The purpose of the appointment of the twelve is twofold. In the first place they are "to be with him"; they are to have close personal fellowship with Jesus. In Mark "those with him" is almost a technical term for discipleship (cf. 5:18-40; 15:41). And from now on the twelve do remain constantly with him. When Jesus sends them out on a mission (6:13-30) he does not engage in any activity in their absence. Twice, it is true, disappointed by their attitude towards him, he withdrew from them to pray (6:46; 14:32-39). But this does not mean leaving them alone. In the long run, it is they who abandon him (14:50). Right through the gospel, in fact, Mark consistently carries through his idea that the twelve are to be "with" Jesus. They are formed by him, entrusted with the "mystery" of the kingdom in order to make it known in due time (4:11,22).

In the second place they are "to be sent out to preach, and have authority to cast out demons." Jesus gives the twelve authority to preach the Good News (cf. 13:10; 14:19) and power like his own over demons; they are associates in his mission. The evangelist has the sending out of 6:7-13 in mind, but his vocabulary shows that he looks beyond it. The Greek words *apostellein*, "to send out," and *keryssein*, "to preach," are terms which the apostolic Church used to describe its mission; Mark is conscious of the post-resurrection missionary situation. The twelve are to preach and to do; the reign of God is proclaimed in word and action together.

The New Testament presents four lists of the Twelve: Mk 3:16-20; Mt 10:2-4; Lk 6:14-16; Acts 1:13. These lists agree substantially as regards eleven of the names, but Luke does not have Thaddaeus (who figures in Mk/Mt). On the other hand, Luke agrees with John in recognizing another Judas distinct from Judas Iscariot (Lk 6:16; Jn 14:22). Despite this discrepancy, and while no two agree on the exact order of names, all four lists set out the twelve in groups of four and the same name always appears at the head of each group: Simon Peter, Philip, and James the son of Alphaeus. We get the impression that while the existence of the twelve, and the nature of their original appointment, were firmly fixed in christian tradition, some of them were little more than names in the tradition. By the time the gospels came to be written there was even some uncertainty as to who one or two of them were.

"Simon whom he surnamed Peter"—from now on the name "Peter" prevails; "Simon" appears again only in 14:37. Our text suggests that *Peter* was given at the time of the appointment of the twelve; according to Jn 1:42 the name was conferred when Simon was first called. The word "Boanerges" is a corrupt transliteration of a Hebrew or

Aramaic name. Mark's "sons of thunder" is an attempt to explain a name he did not understand, although it has a certain fitness (cf. 9:38; Lk 9:54). "Cananaean" probably means one who shared the sentiments of the party later known as the Zealots; cf. Lk 6:15, "Simon who was called the Zealot." The meaning of Iscariot is uncertain; it may mean "the man from Kerioth." Another, perhaps more likely suggestion, is that it is derived from *ish sakariot*, the man in charge of payments, that is, treasurer (cf. Jn 13:29). The presence of a traitor among the twelve is frankly acknowledged by the four evangelists (cf. Mk 14:10,43; Mt 10:4; Lk 6:16; Jn 6:64; cf. Acts 1:13, etc.).

HIS OWN RECEIVED HIM NOT.
3:20-35 (Lk 11:14-18,21-22; 12:10;8:19-21; Mt 12:22-26,29, 31-32, 46-50).

Though the section is made up of three passages (the fears of the family of Jesus vv.20-21, on collusion with Satan, vv.22-30, and on the true kindred of Jesus, vv.31-35), the chiastic structure has shaped it into a unit. The family of Jesus figures in the first and third episodes—setting out to seize him in 3:21 and arriving at where he was in v.31. These episodes represent different traditions, but in the evangelist's eyes they are connected. The insertion of the conflict with the scribes (vv.22-23) into the middle of this material is quite in the style of Mark's "sandwich" arrangement (cf. 5:25-43; 6:7-32; 11:12-25; 14:1-11). The chiastic structure of the section is reasonably obvious:

A.		The friends (family) of Jesus seek him	3:20-21
	B.	Accusation: he is possessed by Beelzebul	3:22a
		C. Accusation: by the prince of demons	3:22b
		D. Logion on Satan	3:23-26
		C'. Response to the second accusation	3:27
	B'.	Response to the first accusation	3:28-29
A'.		The true relatives of Jesus	3:31-35

The passage as a whole illustrates the statement in the prologue of the Fourth Gospel: "He came to his own home, and his own people received him not" (Jn 1:11). The family of Jesus and the religious leaders of the people fail to recognize him and the true source of his activity. His relatives are not his real kindred, those who do the will of God; and the scribes who accuse him of being in league with the devil are guilty of an unforgivable sin. In his own way, Mark wrestles with the problem that tormented the fourth evangelist: that men loved darkness rather than light (Jn 3:19).

Then he went home; [20]and the crowd came together again, so that they could not even eat. [21]And when his friends heard it, they went out to seize him, for they said, "He is beside himself." [22]And the scribes who came down from Jerusalem said, "He is possessed by Beelzebul, and by the prince of demons he casts out the demons."

[23]And he called them to him, and said to them in parables, "How can Satan cast out Satan? [24]If a kingdom is divided against itself, that kingdom cannot stand. [25]And if a house is divided against itself, that house will not be able to stand. [26]And if Satan has risen up against himself and is divided, he cannot stand, but is coming to an end. [27]But no one can enter a strong man's house and plunder his goods, unless he first binds the strong man; then indeed he may plunder his house.

[28]"Truly, I say to you, all sins will be forgiven the sons of men, and whatever blasphemies they utter; [29]but whoever blasphemes against the Holy Spirit never has forgiveness, but is guilty of an eternal sin"—[30]for they had said, "He has an unclean spirit."

[31]And his mother and his brothers came; and standing outside they sent to him and called him. [32]And a crowd was sitting about him; and they said to him, "Your mother and your brothers are outside, asking for you." [33]And he replied, "Who are my mother and my brothers?" [34]And looking around on those who sat about him, he said, "Here are my mother and my brothers! [35]Whoever does the will of God is my brother, and sister, and mother."

The brief narrative 3:20-21, which shows that Jesus' family did not understand him or even believe in him, has no parallel in Matthew or Luke, since both of these evangelists have an infancy narrative in which Jesus' family does know about him. The Greek phrase *hoi par' autou* can mean "neighbors," "friends," "relatives," "family." There is practical consensus that this last meaning fits the context: the family at Nazareth and not merely his "friends" (RSV) are indicated. The family, concerned for Jesus, had decided to intervene; they have come "to seize" him. Their decision shows a lack of sympathy with his aims and conduct. (Cf. Jn 7:5, "For even his brothers did not believe in him.") "He is beside himself"—they fear that he must be out of his mind. They are equivalently suggesting demonic possession (cf. Jn 7:20; 8:48,52; 10:20-21).

For the first time in the gospel we hear of Jerusalem scribes, who certainly represent official Jewish reaction. A title of the god Baal was "*Zabul* (Prince), Lord of the earth," a reminiscence of which is found in 2 Kgs 1:2 and in the Beelzebul of the New Testament. Two charges are aimed at Jesus: he is possessed by Beelzebul, that is, by an evil spirit; and, secondly, his exorcisms are wrought by the power of "the prince of demons," that is, by Satan (v.22b). The accusations are taken up in turn in vv.28-29 and v.27. The charge goes far beyond anything in the conflict stories (2:1-3:6). Jesus is not only an infringer of the Law, not only a blasphemer—he is a tool of Satan. The "blindness of heart" of 3:5 is less blameworthy than this perversity. Yet, for the scribes and Pharisees, their verdict is the only possible one. This man is a friend of sinners, freely sharing table-fellowship with them; he is a proven transgressor of sabbath observance. In both respects this means flouting the Law, the will of God. His miraculous power cannot be from God.

Jesus spoke in "parables," in half-veiled, proverb-like teaching. The Greek word *parabolē* reflects the Hebrew term *māshāl* which can refer either to a "wise saying," or a "riddle" (cf. Mk 4:11-12). It is Mark's theological position that all discourses addressed to "those outside" are "in parables" (cf. 4:33-34; 7:17; 12:1). The charge that Jesus casts out demons by the power of Satan is answered by a denial that Satan is divided against himself. The saying about Satan (vv.24-26) is composed of three parts, each beginning "and if . . ." and originally each having the same structure. Vv. 24-25 illustrate the principle of v.23. The verses stand in parallelism because in Aramaic "house" can also mean realm or domain. The factor involved in v.26 is the inevitably destructive effect of civil war. In the light of the examples given, the break-up of Satan's domain should be evident if the charge of the scribes were true. There ought to be unmistakable signs of the havoc of this alleged civil war. Thus the full implication of the charge (v.22) effectively refutes the charge.

The saying of v.27 must have been added to the preceding saying about Satan at an early date since the association is already found in the different context of Matthew/Luke. The link is natural enough but the verse does introduce a new idea, while it replies to the accusation that Jesus was in collusion with the prince of demons. The underlying metaphor is clear: you cannot rob a strong man's house unless you first overpower the strong man. But the saying itself is certainly allegorical. The influence of Is 49:24-25 is evident. "Can the prey be taken from the *mighty*, or the captives of a tyrant be rescued? Surely, thus says the Lord: 'Even the captives of the mighty shall be taken, and the prey of the tyrant rescued, for I will contend with those who contend with you, and I will save your children.' " Satan is the Strong Man; but Jesus is the "Stronger One" (cf. Mk 1:7) armed with the power of God. The exorcisms prove that Jesus has broken into the house of Satan and has rescued the captives of the tyrant.

The explanatory editorial comment of the evangelist in v.30 shows that the logion of blasphemy against the Holy Spirit (vv.28-29) is to be taken as Jesus' response to the accusation of being possessed by Beelzebul. The saying recurs in a different version and in another context in Mt 12:31-32 and Lk 12:10. "Truly" (literally "amen"), adding emphasis and solemnity to what follows, is found exclusively in sayings of Jesus. The meaning of "blasphemy against the Holy Spirit" is indicated by v.30. It is the act of attributing the exorcisms of Jesus (and, by implication, his whole ministry) wrought by the power of the Spirit (1:8,10,12; 13: 11; Lk 11:20) to the agency of Satan. This is the unforgivable sin, liable to an eternal judgment ("guilty of an eternal sin"). The unpardonable gravity of the sin comes from the fact that, in attributing the activity of Jesus to a demonic influence (3:22a), one refuses to admit that the kingdom of God has come. One thus puts oneself outside of it, refusing the kingdom. The "sin" or "blasphemy" is not so much an offense against the Spirit as a man's refusal of the salvation which God offers to him by the Spirit active in Jesus.

The rabbis also distinguished between sins that could be forgiven either in this world or the future world, and others which were unforgivable—sins so terrible that those who commit them "have no part in the world to come." But Jesus asserts the universality of forgiveness (v.28), and it is the emphatic and heartening assurance of the gospel message that repentance always wins God's forgiveness. The trouble with "blasphemy against the Holy Spirit" is that it is a perversion of mind which chooses to call light darkness. While one persists in that perversion one is impervious to any movement of repentance and so closed to forgiveness. The "unforgivable sin" does not at all exclude the *possibility* of repentance and forgiveness.

The pronouncement story 3:31-35 preserves the saying of Jesus that his true kindred are those who do the will of God. For Mark it is a continuation of vv.20-21. His insertion of the Beelzebul discourse establishes a relationship between the attitude of the brethren of Jesus and the attitude of the religious authorities—his own did not receive him. The mother of Jesus (v.31) does not appear again in Mark, but she is mentioned in 6:3. Those who are sitting around Jesus are in the process of listening to his teaching and thus of placing themselves in his "family." The rhetorical question and reply of Jesus (vv. 33-34) form the climax of the pronouncement story. There is a marked tone of disappointment in the question; the family at Nazareth have shown that they do not understand him (v. 21). Jesus subordinates the bond of kinship to the higher bond of brotherhood. The will of his Father is the motive power and guide of all Jesus' activity: "My food is to do the will of him who sent me" (Jn 4:34). Those who similarly do the will of God enter into a real relationship with Jesus, they belong to the family of God. But the first requirement in doing God's will is to know it; one must learn at the school of Jesus.

In this episode of the family of Jesus and again in 6:3, Mark shows no awareness of the virginal conception tradition and gives no suggestion of any special role of Mary. The passage may be seen to distinguish between those who stood outside the sphere of salvation and those who are within it. Those outside, though they be the Lord's own people, his own kin, are those who do not recognize that his ministry was the work of God. Those within are they who do the will of God, who recognize and accept the ministry of Jesus and gather about him in faith and discipleship. Their following of him might involve the breaking of family ties, but it will gain a closer fellowship with him and with his brethren (10:28-30).

HE SPOKE IN PARABLES.
4:1-32 (Lk 8:4-15; Mt 13:1-51).

The passage on parables (4:1-34) is complex and is composed of a number of clearly defined sections: an introduction (1-2), the parable of the sower (3-9), the purpose of parables (10-12), explanation of the parable of the sower (13-20), wisdom sayings (21-25), the parable of the seed growing to harvest (26-29), the parable of the mustard seed (30-32), and a concluding statement on the use of parables (33-34). We may, with some confidence, form a general picture of how 4:1-34 was built up. The primitive tradition combined the three parables (3-9, 26-29, 30-32); at an early stage the explanation of the parable of the sower (13-20) was supplied. Verses 33-34 could well represent the conclusion of this grouping. The evangelist himself added the passage on the purpose of parables (10-12) and the wisdom sayings (21-25), passages that are reflections on the teaching of parables as such. They explain, from Mark's point of view, why Jesus spoke in parables. Finally, his introduction (1-2) provides a setting for the teaching in parables.

Mark's intent in this passage is to propose a lesson on the hearing of the word about the kingdom. There is notable emphasis on hearing: "Listen" (v.3); "he who has ears to hear, let him hear" (9,23); "those who hear the word" (18; cf. 15-20); "take heed what you hear" (24); ". . . as they were able to hear it" (33). This hearing stands in contrast to a "hearing but not understanding" (12). There is a withdrawing from "those outside" (11), who do not hear and understand, and a turning to those who will receive the "secret of the kingdom" (11,34). In the explanation of the Sower the two levels of understanding are illustrated: the superficial level of "seeing" and "hearing" (12) is exemplified by those who "hear" the word but then fall away (15,16,18). The deeper level, called "perceiving" and "understanding" (12) is exemplified by those who "hear and accept" (20). It is significant that none other than Satan (v.15) blocks the transition from the first level of understanding to the second; he achieves his purpose through tribulation and persecution (17) and by means of the cares and lures of the world (19). Those who attain the second level of understanding receive it as a gift from God (in v.11 the passive form "has been given" implies God as the agent). Once again, we see Satan and the Spirit-filled Messiah locked in struggle. The words of Jesus, too, are weapons in his warfare on God's behalf.

Parable.

Before going on to comment on this section of Mark, it is needful to establish what "parable" is. In the New Testament the Greek word *parabolē* should be understood as a rendering of the Hebrew word *māshāl,* in the process taking on the meaning of *māshāl.* What is this meaning? In Hebrew this word has a whole range of intricate meanings. It could be a representation or a type, a simile or a metaphor, a maxim or proverb or pithy saying, a symbol or a riddle. It had, too, the quality of a "dark saying," something involving mystery. Once we are aware of this Old Testament background to "parable" we cannot help realizing that it is largely encompassed in the New Testament usage of the term. For our immediate purpose, though, we take it in the sense of a short narrative, a story.

It has been customary to set up a sharp contrast between parable and allegory. Parable is commonly described as a story that has one point and one point only. It is held to be distinct from allegory, or prolonged metaphor, in which each detail has symbolic meaning (e.g. Eph 6:13-17). The proper distinction is that parable is a specific literary form, while allegory is a device of meaning. What marks off a parable is that it is a story with a particular religious or ethical purpose: it is always thought-provoking and often is a challenge to decisive action. Every parable has two levels of meaning; it is not story only, but story with meaning and purpose, with challenge. Allegory, on the other hand, is a component of some parables. An allegorical story can be quite other than parable, but there are parables that are allegorical (e.g. the parable of the prodigal son). It is incorrect to base judgments on the authenticity or not of a parable of Jesus on whether or not it contains allegorical traits. It had customarily been assumed that anything smacking of allegory was foreign to Jesus; he would have employed only "pure" parables. Always, Jesus' intent was to challenge attitudes and invite commitment; he was not to be hampered by academic niceties. The assumed rigid separation of parable and allegory is now seen to be invalid. Jesus could have employed allegory. The question of authenticity must be decided on other grounds.

Because a parable must have two levels of meaning, it can thereby function as mysterious speech. The hearer may be unable or unwilling to grasp the secondary (and more important) meaning. While a parable is not necessarily difficult to comprehend it may well be so. Failure to attain the second level of meaning will make the parable seem mysterious. Mark has exploited this mysterious aspect of parable.

4 Again he began to teach beside the sea. And a very large crowd gathered about him, so that he got into a boat and sat in it on the sea; and the whole crowd was beside the sea on the land. 2And he taught them many things in parables, and in his teaching he said to them: 3"Listen! A sower went out to sow. 4And as he sowed, some seed fell along the path, and the birds came and devoured it. 5Other seed fell on rocky ground, where it had not much soil, and immediately it sprang up, since it had no depth of soil; 6and when the sun rose it was scorched, and since it had no root it withered away. 7Other seed fell among thorns and the thorns grew up and choked it, and it yielded no grain. 8And other seeds fell into good soil and brought forth grain, growing up and increasing and yielding thirtyfold and sixtyfold and a hundredfold." 9And he said, "He who has ears to hear, let him hear."

10And when he was alone, those who were about him with the twelve asked him concerning the parables. 11And he said to them, "To you has been given the secret of the kingdom of God, but for those outside everything is in parables; 12so that they may indeed see but not perceive, and may indeed hear but not understand; lest they should turn again, and be forgiven."

13And he said to them, "Do you not understand this parable? How then will you understand all the parables?

[15]The sower sows the word. [15]And these are the ones along the path, where the word is sown; when they hear, Satan immediately comes and takes away the word which is sown in them. [16]And these in like manner are the ones sown upon rocky ground, who, when they hear the word, immediately receive it with joy; [17]and they have no root in themselves, but endure for a while; then, when tribulation or persecution arises on account of the word, immediately they fall away. [18]And others are the ones sown among thorns; they are those who hear the word, [19]but the cares of the world, and the delight in riches, and the desire for other things, enter in and choke the word, and it proves unfruitful. [20]But those that were sown upon the good soil are the ones who hear the word and accept it and bear fruit, thirtyfold and sixtyfold and a hundredfold."

[21]And he said to them, "Is a lamp brought in to be put under a bushel, or under a bed, and not on a stand? [22]For there is nothing hid, except to be made manifest; nor is anything secret, except to come to light. [23]If any man has ears to hear, let him hear." [24]And he said to them, "Take heed what you hear; the measure you give will be the measure you get, and still more will be given you. [25]For to him who has will more be given; and from him who has not, even what he has will be taken away."

[26]And he said, "The kingdom of God is as if a man should scatter seed upon the ground, [27]and should sleep and rise night and day, and the seed should sprout and grow, he knows not how. [28]The earth produces of itself, first the blade, then the ear, then the full grain in the ear. [29]But when the grain is ripe, at once he puts in the sickle, because the harvest has come."

[30]And he said, "With what can we compare the kingdom of God, or what parable shall we use of it? [31]It is like a grain of mustard seed, which, when sown upon the ground, is the smallest of all the seeds on earth; [32]yet when it is sown it grows up and becomes the greatest of all

shrubs, and puts forth large branches, so that the birds of the air can make nests in its shade."

[33]With many such parables he spoke the word to them, as they were able to hear it; [34]he did not speak to them without a parable, but privately to his own disciples he explained everything.

THE PURPOSE OF PARABLES.
4:10-12 (Lk 8:9-10; Mt 13:10-15).

The brief passage 4:10-12 is of great importance, revealing as it does Mark's own peculiar theory on the purpose of parables. The evangelist is preoccupied with the problem of Jewish hostility to and rejection of Jesus and of the christian message of salvation in Christ. He sees it as in some fashion falling under the deliberate decree of God. And so in his eyes teaching in parables, being enigmatic, veils the truth from those who are not meant to have it. But Jesus will instruct in the full meaning of the parables those who are destined to receive the divine gift of the truth.

The phrase "and when he was alone" (v.10) prepares the setting for vv.11-12. "Alone" (*kata monas*) is a synonym of the characteristic Marcan phrase *kat' idian*, "privately," "by themselves" (cf. 4:34; 6:31-32; 7:33; 9:2,28; 13:3). Each time it occurs the expression is used in connection with a revelation or a private teaching reserved for the disciples. "Those who were about him with the twelve"—in the immediate context this group corresponds to the "you" and stands in contrast to the "those outside" of v.11. Mark is reflecting the life and experience of his christian community. Christians are those who understand (or who ought to understand), they are not "those outside."

The saying of v.11-12 is concerned with the purpose of the parabolic form as such. "To you," that is, "those who were about him with the twelve" (v.10): the disciples and, by extension, the christian readers of the gospel. Mark's readers thus take their place among the immediate disciples of Jesus and share a revelation in which "those outside" have no part. "The secret of the kingdom of God" is, literally, "the mystery (*mystērion*) of the kingdom of God." The word *rāz*, "mystery," is found in the late Old Testament writings. In Daniel (Dan 2:19, 28-30) it designates the eschatological plan of God, in particular the coming of the eternal kingdom which will bring to an end all the ephemeral empires of men. The notion of mystery is developed in much the same sense in later apocalyptic writings. "Mystery" is also used to express the Qumran community's interpretation of the law. An interesting point is that these mysteries of the law were revealed only to the sectarians. So, here too, "everything happens in parables" explains to the disciples and the readers why Jesus speaks of himself and of the kingdom in parables, and only in parables (v.34). Clearly, for Mark, *parabolē* has a meaning close to "riddle."

The citation in v.12, of Is 6:9-10 follows the wording of the *Targum*, which is an Aramaic paraphrase of the Hebrew scriptures. In its Isaian setting the saying is a forceful and paradoxical way of proclaiming what is inevitably going to happen: the prophet's preaching will not be heeded. This text was applied by the early Christians in a sense very close to its original significance (see the parallel passages Mt 13:14-15; Lk 8:10). In Jn 12:40 it describes Jewish blindness to the "signs" of Jesus; and in Acts 28:25-27 Paul applies it to the negative Jewish reaction to his preaching. In our text Mark is facing up to the problem of the obduracy of Israel. Why did, by and large, the Jewish contemporaries of Jesus not hear his message, not come to understand him? And why did the Jewish people continue to resist the preaching of Mark's community? Mark's answer is stark: their rejection of the gospel was within God's plan. Nor is he alone in this view. Early christian thinkers tended to account for the rejection of the teaching of Jesus and the apostles by asserting that such was the will of God (cf. Rom 9:18-29; 10:16-21; 11:7-10; Jn 12:37-41; Acts 28:25-28). Mark's distinctive contribution is to exploit the mysterious aspect of parable in that direction. Ultimately he is, in tortuous fashion, asserting that Israel's inexplicable behavior has a divine purpose. It is Paul's conviction also, expressed in a similarly labored manner (Rom 9-11). Of course, the New Testament writers, like their Old Testament predecessors, maintained the view that people bear the responsibility for their actions, and this responsibility was not taken to be made void by the doctrine of determination. In accord with the deterministic will of God, Mark proposes that Jesus had taught in mysterious parables; to the disciples alone is given the secret of the kingdom. Through them his teaching will be preserved and passed on. Yet, Mark will go out of the way to insist that the disciples did not really comprehend Jesus or his teaching. His statement that God had granted the secret of the kingdom to some while hiding it from others relates to the situation of his day and looks beyond the precise problem of Israel. He has in mind the situation illustrated in the explanation of the parable of the sower (vv.14-20). He is sure that God alone can open hearts to the word and bring it to harvest.

THE PARABLE OF THE SOWER AND ITS EXPLANATION.
4:1-9, 13-20 (Lk 8:4-8, 1-15; Mt 13:1-9,18-23).

The text of the parable (vv.1-9) is notably semitic and the lines of it are very simple and clear. But because we can no longer determine its setting in the ministry of Jesus we cannot be sure of its original meaning. It is commonly taken to be a parable of the kingdom; but it is not at all clear that it was ever meant to be such. What is beyond doubt is that, for Mark, it is a parable of the word—we have drawn attention to his insistence on hearing and understanding. It is quite likely that this, too, was Jesus' intent. It certainly cannot be said that Mark has turned the parable from its original purpose. In following his line we are not only being true to his text but have a good chance of hearing the parable aright.

Structurally, the parable falls into two parts: the first is negative—the grain and seedlings and young plants perish; the second is positive—the rest of the grain flourishes and the yield is striking. "Listen" (v.3) echoes the "Hear" of

Dt 6:4. For Mark the admonition highlights, from the outset, the importance of "hearing" throughout this narrative (cf. v.9) and also suggests that parables are meant to provoke thought. "As he sowed"—the scene is vivid: one can picture the sparrows gathering to peck away at the fallen grain. The situation depicted here (vv.4-7) is typically Palestinian. In Palestine sowing comes before plowing (as with us the seed is scattered before harrowing); hence it is natural for the farmer to sow apparently helter-skelter as he does. He sows intentionally on the casual path which the villagers have trod through the stubble because it is going to be plowed up (and the seed plowed in at the same time). He sows intentionally among the withered thorns because these, too, are going to be plowed up. He cannot avoid the rocks that jut through the thin soil. In vv.5-6 the withering is due to the same cause which led to rapid growth: the shallowness of the soil which did not permit the plant to strike roots. The thorns grew faster and higher than the wheat and "choked" it, a strong, descriptive word (v.7). A vivid agricultural vignette, yes; but this is parable and necessarily has a second, metaphorical level of meaning. And the solemn call to hear (v.9) points to that meaning. The parable is allegory as its explanation (vv.14-20) insists. Its main concern is the word and the hearers of the word. The hearer is exhorted to receive the word in faith and keep it with steadfastness. And the "word" is not only Jesus' proclamation of the coming kingdom but, more immediately for Mark, the proclamation of the christian message. Here, too, is the counter to the determinism of vv.11-12, stressing human responsibility and the need for a response to the proclamation. The questions of Jesus in v.13 point to another dimension of the parable: it is the key to understanding all the other parables. It is so because it is concerned with the presupposition of all parables, the word sown by Jesus. It is, then, a parable not only on the hearing of the word but on the right hearing of parables.

The Marcan link-formula "And he said to them," joins the explanation of the Sower to the evangelist's insertion on the use of parables. There is a contradiction, or so it would appear, between vv. 11 and 13: on the one hand it is affirmed that the disciples cannot understand without a specific "gift" of God, while in v.13 they are blamed for their lack of understanding. In fact, both affirmations are aspects of the special theology of Mark and aspects of the same eschatological reality. The slowness of the disciples to understand only sets in relief the greatness of the revelation that is granted to them. Besides, the disciples by themselves cannot come to see the mystery of the kingdom; Jesus must open their eyes (cf. 8:22-26; 10:46-52). The tenor of the question (v.13) would appear to be: if you have failed to understand this parable (the sower) about hearing the word (vv.3,9), how are you going to understand the parables in general?

The explanation of the sower (vv.14-20) is a commentary which takes up and explains each phrase of the parable. In v.14 "the sower" is the sower of the parable and is not further identified. "The word" (*ho logos*), used absolutely, is a technical term for the gospel, coined and currently employed, by the early Church (cf. 1 Thess 1:6; Col 1:5; 1 Pt 2:8; Jas 1:21). In the synoptics, however, it is very significant that the absolute use of *ho logos* by Jesus occurs only in the explanation of the parable of the sower (eight times in Mark, five times in Matthew, and three times in Luke). In v.15 the phrase, "some seed fell along the path" of 4:4 is taken up. Here the interest is on the hearers of the word; the type of soil, "along the path," is taken to represent a class of hearers. The thieving birds are powers of evil; Luke (8:12) explains Satan's intent "that they may not believe and be saved."

In vv.16,18 and 20 it is *human beings* who are sown: the emphasis has moved to the hearers of the word. The explanation takes up (v.16) the case of the seed which "fell on rocky ground" (4:5). The enthusiastic joy of the hearers is like the precocious growth of the seedling, and it is equally ephemeral. The use of *hriza*, "roots," meaning internal stability (cf. Col 2:7; Eph 3:17), and the term *proskairos*,

"for a while" (cf. 2 Cor 4:18; Heb 11:25) do not occur elsewhere in the synoptics. From v.17b onward the experiences
of the early christian community are reflected, beginning
with troubles and persecution on account of the word. In
vv.18-19 it is the turn of the seed which "fell among thorns"
(4:7). Cares, delight, desire: for this third group the obstacles come from within man. Finally, v.20, is the turn of
the seed which "fell into good soil" (4:8). These hear the
word, accept it, and yield fruit.

Noteworthy is the attention to the various types of soil—
and the variation extends to the good soil. But this was
already a feature of the parable. The explanation builds
on what is already there; it does not give a new and different
twist. This is evident if we look again at the explanation.
The seed is the gospel preaching; this word is sown in the
hearers, it is "seeded" in them (4:15). Four categories of
hearers are distinguished in terms of the place where the seed
has fallen: "along the path," "upon rocky ground," "among
thorns," and "upon the good soil." The fate of the word is
different in each case. Satan comes and snatches the word
as it is preached (v.15). Initial joy at the hearing of the word
will not compensate for lack of root. These are men of the
moment who will not persevere in the face of tribulation
and persecution. The description of the third category is
the psychological analysis of a moralist who leans in great
part on the explicit teaching of Jesus; much of it is redolent
of the Sermon on the Mount. The fourth category is marked
only by the manner in which these hearers receive the word:
it is enough to be good soil, to be receptive, in order to bring
forth fruit. This application is not unfaithful to the parable,
once that is seen for what it is; for it only takes the subjective
aspect of the proclamation and applies it to the hearers.
They are shown that the story of the sower does concern
them. They are expected to be receptive to the proclaimed
word of God.

The explanation is a product of the early church. It came
about because christians discovered to their shock and sorrow the truth that few really believed Jesus' message. They

asked the burning question: how could it be that there was such a gulf between them and those who could not see? They found an answer in the words of the parable. Do not be dismayed by this experience. How could you expect it to be otherwise? Think what happens when the sower scatters his seed. Not every seed bears fruit. Much is lost for one reason or another. This understanding then led them to delineate the various oppositions to the word which they saw happening around them in terms of the twofold description they already had to hand in the parable. Many men are like the men on the path: the word cannot reach them, as if the devil swiped it away at the very moment of receiving. Or, many men seem like shallow, luxuriant growth: they are ready enough to receive, but they cannot persist. They have not had to face resistance and so are not equal to resistance. Or, many men are like seed under thorns: they hear, but the word loses its significance because they are choked up by cares and distractions. The major concern of the explanation is the structure of human life itself. The shallow mind, the hard heart, the preoccupations of the world, persecution—all these are precisely the obstacles which could frustrate the growth of faith. The explanation presumes a period when christian faith was tested by cares, the deceit of riches, and persecution. It offers a warning and an encouragement to Christians in such conditions.

WISDOM SAYINGS.
4:21-25 (Lk 8:16-18; 11:33; 6:38; 12:2; 19:26; Mt 5:15; 10:26; 7:2; 13:12; 25:29).

This is a passage built up of five separate logia arranged in the pairs vv.21-22 and vv.24-25 with v.23 as a connecting link relating them to the parable of the sower (cf. 4:9). The formula, "And he said to them" (vv.21,24), indicates that they are Marcan insertions; the formula also suggests that the sayings already stood in pairs. Similarity of subject matter links the sayings of vv.21-22. For Mark the resultant "parable" clarifies his viewpoint expressed in 4:11-12. Just as it is the function of a lamp to give light, so the parables of Jesus are meant to enlighten. The "hid and secret" of v.22 recall the "mystery" of v.11; it is conceded that the mystery of the kingdom is hidden for a time—but only for a time. What is now hidden will eventually be revealed to all. The evangelist's meaning probably is that though the mystery of the kingdom was hidden during the ministry of Jesus, it was destined to be proclaimed abroad after the resurrection (cf. 9:9). Mark may mean something more. He wrote not that the lamp "is brought in" but, literally, that it "comes." Jesus (the lamp) has come, is hidden for a while, but cannot remain hidden. The mystery has been given to the disciples in order that (though for the present they do not understand) they may make it known. Of course, either meaning of the saying seems rather forced and artificial because each of these sayings originally had a different meaning and context (cf. for v.21, Lk 11:33; Mt 5:15; and for v.22, Lk 12:2; Mt 10:26). The solemn warning of 4:23 echoes 4:9; here it is meant to emphasize the responsibility of disciples. It underlines the message of vv.21-22 and suggests that the time had come to proclaim the gospel plainly before men.

The second pair of sayings (vv.24-25) is, in the setting, more obscure. "Take heed what you hear" means, carefully consider what you hear, weigh its meaning. The proverbial saying (v.24b) gives the reason for heeding. This saying occurs in Mt 7:2 and Lk 6:38 in a context of judgment—you will be judged in the measure you judge others—and it is obviously at home in that context. But Mark sets it in relation to the parables and its sense, for him, seems to be: your attention to the teaching will be the measure of the profit you will receive from it. The second saying (v.25) may have been a popular proverb. The other synoptists have the saying again after the parable of the Talents/Pounds (Mt 25:.9; Lk 19:26). Here Mark seemingly takes it to mean that the spiritual insight which denotes openness to the teaching of Jesus (v.24) will be deepened by God (the passive, "will be given," implies God as the agent). And, conversely, indifference to the message of the parable will lead to a loss of whatever insight one may have had.

It is obvious that none of these sayings originally referred to the parabolic teaching of Jesus. Mark has chosen to connect them with his own parable theory; his insertion of them here makes that much clear at least. For the rest, we cannot be sure of the precise meaning they held for him.

THE GROWING SEED AND THE MUSTARD SEED. 4:26-32 (Lk 13:18-19; Mt 13:31-32).

The parable of the seed growing to harvest (vv.26-29) is peculiar to Mark. We do not know its original context. It seems best to take it as a parable of contrast between the inactivity of the sower and the certainty of the harvest. The sower goes his way; his life follows its normal ordered round (v.27). All the while the seed sprouts and grows without his taking anxious thought. In fact, there is nothing the sower can do because "the earth produces of itself"— this is very emphatically stated (v.28). The seed grows from blade, to ear, to full grain: its growth is irresistible. Then, one day, the time again comes for the intervention of the farmer (v.29). The grain is ripe and "at once" he proceeds to harvest it. "Put in the sickle, for the harvest is ripe" (a glance at Joel 3:13) refers to the final judgment: this pastoral scene is really concerned with the coming of the kingdom (cf. Rev 14:14-20). And God it is who brings about that coming, that growth. Paul had learned the lesson of the parable: "I planted, Apollos watered, but God gave the growth. So neither he who plants nor he who waters is anything, but only God who gives the growth" (1 Cor 3:6).

It may be that, originally, the parable was Jesus' reply to those who impatiently looked for a forceful intervention of God or of his kingdom; or it may have been meant to give assurance to those of the disciples who were discouraged because nothing seemed to be happening. Mark, at least, takes it in the latter sense. Jesus encourages his disciples: in spite of hindrance and apathy the seed was being sown. Its growth is the work of God who will bring it to harvest.

The parable of the mustard seed (vv.30-32) is another parable of contrast; but again the idea of growth must be given due weight. The contrast between insignificant beginning and mighty achievement is primary—but the seed does grow into a plant. The rabbis usually began their parables with the words: "A parable: it is like . . . ," which was a conventional abbreviation of: "I will tell you a parable. With what may the matter be compared? It is the case with it as with . . . ." Our text (v. 30) is quite like the rabbinical formula. (Cf. Lk 13:20-21.) "It is the case with it (the kingdom) as with a grain of mustard seed": it follows that it is not the seed itself but what happens to the seed that is significant, and the kingdom is like the great shrub that grows out of the seed. The small beginnings of the kingdom are carefully emphasized: every word depicts its smallness.

By contrast, in v.32, every word now paints the greatness of the shrub. In favorable conditions the tiny mustard seed could grow into a shrub some eight or ten feet high. In Dan 4:12; Ezek 17:23; 31:6 a tree sheltering the birds is a symbol of a great empire offering protection to its subject peoples—Mark seems to have the gentiles in mind. The proclamation of the kingdom will bring all nations within the scope of the kingdom.

The parable of the mustard seed would have been the answer of Jesus to an objection, latent or expressed: could the kingdom really come from such inauspicious beginnings? His reply is that the little cell of disciples will indeed become a kingdom. And, in the last analysis, if the kingdom does reach its full dimension, it is not due to anything in the men who are the seed of the kingdom; the growth is due solely to the power of God (cf. 1 Cor 3:6-7). This is why Jesus can speak with utter confidence of the final stage of the kingdom. And that is why this parable is a call to patience.

THE USE OF PARABLES.
4:33-34 (Mt 13:34-35).

"With many such parables"—the parables just given are only a selection, a few out of many. "The word" is the good news of the kingdom as in 2:2. "As they were able to hear"—the parabolic teaching of Jesus was adapted to the capacity of the hearers. The verse might be taken as putting neatly both the fact of Jesus' use of parables and the purpose of this preaching in parables. The first part of v.34 does more than repeat in negative form the positive statement in v.33; it affirms that Jesus spoke *only* in parables to the crowds. Indeed, from the whole verse it emerges that he refused to address the crowd in any other way and reserved explicit teaching for his disciples alone. One cannot fail to discern Mark's special position according to which the "parable" is a deliberately obscure literary form whose meaning must be specially revealed. This becomes explicit in v.34b. The phrase *kat' idian*, "privately," as we have seen, always in Mark indicates a revelation or a private teaching reserved for the disciples (cf. 4:10). These concluding verses clearly reflect the evangelist's theological outlook and concludes what he has to say about the use of parables.

A GROUP OF MIRACLE STORIES.
4:35 - 5:43.

The parable section 4:1-34 is followed by a group of miracle stories which reveal the power of Jesus. The three narratives are vivid, the stories being related with a wealth of detail. Following on the day of parables, the group of miracles continues the preparation of the disciples for their missionary apostolate (6:7-13). Jesus shows them that the mission is rooted in his power over the elements, over devils, and over death, and that, at least by an initial and symbolic action, the mission spreads into pagan territory beyond the frontiers of Israel.

WHO THEN IS THIS?
4:35-41 (Lk 8:22-25; Mt 8:23-27).

³⁵On that day, when evening had come, he said to them, "Let us go across to the other side." ³⁶And leaving the crowd, they took him with them, just as he was, in the boat. And other boats were with him. ³⁷And a great storm of wind arose, and the waves beat into the boat, so that the boat was already filling. ³⁸But he was in the stern, asleep on the cushion; and they woke him and said to him, "Teacher, do you not care if we perish?" ³⁹And he awoke and rebuked the wind, and said to the sea, "Peace! Be still!" And the wind ceased, and there was a great calm. ⁴⁰He said to them, "Why are you afraid? Have you no faith?" ⁴¹And they were filled with awe, and said to one another, "Who then is this, that even wind and sea obey him?"

The opening temporal statement (vv.35-36) is editorial; the narrative (vv.37-41) is a miracle story arranged in three scenes. The first contrasts the plight of the storm-tossed boat with the tranquil sleep of Jesus (vv.37-38a). The second contrasts the abject terror of these professional fishermen with the sovereign calm of the Master who commands winds and waves with authority (vv.38b-39). In the third place, we are shown the reaction of the disciples to Jesus: they are awe-struck by this display of cosmic power (v.41). The apostrophe of Jesus in v.40, underlining the lack of confidence on the part of the disciples, brings out the catechetical interest of the narrative.

We need to have in mind that certain Old Testament ideas and passages form the background of the narrative. Control over the sea and the calming of storms are characteristic signs of divine power (Job 7:12; Pss 74:13; 89:8-9; 93:3-4; Is 51:9-10). Calming of a storm at sea is a major proof of God's loving care (Ps 107:23-32). It is also noteworthy that peaceful and untroubled sleep is a sign of perfect trust in God (cf. Prov 3:23-24; Pss 3:5; 4:8; Job 11:18-19). Of particular interest is the passage in Jonah (1:4-15) which seems to have influenced the form of the Marcan story.

Mark's narrative is a miracle story with a catechetical point. We may distinguish between the two interests which indicate stages in the evolution of the narrative. We have noted that, in biblical thought, God alone can control the waters of the sea and the storm. Furthermore, these elements can be the image, and the home, of evil powers; here Jesus "exorcises" these infernal forces. Again, in view of the Old Testament background, it could be expected that the story would have closed with praise of God "who had given such power to men"; instead, the limelight is on Jesus. The disciples have seen a work that only God can accomplish. In the light of their monotheistic faith they must ask, in awe and perplexity, who this man is who can do a work of God.

The reproach of v.40 transforms the miracle story into a catechetical lesson; though from the beginning, doubtless, the episode was seen as one which raised the question of the identity of Jesus, and as a teaching on faith. Jesus blames the disciples for their lack of confidence. The term *deiloi*, "afraid," is very strong, expressing total disarray. During the storm the disciples had failed in that confidence in God of which the tranquil sleep of the Master was a visible sign. However, Jesus accuses them especially of lack of confidence in his person (cf. Jn 14:1). By his tranquil sleep, his reproach, and his stilling of the storm, Jesus exhorts his disciples to have trust in him at all times and in all circumstances.

But, after all, it is not the little handful of disciples in that lake drama who are chiefly in question. The cry, "Master, are we to perish for all you care?" (v.38) suggests that the disciples are in a danger which does not threaten their master. This scene where the disciples are awake and in danger while their Master "sleeps" reflects the post-Easter experience of the Church. Christians may feel that the Lord has no care for them, has abandoned them, and the Church may seem to be at the mercy of the forces pitted against it.

Individuals and communities who feel so earn the rebuke: "Have you no faith?" It is enough that he should "awaken," that they should have faith and trust in his presence, for the storm of their fear to be stilled. Mark has painted an episode in the life of Jesus in colors of early Christianity. Just as John's Apocalypse was written to illustrate the encouraging declaration of Christ, "Have confidence, I have overcome the world" (Jn 16:33) so, in its way, this miniature gives the same assurance.

Evidently, it is not easy to establish what really happened on the lake; the story has been much embellished. Though, in Mark, the passage stands as a miracle story, it is by no means certain that the basic incident was a miracle in the strict sense. Rather, we seem to have a combination of circumstances in which the disciples, and Jesus himself, perceived a message, one which had the impact of a revelation. It is also to be noted that our passage offers certain close contacts with the narrative of the walking on the waters (6:45-52); and it, too, raises the question of what really happened.

AN OPENING TO THE GENTILES.
5:1-20 (Lk 8:26-29; Mt 8:28-34).

The power of Jesus over nature has been demonstrated; now once again (cf. 1:23-27) it is shown that he has power over evil spirits, and the narrative meticulously brings out the range of Jesus' power. He is faced with an extreme case of mental derangement—the demonic source of sickness in general was popularly acknowledged to be most obvious in cases of insanity—and all attempts to deal with it had proved ineffective. Indeed, Jesus has to cope, not with a single demon, but with a host of evil. But, in the presence of Jesus, the devils are helpless (5:7, 10-12), his simple word of command puts them to flight. Those who had known the demoniac are apprehensive of the supernatural power shown by the healer (vv.16-17). The narrative is skillfully presented as a little drama in four acts: the interest shifts from the afflicted man (1-10), to the herd of swine (11-13), then to the man's fellow-countrymen (14-17), and back again to the man and Jesus by the lakeside (18-20).

The core of 5:1-20 is an exorcism story which has been embellished with legendary details. It can readily be seen that the episode of the swine is not essential to the main story at all. However, for the evangelist, the resultant dramatic narrative is full of significance. For this is no ordinary exorcism. The man is subject to an unusually severe form of demonic possession (vv.2-5), explained by the fact of multiple possession (v.9). All goes to demonstrate the overwhelming power of Jesus which not only rids the man of his evil guests, but cleanses the land of them (vv. 10-13). The afflicted one's fellow-countrymen bear witness to the extraordinary power that had been at work (vv.14-17). The exorcism has taken place in gentile territory; in this land, cleansed by Jesus himself, the healed man becomes a precursor, heralding the preaching of the Good News to the gentiles (vv.18-20).

> **5** They came to the other side of the sea, to the country of the Gerasenes. [2]And when he had come out of the boat, there met him out of the tombs a man with an unclean spirit, [3]who lived among the tombs; and no one could bind him any more, even with a chain; [4]for he had often been bound with fetters and chains, but the chains he wrenched apart, and the fetters he broke in pieces; and no one had the strength to subdue him. [5]Night and day among the tombs and on the mountains he was always crying out, and bruising himself with stones. [6]And when he saw Jesus from afar, he ran and worshiped him; [7]and crying out with a loud voice, he said, "What have you to do with me, Jesus, Son of the Most High God? I adjure you by God, do not torment me." [8]For he had said to him, "Come out of the man, you unclean spirit!" [9]And Jesus asked him, "What is your name?" He replied, "My name is Legion; for we are many." [10]And he begged him eagerly not to send them out of the country.

¹¹Now a great herd of swine was feeding there on the hillside; ¹²and they begged him, "Send us to the swine, let us enter them." ¹³So he gave them leave. And the unclean spirits came out, and entered the swine; and the herd, numbering about two thousand, rushed down the steep bank into the sea, and were drowned in the sea.

¹⁴The herdsmen fled, and told it in the city and in the country. And people came to see what it was that had happened. ¹⁵And they came to Jesus, and saw the demoniac sitting there, clothed and in his right mind, the man who had had the legion; and they were afraid. ¹⁶And those who had seen it told what had happened to the demoniac and to the swine. ¹⁷And they began to beg Jesus to depart from their neighborhood. ¹⁸And as he was getting into the boat, the man who had been possessed with demons begged him that he might be with him. ¹⁹But he refused, and said to him, "Go home to your friends, and tell them how much the Lord has done for you, and how he has had mercy on you." ²⁰And he went away and began to proclaim in the Decapolis how much Jesus had done for him; and all men marveled.

The narrative is very smoothly linked to the preceding one (5:1); after the stilling of the storm the boat completes its journey (cf. 4:35). "Gerasenes"—textual variants are "Gergesenes," and "Gadarenes" (as in Matthew). The reason for the variants is the distance of Gerasa (30 miles to the south-east) from the lake, while v. 14 suggests that a town was close at hand. Likely, the original exorcism story was set near Gerasa and not by the lake. Demons were popularly believed to haunt cemeteries and tombs (v.2). The descriptive passage (vv.3-5) bears the stamp of Mark's vocabulary. Its vividness, which involves some apparent overcrowding and some repetition, serves to underline the importance of the incident.

As the narrative now stands, v.6 marks the resumption of the story after the parenthesis of vv.3-5. The demon is aware of an extraordinary spiritual force, so he, through the demoniac, "worshiped" (literally, "went down on his knees"). The use of the name, "Jesus, Son of the Most High God" (v.7) was probably a despairing attempt to render the exorcist powerless. It is the evangelist's view, however, that demons, with their preternatural insight, perceive something of the true nature of Jesus. "The Most High God," a gentile designation of the God of Israel (cf. Dan 3:26; 4:2; Acts 16:17) comes fittingly from a gentile demon. "I adjure you by God" is a formula used in Jewish exorcisms; there is a certain irony in its use here by the demon in addressing Jesus. "Do not torment me"—not only the torment of being driven out of his victim. Matthew (8:29) has caught the implication: "Have you come to torment me before the time?" The unclean spirit recognizes that definitive torment awaits him.

The tables are turned on the demon: Jesus demands to know his name and wins an immediate response (v.9). "Legion" does seem to mean that a whole army of demons had taken possession of the man; for other examples of possession by more than one devil, cf. Mk 16:9; Lk 8:2; Mt 12:45 = Lk 11:26. Demons were popularly supposed to be attached to a particular locality from which they were loth to be removed; cf. Lk 11:24. This demon has surrendered and is now desperately pleading for terms (v.10). The episode of the swine is patently folk narrative with a typically earthy humor. The demons had, seemingly, won a concession, but it proved to be their undoing. We are to take it that they perished with the pigs. No Jew would have shed a tear over the destruction of a herd of pigs— fitting habitat for demons indeed. For Mark the incident is important as he shows the reader that this exorcism goes far beyond the deliverance of the unhappy possessed one. It is the expulsion of a horde of demons from the country, a veritable victory of Jesus over the kingdom of Satan.

The scene changes (vv.14-20). It is not surprising (as the narrative runs) that the herdsmen fled, nor that people quickly came to verify their extraordinary story. These newcomers become filled with superstitious terror of

Jesus' awesome power. The contrast of v.15 with vv.3-5 is typical of exorcism stories, the contrast between the violence and destructiveness of the demon towards the human he possesses and the tranquility of the liberated person and his communion with Jesus. The concluding verses 18-20 are theologically eloquent for Mark. The man begs "that he might be with" Jesus, that is, that he might be a disciple. Jesus' refusal of the man's generous offer made in thankfulness is by no means ungracious, nor, indeed, is it really a refusal. He will not take the man with him in his immediate circle of disciples because he has a special mission for him: he is to be the first missionary to the gentiles. And that is why, though the man is asked to tell what God had done for him (v.19), what he in fact does is to "proclaim" (cf. 1:14; 3:14) the work of Jesus. The idea of the christian message to the gentiles is close to the surface.

YOUR FAITH HAS SAVED YOU.
THE DAUGHTER OF JAIRUS AND THE WOMAN
WITH AN ISSUE OF BLOOD.
5:21-43 (Lk 8:40-56; Mt 9:18-26).

The dovetailing of one story with another is a feature of Mark's style; it is his "sandwich" technique (e.g. 3:19b-21, [22-30], 31-35; 11:12-14, [15-19], 20-25). However, nowhere else does an insertion so clearly separate two parts of a single story as it does here. We must note that this interpolation procedure in Mark implies that the narratives should be interpreted in relation to each other; this is evident, for instance, in 3:19-35 and 11:12-25. Here, too, the stories are interwoven. The closing words of the first part of the daughter of Jairus story (v.24) prepare the way for the story of the woman, and the words, "while he was still speaking" (v.35), form a neat link with the second part of the main story.

²¹And when Jesus had crossed again in the boat to the other side, a great crowd gathered about him; and he was beside the sea. ²²Then came one of the rulers of the synagogue, Jairus by name; and seeing him, he fell at his feet, ²³and besought him, saying, "My little daughter is at the point of death. Come and lay your hands on her, so that she may be made well, and live." ²⁴And he went with him.

And a great crowd followed him and thronged about him. ²⁵And there was a woman who had had a flow of blood for twelve years, ²⁶and who had suffered much under many physicians, and has spent all that she had, and was no better but rather grew worse. ²⁷She had heard the reports about Jesus, and came up behind him in the crowd and touched his garment. ²⁸For she said, "If I touch even his garments, I shall be made well." ²⁹And immediately the hemorrhage ceased; and she felt in her body that she was healed of her disease. ³⁰And Jesus, perceiving in himself that power had gone forth from him, immediately turned about in the crowd, and said, "Who touched my garments?" ³¹And his disciples said to him, "You see the crowd pressing around you, and yet you say, 'Who touched me?'" ³²And he looked around to see who had done it. ³³But the woman, knowing what had been done to her, came in fear and trembling and fell down before him, and told him the whole truth. ³⁴And he said to her; "Daughter, your faith has made you well; go in peace, and be healed of your disease."

³⁵While he was still speaking, there came from the ruler's house some who said, "Your daughter is dead. Why trouble the Teacher any further?" ³⁶But ignoring what they said, Jesus said to the ruler of the synagogue, "Do not fear, only believe." ³⁷And he allowed no one to follow him except Peter and James and John the brother of James. ³⁸When they came to the house of the ruler of the synagogue, he saw a tumult, and people weeping

and wailing loudly. ³⁹And when he had entered, he said to them, "Why do you make a tumult and weep? The child is not dead but sleeping." ⁴⁰And they laughed at him. But he put them all outside, and took the child's father and mother and those who were with him, and went in where the child was. ⁴¹Taking her by the hand he said to her, "Talitha cumi"; which means, "Little girl, I say to you, arise." ⁴²And immediately the girl got up and walked; for she was twelve years old. And immediately they were overcome with amazement. ⁴³And he strictly charged them that no one should know this, and told them to give her something to eat.

Mark sets the scene simply on the western shore of the lake after Jesus had crossed from "the country of the Gerasenes" (v.21). A great crowd by the lakeside is typical (cf. 3:8-9; 4:1). The suppliant, Jairus, was an *archisynagogos,* the director of synagogue worship (v.22). Personal dignity forgotten, in his sorrow and concern he falls at the feet of Jesus (cf. 7:25). The little girl is at the point of death, already beyond any earthly help. In these narratives the raising of the dead girl and the cure of the woman are accomplished by physical contact with Jesus; here the father requests Jesus to impose his hands on the little girl. "That she may be made well *(sōzō)* and live *(zaō).*" At the catechetical level of the story the words mean: "that she may be saved and have (eternal) life." Jesus set out at once with Jairus. Mention of the thronging crowd prepares the way for the story of the woman.

The unfortunate woman (vv.25-26) not only had to bear her infirmity for twelve years but had suffered much at the hands of different doctors. She had heard "the reports about Jesus" *(ta peri tou Iēsou),* that is, the report of his powers of healing (vv.27-28). However, the phrase frequently refers to the post-Easter proclamation of Christ (cf. Lk 24:19,27; Acts 18:25; 23:11; 28:31) and would have been so understood by christian readers. The woman acted as unobtrusively as she could because her malady rendered her ceremonially unclean (cf. Lev 15:25). She shares the belief that the mere touching of his garments will achieve her cure (cf. 3:10; 6:56); here it is three times asserted that this physical contact was efficacious (vv.27,28,30. Cf. Acts 19:11-12; 5:15). The woman's faith is evident, but it is still imperfect. She believes that Jesus possessed a supernatural power of healing which somehow resided in him and could flow from him without his being aware of it. The rest of the story will show that he is conscious of and in control of the power he wields.

The hemorrhage ceased at once and the woman is aware of the cure. Jesus, too, knows that healing power has gone forth from him. (Cf. a similar conception in Lk 5:17—"and the power of the Lord was with him to heal.") The remark of the disciples (v.31) shows their familiarity with Jesus; curt, and not at all respectful, it is softened by Luke and omitted by Matthew. For Mark, however, the reaction of the disciples to Jesus' activity is important. He has drawn our attention to it by his bracket: "she was healed of her disease," "be healed of your disease" (vv.29,34). It is an instance of their lack of sensitivity to him and to what he achieves. The woman understands that Jesus' question refers to what had happened to her. When she now fully realizes that she has indeed been cured, she comes forward "in fear and trembling"—a religious sentiment (cf. 1 Cor 2:3; 2 Cor 7:15; Eph 6:5; Phil 2:12). Jesus reassures the woman; he addresses her affectionately as "daughter" and he attributes the cure to her faith (cf. 10:52). Her believing confidence had enabled her to take the risk involved in reaching out towards Jesus and ultimately establishing a bond with him. She is no longer fearful but can go her way in peace. "Your faith has made you well"—this can just as readily be rendered, with christian overtones: "your faith has brought you salvation."

"While he was still speaking there came. . ."; the transition is adroit (v.35). The messengers not only inform Jairus of the death of his daughter but observe that there is no point in taking Jesus any further on a fruitless journey.

We get the impression that they were not very enthusiastic about Jairus' action in the first place. They had no expectation that Jesus could raise the dead. Jairus, who had faith in Jesus when his daughter was at the point of death (v.23), is now bidden to have faith in Jesus' power to raise the dead. Jesus takes with him only the inner circle of the twelve, the three intimate disciples who will be with him also at the transfiguration (9:2), in Gethsemane (14:33) and on the Mount of Olives (13:3). Their presence here tells us that, for the evangelist, the raising of the dead girl was, in some sense, an epiphany of Jesus, a glimpse of his true nature.

The "tumult" (v.39) with loud wailing may point to the presence of professional mourners. "The child is not dead but sleeping"—the statement is enigmatic. While "sleep" *(katheudien)* means "death" in such texts as Dan 12:2, 1 Thess 5:10, and Eph 5:14, the verb "to sleep" is here placed in contrast with "to be dead." It is certain that the evangelist viewed the incident as a raising from the dead. What Jesus declares is that death is not the end of everything but only a "sleep" from which one is awakened at the resurrection. In this sense, "to sleep" *(koimasthai)* was, among Christians, a euphemism for death (e.g. Mt 27:52; 1 Cor 11:30; 15:16; 1 Thess 4:13-15). The scornful laughter of those present (v.40) reflects their certainty that the child was indeed dead. "He put them all outside": a contrast between "those outside" and "those with him" (cf. 4:11). Mark frequently retains an Aramaic word or phrase (cf. 3:17; 7:11,34; 11:9-10; 14:26; 15:22,24) as he does here with the phrase: *Talitha cumi.* Apart from 11:9-10 (Hosanna) he always translates these terms for the benefit of his readers. "Arise"—the verb *egeirein* is used of the resurrection of Jesus in 14:28 and 16:6. The girl "got up": she arose. Here the verb is *anistēmi,* also used of the resurrection of Jesus (8:31; 9:9,31; 10:34). The expression of amazement is unusually strong (cf. 2:12); the eyewitnesses are convinced that they have seen something wholly exceptional and unexpected. In the circumstances of the miracle which cannot be kept from the crowds, there is something forced about the command to preserve secrecy (v.43): the works of Jesus cannot remain hidden. The instruction to give food to the girl is a lifelike touch which witnesses to the sympathetic compassion of Jesus as well as to his sense of the sober realities of the situation.

The themes of salvation and faith are the major themes of this two-faceted story. Jairus is persuaded that at Jesus' touch his daughter will be "made well" (v.23) and the woman is convinced that if she touches Jesus' garments she will be "made well" (v.28). Each time the Greek verb used is *sōzō* which also means "to save." More pointedly, in v.34, Jesus reassures the woman, telling her, "Your faith has made you well"—has "saved" you. Mark has in mind more than bodily healing. Salvation stands in close relation to faith. Jesus exhorts the father of the dead girl, "Do not fear, only believe" (v.36). Furthermore, the evangelist lets it be understood that the narrative of the daughter of Jairus has to do with resurrection. The verbs "to arise" and "to raise up," we have seen, are used to describe the resurrection of Jesus. The christian reader could not fail to grasp the overtones of terms that had already found their way into the vocabulary of the Christian. A confirmation of the theological significance of the raising is the presence of the three privileged witnesses, Peter, James, and John. Jesus raises the dead girl to life because he is "the resurrection and the life" (Jn 11:25). For Mark and his readers Jesus is the Son of God already mediating the power of his resurrection; he is the Lord, the source of saving power (v.30). And the narrative is a lesson of salvation by faith.

Faith comes to fulfillment only in personal encounter with Jesus, only when one enters into dialogue with him. Jairus believed that Jesus had power to heal one at the point of death, when all earthly means had failed. But Jesus looked for a deeper faith: faith in him as one who could raise from the dead, a faith that must find expression in the midst of unbelief. The woman, too, had faith in the power of Jesus. She, too, is asked to have a deeper, fuller faith in him; she meets his gaze and comes to kneel at his feet. And through faith in Jesus she and the little girl are *saved*. The lesson cannot be missed. The Christian is asked to recognize that faith in Jesus can transform life and is a victory over death. But this faith is not something vague or impersonal. One must come to him, seek him out. One must kneel at his feet, not abjectly, but in the intensity of one's pleading (v.22) or in humble thankfulness (v.33). This Jesus will give to him who believes that peace the world cannot give (v.34). He will assure him of life beyond death (v.41).

A PROPHET HAS NO HONOR IN HIS OWN COUNTRY. 6:1-6a (Mt 13:53-58; cf. Lk 4:16-30).

This episode has deep meaning for the evangelist and he has placed it carefully at this point in his gospel. A poignant situation in the early days of the church was, as we have observed, the fact that while the gentiles, by and large, were accepting the Good News, the Jewish people rejected it (cf. Rom 9-11). Already, in Mark, the bitter opposition of the authorities has been demonstrated (2:1-3:6), and we have seen that Jesus was misunderstood by his family (3:20-35). Now, at the close of the Galilean ministry, his own townspeople are challenged to make up their minds about his claim, and they take offence at him. Their rejection of him is an anticipation of his rejection by the Jewish nation (15:11-15). That final rejection of him is possible because the blindness of men to God's revelation had been present from the start (cf. Jn 1:10-11).

> **6** He went away from there and came to his own country; and his disciples followed him. ²And on the sabbath he began to teach in the synagogue; and many who heard him were astonished, saying, "Where did this man get all this? What is the wisdom given to him? What mighty works are wrought by his hands! ³Is not

this the carpenter, the son of Mary and brother of James
and Joses and Judas and Simon, and are not his sisters
here with us?" And they took offense at him. ⁴And Jesus
said to them, "A prophet is not without honor, except
in his own country, and among his own kin, and in his
own house." ⁵And he could do no mighty work there,
except that he laid his hands upon a few sick people
and healed them. ⁶And he marveled because of their
unbelief.

"To his own country," literally, "his native town"
(v.1). This is Nazareth, cf. Lk 4:23-24. Mark (1:9,24) and
John (1:46) imply that Jesus was known as a Nazarene.
"His disciples followed him": not a private but a formal
visit to his home town. We find Mark's typical emphasis
on the teaching of Jesus (the sabbath offers him an
occasion) and on the astonishment of his hearers (cf. 1:22).
"Many": not all were impressed and the undercurrent of
dissatisfaction eventually prevailed (v.3). The hearers
wonder at the origin ("where") of his teaching and the
nature ("what") of his wisdom. They had heard of his
mighty works (such as those of 4:35-5:43). They are on
the verge of asking the right question about him. But they
cannot bring themselves to believe in the greatness or
in the mission of a man who is one of themselves.

In v.3 there is a brusque change as admiring astonishment yields to frank hostility. "The carpenter," the Greek
word *tektōn* stands for a worker in stone, wood, or metal.
"The son of Mary": the designation occurs nowhere else
in the New Testament. It was contrary to Jewish custom
to refer to a man by his mother's name; it might mean that
Mary was known to be a widow. Matthew (13:15) has "the
son of the carpenter" and the same reading is found in
important manuscripts of Mark's Gospel. However, the
reading, "the carpenter, the son of Mary," is more likely
to be the right one. "Brothers" and "sisters" of Jesus are
mentioned in v.3. There are three main views as to what
the text means: (1) that they were full blood brothers and

sisters of Jesus (Helvidius); (2) that they were children of Joseph by a former wife (Epiphanius); (3) that they were cousins of Jesus (Jerome). For all who accept the perpetual virginity of Mary the first view is obviously excluded; and the second has very much the air of an *ad hoc* solution. In favor of the third position is the fact that the term "brother" regularly has a broader meaning in the Old Testament. And the interpretation is supported by the fact that two of the "brothers" mentioned here, James and Joses, are elsewhere (15:40) said to be sons of another Mary. Thus, though one's interpretation (these are cousins of Jesus) is prompted by factors outside of Mark, his text can bear that interpretation. The names of the four brothers are given only here and in Mt 13:55. None of them was among the twelve, though they shared names with some of the twelve.

"They took offence": the offence was that Jesus was one of themselves. We might note, too, the Jewish belief that the Messiah, before entering upon his office, would be hidden (cf. Jn 7:27). Also, by Mark's time, *skandalon* had practically become a technical term to describe the obstacle which some found in Christ and which prevented them from going on to full christian faith and discipleship (cf. Rom 9:32-33; 1 Pet 2:8; 1 Cor 1:23). The proverb of v.4 is found also in Mt 13:57; Lk 4:24; Jn 4:44 and, in one form or another, was current in the ancient world. Jesus implicitly assumes the role of the prophet. "He could do no mighty works there"—Luke has omitted the statement and Matthew has softened it. Jesus always demanded faith in himself before he worked a miracle: because a miracle is a sign of the kingdom and without faith would lack significance. Want of faith in Nazareth means that an opportunity of doing a mighty work was not there. But not all had rejected him: "a few" had the needful disposition.

The people of Nazareth were impressed by Jesus' wisdom and did not deny the reality of his mighty works. In their own way they ask the right question, "Who, then, is this?"

(cf. 6:2; 4:41). But they do not press on to faith in him. Instead they take offence at him; his humble origin conflicts with their expectation of a glorious Messiah. Perhaps their attitude is not so surprising after all: such treatment of him was of a piece with the general treatment of prophets. Because of his townspeople's lack of faith he can do no mighty work for them, just as he could not ultimately do what he longed to do for his whole people (cf. Lk 13:34; 19:42). Mark's message seems to be that if Christians were understandably troubled by Israel's lack of faith, they must remember that their Master, too, had marveled at this unbelief.

C. DISCIPLESHIP AND MISSION. 6:6b-8:30.

THIS SECTION does have some sort of unity, but one cannot provide it with a neat title that is wholly apt. One might say that Jesus, rejected by his own townspeople, now devotes himself to his disciples, so the title might be: Jesus and His Disciples. This is true, after a fashion. The section begins with the mission of the twelve and closes with the confession of Peter at Caesarea Philippi, and the disciples figure prominently throughout. But, apart from the opening and closing episodes, the emphasis is on their lack of understanding, which becomes more and more pronounced. And the evangelist does show considerable interest in the gentile mission which must, therefore, be regarded as a major theme. At any rate, this unit, like the previous two, begins with a summary statement of the activity (teaching) of Jesus (6:6b) and concludes with the adoption of an attitude towards him (8:27-29).

THE MISSION OF THE TWELVE AND THE DEATH OF THE BAPTIST.
6:6b-31 (Lk 9:1-10; Mt 9:35; 10:1-14; 14:1-12).

6b And he went about among the villages teaching.

7And he called to him the twelve, and began to send them out two by two, and gave them authority over the unclean spirits. ⁸He charged them to take nothing for their journey except a staff; no bread, no bag, no money in their belts; ⁹but to wear sandals and not put on two tunics. ¹⁰And he said to them, "Where you enter a house, stay there until you leave the place. ¹¹And if any place will not receive you and they refuse to hear you, when you leave, shake off the dust that is on your feet for a testimony against them." ¹²So they went out and preached that men should repent. ¹³And they cast out many demons, and anointed with oil many that were sick and healed them.

¹⁴King Herod heard of it; for Jesus' name had become known. Some said, "John the baptizer has been raised from the dead; that is why these powers are at work in him." ¹⁵But others said, "It is Elijah." And others said, "It is a prophet, like one of the prophets of old." ¹⁶But when Herod heard of it he said, "John, whom I beheaded, has been raised." ¹⁷For Herod had sent and seized John, and bound him in prison for the sake of Herodias, his brother Philip's wife; because he had married her. ¹⁸For John said to Herod, "It is not lawful for you to have your brother's wife." ¹⁹And Herodias had a grudge against him, and wanted to kill him. But she could not, ²⁰for Herod feared John, knowing that he was a righteous and holy man, and kept him safe. When he heard him, he was much perplexed; and yet he heard him gladly. ²¹But an opportunity came when Herod on his birthday gave a banquet for his courtiers and officers and the leading men of Galilee. ²²For when Herodias' daughter came in and danced, she pleased Herod and his guests; and the king said to the girl, "Ask me for whatever you wish, and I will grant it." ²³And he vowed to her, "Whatever you ask me, I will give you, even half of my kingdom." ²⁴And she went out, and said to her mother, "What shall I ask?" And she said, "The head of John the baptizer." ²⁵And she came in immediately with haste to the king, and asked, saying, "I want you to give me at once the head of John the

Baptist on a platter." [26]And the king was exceedingly sorry; but because of his oaths and his guests he did not want to break his word to her. [27]And immediately the king sent a soldier of the guard and gave orders to bring his head. He went and beheaded him in the prison, [28]and brought his head on a platter, and gave it to the girl; and the girl gave it to her mother. [29]When his disciples heard of it, they came and took his body, and laid it in a tomb.

[30]The apostles returned to Jesus, and told him all that they had done and taught. [31]And he said to them, "Come away by yourselves to a lonely place, and rest a while." For many were coming and going, and they had no leisure even to eat.

Jesus has been rejected by his own people. Now he turns his attention to the twelve. He had chosen them "to be with him" (3:14) and so he had concentrated on instructing them. But he had chosen them, too, "to be sent out to preach"; the time has come for them to take an active part in the ministry. Mark evidently meant the incident (6:6b-13, 30-31), though preparatory and provisional, to be seen as the basis of christian missionary activity. Yet, the passage stands almost in isolation and we learn nothing of the extent or effect of this mission. He carefully avoids the statement, present in Matthew and Luke, that the disciples proclaimed the kingdom of God for, in Mark's perspective, the disciples have not yet understood the true nature of the kingdom. Like the Baptist, (1:4) they preached "that men should repent."

The brief editorial summary (v.6b) is transitional; Jesus makes another circuit of the villages of Galilee (cf. 1:38-39; 5:14; 6:56). The sending out of the disciples "two by two" follows Jewish practice; cf. Lk 10:1. They are to take nothing with them for the journey, no food, no bag to carry provisions, no money to buy food, no change of clothes. During their visit to a village they will remain in the house where they first found hospitality and not move to more congenial quarters. If they are not received they will give solemn warning. "Shake off the dust that is on your feet." This is a symbolic action indicating that the place is as good as heathen. Jews shook off heathen dust on re-entering Palestine. "For a testimony against them," that is, as a warning to them: the gesture is intended to make them think again and lead them to repentance.

In a summarizing passage (vv.12-13) Mark's reference to a preaching of repentance is deliberate: in his plan the preaching of the imminence of the kingdom is reserved to Jesus; the disciples, like the Baptist, prepare for Jesus' proclamation. Besides, Mark may wish to distinguish their "preaching" from the full christian gospel which can be proclaimed only after the Easter event. They also shared in the exorcising and healing work of Jesus. Oil was used in medical treatment (cf. Lk 10:34), hence its symbolical value in miraculous healing. James (5:14-15) shows that healing by anointing was known in the early Church. The practice attested here may well be at the origin of the later practice, and eventually of the sacrament of the anointing of the sick.

HEROD AND THE BAPTIST—THE SHADOW OF THE CROSS. 6:14-29 (Lk 9:7-9; Mt 14:1-12).

Between the sending of the twelve (vv.6b-13) and their return (vv.30-31) Mark has, in customary fashion, inserted another episode: the death of the Baptist. The shadow of the cross falls starkly across the gospel because the death of the precursor is a presage of Jesus' fate. We are also to understand that just as this initial apostolic mission coincides with the death of the forerunner, so the death of Jesus himself will give birth to the christian mission.

a) Herod. 6:14-16 (Lk 9:7-9; Mt 14:1-2).

"Herod" is Herod Antipas, son of Herod the Great and Malthake. He was tetrarch (likely, popularly called "king")

of Galilee and Perea from 4 B.C to 39 A.D. He had
heard a report of the disciples' activity throughout Galilee
(v.13), which had given a boost to the renown of Jesus
(v.14). There were various opinions as to who Jesus himself
might be: John the Baptist *redivivus,* Elijah, a prophet.
Though John, in his lifetime, was not accredited with
miracles, popular estimation would readily accept the
evidence of miraculous powers in a Baptist risen from the
dead. The expectation of a return of Elijah (based on Mal
3:1; 4:5) was widespread in Palestine at the time of Jesus
(cf. Mk 1:2; 9:9-13). In the gospels it is generally the Baptist
and not Jesus who is regarded as an Elijah-figure. Others
felt that Jesus was a figure like one of the Old Testament
prophets. (Contrast Luke (9:8): others said "that one of
the old prophets had risen.") Later, in Mk 8:28, these
popular opinions are again listed. Herod is said to have
shared the naive view which identified Jesus with John; his
opinion is highlighted by the repeated "Herod heard of
it" (vv.14,16). Luke's version is more in keeping with the
character of "that fox" (Lk 13:32): "John I beheaded,"
that is to say, that accounts for him (Lk 9:9). Mark's interest
is to present the execution of the Baptist as a foreshadowing
of the death of Jesus. Herod's concern at the prominence
of Jesus is entirely credible. He had just got rid of one
potential source of trouble, now another and even more
dangerous "trouble-maker" has emerged.

b) The Death of the Baptist. 6:17-29 (Mt 14:3-12; cf. Lk
   3:19-20).

The story of the Baptist's execution is the only narrative
in Mark which is not directly a story about Jesus. And yet
it, too, is concerned with him, for it aims to present John
as the precursor whose death prefigured the death of Jesus
(cf. 9:11-13). The story has been colored by reminiscences
of Old Testament precedents. One can think of Jezebel,
who sought Elijah's death (1 Kgs 19:2), for the Baptist,
we have noted, was seen as an Elijah figure. Then, the
influence of the book of Esther is undoubted. This is rather

surprising because the characters do not correspond: the wicked Haman and John, the virtuous Esther and Salome have nothing in common. It may well be that in this popular and vivid tale of the Baptist's death reminiscences of Jezebel and Esther are involuntary rather than studied.

The credibility of the Marcan story has been challenged on the grounds that it conflicts with Josephus' testimony. According to Josephus, John was imprisoned in the fortress of Machaerus on the east of the Dead Sea and was put to death there. Mark gives the impression that the scene of the banquet (and so of death of John) was Herod's Galilean capital of Tiberias. Josephus alleges a political motive for John's imprisonment and execution: his fear of a messianic movement sparked off by the Baptist's preaching. For Mark, the motivation is John's denunciation of Herod's marriage, which aroused the implacable hatred of Herodias. It is noteworthy that the differences between Mark and Josephus center on the theme of the banquet and the role of Herodias and so stem mostly from the parallelism of the Marcan story with the stories of Jezebel and Esther. And there is the matter of an Herodian princess dancing like a slave-girl. The explanation seems to be that Mark has woven colorful and legendary details into his broadly historical narrative of the fate of John the Baptist.

"In prison" (v.17)—there is no indication of place in Mark. From Josephus (*Antiquities* XVIII. 5.2) we learn that it was the fortress of Machaerus, east of the Dead Sea, in the extreme south of Herod's territory of Peraea. Herodias was the daughter of Aristobulus, son of Herod the Great, and so was Antipas' niece, and she had been the wife of his half-brother, Herod. Antipas had married a daughter of the Nabatean king Aretas IV but had divorced her in favor of Herodias. In Mark (v.17) Herodias appears as the wife of "Philip." This is a readily understandable mistake. Philip the tetrarch (Lk 3:1) later married Salome, daughter of Herodias. The confusion here is between Herodias' husband (Herod) and son-in-law (Philip). The situation was undoubtedly sufficiently murky to merit the attention of the prophet. And Josephus informs us that the prime cause of scandal among the people was the open adultery of Antipas and Herodias before their divorce and marriage. In the account of the death of John, v.17 especially is an analogue of the fate of Jesus. John is arrested (seized) as Jesus was arrested in Gethsemane (14:46); he was bound, like Jesus (15:1). And, in v.19, it had been already decided to kill the Baptist (cf. 3:6).

The imprisonment of John was not enough for Herodias; like Jezebel who engineered the death of Naboth (1 Kgs 21), she plotted his death. Herod "feared," "stood in awe of," John—just as the disciples (4:41; 9:32; 10:32), the people (5:15), and the healed woman (5:33) stood in awe of Jesus. "A righteous and holy man"—in Acts 3:16 Jesus is "the holy and righteous one." There is a deliberate intent to compare John and Jesus. Antipas' attitude to John is remarkably like that of Ahab to Elijah (1 Kgs 21:17-29); it is Jezebel, not Ahab, who plots Elijah's death (1 Kgs 19:1-2). Antipas seized the opportunity of meeting his prisoner and heard him with mixed feelings. He "heard him gladly"; cf. 12:37, the same reaction of the crowd to Jesus.

Herodias bided her time and her chance came on Herod's birthday. Antipas' banquet is like that of Ahasuerus (Xerxes), who "gave a banquet for all his princes and servants" (Est 1:3). Herodias' daughter is Salome. She "came in," so doing what queen Vashti refused to do (Est 1:12). "She pleased Herod"—cf. Est 2:9: "And the maiden Esther pleased him." The king's offer is a familiar feature of such stories. Cf. Est 5:3: "And the king said to her, What is it, Queen Esther? What is your request? It shall be given to you, even to the half of my kingdom." The delighted girl seeks her mother's advice and Herodias grasps her chance without hesitation. Conscious of the fact that he is, for the moment, in her power, the girl speaks impertinently to the king. Though the gruesome detail of the head being presented to her "on a platter" is obviously meant to be her own contribution, one can, with a smile, appreciate the reluctance of the Victorian, H.D. Swete, to accept it as such: "This piece of grim irony was due, it may be hoped, to the older woman."

The sorrow of Antipas is in keeping with his attitude to the Baptist (v.20). He finds himself trapped. The execution was carried out on the spot. "He went and beheaded him"; compare the terse reference to Jesus' execution, "and they crucified him" (15:24)—in each case the grim event is described as starkly as possible. The Baptist's disciples (cf. 2:18) see to his burial. "His body," literally "corpse" (*ptoma*)—in 15:45 the same word is used of the body of Jesus. But there the resemblance ends. The disciples of Jesus had fled (14:50); another had buried his body (15:43-46). The passion of the precursor ends in death, that of the Messiah in resurrection.

THE RETURN OF THE TWELVE.
6:30-31 (Lk 9:10; Mt 14:13a).

In a short passage, which clearly displays his style, Mark rounds off his account of the mission of the twelve. The narrative is, at the same time, a prelude to the next scene and, indeed, to the following section. Emphasis has shifted to the instruction of the disciples and Jesus' desire to be alone with them. This desire prepares for the retirement to a "desert place" where the miracle of the loaves can take place. Here only in Mark are the twelve called "apostles." It might seem that the missionary journey had achieved their advancement from discipleship to apostleship. But they will be fully apostles only when they are sent out by the risen Lord. After their missionary labors the twelve needed to rest. More significant is the fact that Jesus wants them to be "by themselves." This Greek expression (*kat idian*) occurs seven times in Mark (4:34; 6:31,32; 7:33; 9:2,28; 13:3) always in a redactional passage, and is each time used in reference to a revelation or an instruction reserved for the disciples.

THE ARRANGEMENT OF 6:32 - 8:26.

Any endeavor to understand Mark must take seriously his arrangement of his material. We must note, then, that the episodes of 6:32 - 8:26 are ordered in two parallel series of events.

Feeding of the 5,000 (6:35-44)	Feeding of the 4,000 (8:1-9)
Crossing of the Lake (6:45-52)	Crossing of the Lake (8:10)
Controversy with Pharisees (7:1-23)	Controversy with Pharisees (8:11-13)
The Children's Bread (7:24-30)	The One Loaf (8:14-21)
Healing of a Deaf Mute (7:31-37)	Healing of a Blind Man (8:22-26)

The first multiplication of loaves takes place in Galilee and its beneficiaries are Jews. Moreover, the number twelve (6:43) evokes the twelve tribes of Israel, the chosen people. But the second feeding takes place, according to Mark, in Decapolis (cf. 7:31), that is, in largely pagan territory. One may assume that, this time, those who benefit from the miracle are gentiles. Following on the Jews, the gentiles too are called to share in the feeding, a prefiguration of the eucharistic meal and of the messianic banquet.

The episodes inserted between the two feeding miracles are, in varying degrees, meant to prepare for the call of the gentile to salvation. The two complementary episodes, on the tradition of the elders and on defilement, aim at showing that the "purity" of a man does not lie in the observance of external rites but in righteousness of the "heart." In this sense, a gentile is as "clean" as a Jew if he obeys the demands of his conscience, and nothing prevents him from participating in the eucharistic meal once he has seen in Jesus the one who gives life to the world.

This principle is illustrated in the healing of the daughter of the Syro-Phoenician woman, a gentile. At first, it is true, Jesus seems to refuse to work a miracle on behalf of a gentile. He declares: "Let the children first be fed" (7:27) that is, the children of Israel. The verb "be fed" recalls the story of the loaves (6:42; 8:8). But, in declaring that she will be content with the "crumbs" from the meal (7:28), the woman finally wins healing for her daughter. The lesson is clear. If Jesus himself has received gentiles to salvation how could his disciples refuse to admit them? He himself had expelled the "unclean spirit" which possessed the daughter of a gentile woman (7:29). Mark then adds the story of the healing of a deaf-mute. A native of Decapolis (7:31) that man (in Mark's eyes at least) is a gentile too. His cure could have symbolic intent: the gentiles, once deaf and dumb toward God, are now made capable of hearing God and of rendering him homage. And so they can participate in the eucharistic meal. The second multiplication of loaves is a sign for gentiles.

THE FEEDING OF THE FIVE THOUSAND.
6:32-44 (Lk 9:10-17; Mt 14:13-21; cf. Jn 6:1-15).

All four gospels carry the story of the multiplication of loaves; Mark (6:32-44; 8:1-10) and Matthew (14:13-21; 15:29-38) have two accounts of a miraculous feeding. There are several arguments for regarding these two accounts in Matthew and Mark as variant forms of the same incident. And it seems best to take it that the fourth evangelist (Jn 6:1-15) drew on an independent tradition quite like that of Mark's and Matthew's second account.

In the teaching tradition of the christian community the relevance of the multiplication of loaves to the eucharist, the bread of God's people, was quickly recognized. We find close parallels in gesture and wording between both synoptic accounts and the narratives of the Last Supper. John's account, too, shows some adaptation. And, of course, in his plan, the multiplication of loaves is the starting point of his Bread of Life discourses, notably the explicitly eucharistic discourse of 6:51-58. It is evident then, that the story of the feeding was treasured in the early communities not only because it related a mighty work of Jesus, but also because of its symbolic relation to the eucharist.

In 6:32-44 Mark leaves aside any expression of wonder or amazement on the part of those present (cf. Jn 6:14) because he does not choose to stress the aspect of "wonder." His point is the blindness of men, how blind they can be to God's relevation, even in the light of Jesus' most striking miracles; and he is particularly concerned at the blindness of the disciples (cf. 8:17-21). Mark brings out his intent by means of biblical allusions. The miracles take place in a "desert place," thus evoking the Exodus and the manna, the bread from heaven. Jesus is the good shepherd of Ezekiel 34 who feeds his sheep. As Elisha had fed a group of one hundred men with twenty barley loaves (2 Kgs 4:42-44), so Jesus feeds the multitude; but he far surpasses the feat of Elisha, for he starts with only five loaves (and two fish) and feeds five thousand. He pronounces a blessing over the bread and has it distributed to all present: he is host at a meal, host at an anticipated Messianic Banquet. Furthermore, he takes . . . blesses . . . breaks . . . gives as at the Last Supper: he anticipates the eucharistic meal. The twelve are associated with him in this symbolic eucharistic celebration. This first multiplication of loaves takes place in Galilee and involves only Jews: it is a sign to the chosen people.

> [32]And they went away in the boat to a lonely place by themselves. [33]Now many saw them going, and knew them, and they ran there on foot from all the towns, and got there ahead of them. [34]As he landed he saw a great throng, and he had compassion on them, because they were like sheep without a shepherd; and he began to teach them many things. [35]And when it grew late, his disciples came to him and said, "This is a lonely place, and the hour is now late; [36]send them away, to go into the country and villages round about and buy themselves

something to eat." 37But he answered them, "You give them something to eat." And they said to him, "Shall we go and buy two hundred denarii worth of bread, and give it to them to eat? 38And he said to them, "How many loaves have you? Go and see." And when they had found out, they said, "Five, and two fish." 39Then he commanded them all to sit down by companies upon the green grass. 40So they sat down in groups, by hundreds and by fifties. 41And taking the five loaves and the two fish he looked up to heaven, and blessed, and broke the loaves, and gave them to the disciples to set before the people; and he divided the two fish among them all. 42And they all ate and were satisfied. 43And they took up twelve baskets full of broken pieces and of the fish. 44And those who ate the loaves were five thousand men.

The details of 6:33 are quite vague and the destination is unknown. For the evangelist the important factor is that the disciples reach a "desert" place and that they are by themselves (*kat' idian*). Jesus' attempt to seek solitude for himself is frustrated, but he is not annoyed. Instead, he is deeply moved by the earnestness of the crowd and by their need. The image of a shepherdless people is found in Num 27:17; 1 Kgs 22:17. Jesus sees himself in their regard as the messianic shepherd (Ezek 34; Jn 10:1-18) who will feed his sheep (Ezek 34:13-14; Jn 10:9). The motif of the sheep without a shepherd foreshadows the moment when the shepherd will be stricken and his sheep scattered (14:27). The people's most pressing hunger was spiritual and he began to teach them. It is interesting that in John's first discourse on the bread of life (Jn 6:35-50) the "bread" is Jesus' teaching, his revelation.

The significance of the *desert* place begins to emerge (vv. 35-36): as a setting for the gift of miraculous bread (vv.41,44) it recalls the manna (Ex 16:12-35). By question and answer (v.37) Mark surely intends to bring out the disciples' lack of understanding. The desert setting and the good shepherd theme ought (in Mark's eyes) to have inspired them with trust in Jesus' power. Their reply (toned down in Matthew and Luke) is sarcastic: "Fine . . . but where are we going to get the money!"—a reaction like that of Moses (cf. Num 11:13, 21-22). The disciples had some provisions, presumably in the boat. The loaves were likely of barley (cf. Jn 6:9) and the fish cured. There is a striking parallel in 2 Kgs 4:42-44. Elisha had been brought twenty barley loaves. He proposed to feed a hundred men and his servant objected that the available bread was inadequate. Elisha is confident that the Lord will take care.

In vv.41-42 the motif of the messianic feast is sustained: Jesus acts as a host. It was customary for a Jewish host, at the start of a meal, to pronounce a blessing over the bread and then to break it and distribute it to his guests. If the number was large, others would help in the distribution. The disciples do play an active role; Jesus has shown them how to be shepherds. "Took . . . blessed . . . broke . . . gave" is consciously eucharistic terminology; the agreement with 14:22 is unmistakable. This explains, too, the rather awkward reference to the fish in v.41: because of the eucharistic significance the emphasis is on the loaves; the distribution of the fish has to be relegated to a parenthesis. "He looked up to heaven"—the origin of the words in the Roman Canon: "and looking up to heaven." In 2 Kgs 4:44 we read, "And they ate, and had some left, according to the word of the Lord." Here (v.43) more is left over at the end than was there at the beginning—a greater than Elisha is here. "Twelve baskets"—the number twelve evokes the number of the tribes of Israel. The story ends without any of the expressions of wonder customary at the close of a miracle story. Mark regards the incident as a messianic sign bearing on the mystery of Jesus' person (cf. 8:19).

THE WALKING ON THE SEA.
6:45-52 (Mt 14:22-33; Jn 6:16-21).

> [45]Immediately he made his disciples get into the boat and go before him to the other side, to Bethsaida, while

he dismissed the crowd. [46]And after he had taken leave of them, he went into the hills to pray. [47]And when evening came, the boat was out on the sea, and he was alone on the land. [48]And he saw that they were distressed in rowing, for the wind was against them. And about the fourth watch of the night he came to them, walking on the sea. He meant to pass by them, [49]but when they saw him walking on the sea they though it was a ghost, and cried out; [50]for they all saw him, and were terrified. But immediately he spoke to them and said, "Take heart, it is I; have no fear." [51]And he got into the boat with them and the wind ceased. And they were utterly astounded, [52]for they did not understand about the loaves, but their hearts were hardened.

The incident of the walking on the waters is closely connected with the feeding of the five thousand in the synoptics (Mk/Mt) and in John. "He made his disciples get into the boat" (v.45)—there is a sense of urgency and constraint. Jesus forces his disciples to cross the lake. He had prepared them for a gentile mission; now he expects them to lead the way. But, as it turns out, they fail, because they had not grasped the significance of that former journey (4:35-41). That Mark does mean to imply a journey to the east side of the lake is clear from the phrases "the other side" (v,45) and "when they had crossed over" (v.53). This is so despite reference to Bethsaida, (to the east of the Jordan mouth), and Gennesareth, (to the west, near Capernaum). "He went into the hills to pray" just as in 1:35 and 14:35,39. On both these occasions, as here, the true nature of Jesus' messiahship is involved and he has to contend with the incomprehension of his disciples (1:36-37; 6:52; 14:40). These are moments of the apparent failure of his mission.

There is no suggestion of a storm (as in 4:37): the disciples labored against a contrary wind. The incident of the walking on the waters is certainly mysterious. Again (cf. 4:37-39) we may ask: "What really happened?" The Greek *epi tēs thalassēs* (Mk 6:48-49; Mt 14:26; Jn 6:19) is ambiguous and can mean "on the sea(shore)," "by the sea" (Jn 21:1) or "on the

sea." One may well take the view that the underlying incident was of a non-miraculous character while acknowledging that Mark viewed the walking on the waters as a
miracle. "Walking on the sea": this appearance of Jesus
on the waters is reminiscent of the awesome apparitions
of Yahweh to Israel (cf. Job 9:8, "(God) who trampled the
waves of the sea," also Job 38:16; Ps 77:19; Sir 24:5). "He
meant to pass by them" (v.48)—cf. Job 9:11: "Lo, he (God)
passes by me, and I see him not." This too may suggest an
epiphany of Jesus' messianic glory. But in the Emmaus
story of Lk 24:28, the similar phrase "he appeared to be
going further," is meant as a test for the two disciples, with
everything depending on whether they would press Jesus
to stay with them. Similarly here the disciples' faith is being
tested; they failed to recognize Jesus' true nature.

"They thought it was a ghost" (cf. Lk 24:37). The disciples' reaction is part of the theme of misunderstanding.
Yet, they were not fancying something, for "all saw him."
"It is I"; the Greek phrase *egō eimi*, in this epiphany context,
may have some suggestion of the Johannine "I am" sayings.
The words "I am" were used as a name for God in the Old
Testament, signifying God's saving presence among his
people. In light of the eucharistic overtones (v.41) in
this passage, this comforting "It is I" may be meant to
reassure Christians that their Lord is indeed present at the
Lord's Supper, that they do meet him at the breaking of
bread (cf. Lk 24:35). "And the wind ceased": Jesus, as in
4:39, is master of the elements.

"Their hearts were hardened" (v.52) is a strong statement, meaning blindness of heart; it is used of the Pharisees
in 3:5. They have practically put themselves among "those
outside" (4:11). The disciples' lack of understanding bears
on the significance of the feeding miracle; they will fail,
too, to grasp the meaning of the other miracle of loaves
(cf. 8:14-21). We shall see that what they have failed to grasp
is that Jesus brings about the unity of Jew and gentile: he
is the "one loaf" for them (8:14). His calming of storm
(4:39) and stilling of the wind (6:51) were designed to smooth
the path to the gentiles. Because they had not really come to

know him (v.49) the disciples did not perceive the universal scope of his mission. If they are astonished it is because they have not yet really understood at all. In this way Mark invites his readers to a salutary reflection on the meaning of the multiplication of loaves.

SUMMARY.
6:53-56 (Mt 14:34-36).

> [53]And when they had crossed over, they came to land at Gennesaret, and moored to the shore. [54]And when they got out of the boat, immediately the people recognized him, [55]and ran about the whole neighborhood and began to bring sick people on their pallets to any place where they heard he was. [56]And wherever he came, in villages, cities, or country, they laid the sick in the market places, and besought him that they might touch even the fringe of his garment; and as many as touched it were made well.

The passage is wholly editorial, a typical Marcan summary, a generalized description of Jesus' healing activity. However, the first item, the landing (v.53) does establish a connection with the foregoing narratives, for the sequence feeding—crossing—landing is well attested (Mk 6:30-56; 8:1-10; Jn 6:1-25) and is obviously traditional. "Gennesaret" is a town beside the lake, west of Capernaum. In fact, the landing-place after the feeding varies in different versions of the story: Dalmanutha (Mk 8:10), Gennesaret (6:53), Capernaum (Jn 6:24). It is idle to seek a precise geographical location. "That they might touch even the fringe of his garment"—see 5:27-28. The summary, as might be expected, has numerous borrowings from and echoes of other Marcan passages.

HE DECLARED ALL FOODS CLEAN.
7:1-23 (Mt 15:1-20).

A precise incident lies behind this dispute with the Pharisees and scribes: they had observed that the disciples of

Jesus did not perform the ritual washing of hands before meals. In their eyes, this constituted a transgression of the "tradition of the elders," the *Halakah*, the oral law. Jesus responds to the criticism. He does not confine himself to the precise point of ritual purification but turns the debate on to a wider issue. He cites Is 29:13 against the Pharisees, drawing a parallel between the "precepts of men" of which Isaiah speaks, and the "tradition of men" on which the Pharisees count. Implicitly, he accuses them of putting their tradition on the same level as, or even above, the Law of God. Jesus rejected the *Halakah* because it was the work of men and because it could conflict with the law of God. This oral law had put casuistry above love.

The principle of clean and unclean was at the root of Jewish preoccupation with ritual purification. A saying of Jesus (v.15) points out that sin, which alone defiles a man, comes from within oneself; it is more important to be concerned about evil thoughts and sinful deeds than about ceremonial purity. The broad implication of the saying, which set aside the law of cultic purity, was recognised in a gentile-christian setting (vv.18-23). It is made clear to these Christians that being followers of Christ does not involve the observance of Jewish practices. The door is truly open to all.

The deepest reason why the Marcan Jesus rejected the "tradition of the elders" and annulled the whole concept of cultic impurity, is because another and more efficacious economy has come into being. The argument of 7:14-23 is remarkably close to that of Heb 9-10. Like the author of the epistle, Jesus shows that legal discrimination between clean and unclean is incapable of truly purifying the heart of man; for it cannot be more than a provisional expedient. And if Jesus can *now* pronounce the disposition obsolete it is for one reason: because the definitive order has brought the provisional order to an end. This is not formulated but it is presupposed, and Mark suggests this meaning by the reproach of 7:18. Jesus' abolition of the Jewish tradition of clean and unclean manifests to whomever can understand that a new order has emerged (cf. 2:21-22). Mark's full treatment of the matter is a measure of its importance for him and for his community. The passage falls naturally into three parts: on ritual purification (7:1-8); on Corban (7:9-13); on defilement (7:14-23).

> 7 Now when the Pharisees gathered together to him, with some of the scribes, who had come from Jerusalem, ²they saw that some of his disciples ate with hands defiled, that is, unwashed. ³(For the Pharisees, and all the Jews, do not eat unless they wash their hands, observing the tradition of the elders; ⁴and when they come from the market place, they do not eat unless they purify themselves; and there are many other traditions which they observe, the washing of cups and pots and vessels of bronze.) ⁵And the Pharisees and the scribes asked him, "Why do your disciples not live according to the tradition of the elders, but eat with hands defiled?" ⁶And he said to them, "Well did Isaiah prophesy of you hypocrites, as it is written,
>
> 'This people honors me with their lips, but their heart is far from me; ⁷in vain do they worship me, teaching as doctrines the precepts of men.' ⁸You leave the commandment of God, and hold fast the tradition of men."
>
> ⁹And he said to them, "You have a fine way of rejecting the commandment of God, in order to keep your tradition! ¹⁰For Moses said, 'Honor your father and your mother'; ¹¹but you say, 'If a man tells his father or his mother, what you would have gained from me is Corban' (that is, given to God)—¹²then you no longer permit him to do anything for his father or mother, ¹³thus making void the word of God through your tradition which you hand on. And many such things you do."
>
> ¹⁴And he called the people to him again, and said to them, "Hear me, all of you, and understand: ¹⁵there is nothing outside a man which by going into him can defile him; but the things which come out of a man are what defile him." ¹⁷And when he had entered the

house, and left the people, his disciples asked him about the parable. [18]And he said to them, "Then are you also without understanding? Do you not see that whatever goes into a man from outside cannot defile him, [19]since it enters, not his heart but his stomach, and so passes on?" (Thus he declared all foods clean.)[20] And he said, "What comes out of a man is what defiles a man. [21]For from within, out of the heart of man, come evil thoughts, fornication, theft, murder, adultery, [22]coveting, wickedness, deceit, licentiousness, envy, slander, pride, foolishness. [23]All these evil things come from within, and they defile a man."

a) On Ritual Purification. 7:1-8 (Mt 15:1-2, 7-9).

The controversy setting in 7:1-2 is like that in 2:18 and 2:23-24. At first sight there appears to be no close link with the preceding episode. Yet, when we recall the interest in the gentile mission from chapter 5 on, we appreciate that the matter of Jewish observance has become an issue. The "scribes who had come from Jerusalem" (cf. 3:2) represent official Jewish reaction. The question to be settled is whether the gentiles have to conform to Jewish tradition. While, strictly speaking, the ritual washing of hands before eating was of obligation only for priests, the Pharisees had extended the practice. Mark adds an explanatory note for his gentile readers (vv.3-4); the tone of it is hostile to these observances. The "tradition of the elders" is the unwritten tradition of legal interpretations handed down by generations of leading rabbis and was regarded by the Pharisees to be as binding as the written Torah; it constituted the oral law or *halakah* (cf. Gal 1:14; Col 2:8,22). These interpretations, transmitted orally in the rabbinical schools, were fixed in writing during the second century of our era in the Mishnah and Talmud. By the time of Jesus the prescriptions were already so numerous that observance of the Torah had become an impossible burden (cf. Lk 11:46,52; Mt 23:4,13; Acts 15:10). Only the specialists, the scribes, could hope to know them all, let alone observe them, while the "people of the land," ordinary folk, were in inevitable ignorance (Jn 7:49). In Mark's Gospel, Jesus takes strong exception to the excesses of the Halakah.

Jesus' answer to the challenge of the Pharisees and scribes (v.5) is in two parts: vv.6-8 and vv.9-13. Matthew has both, but in inverse order (Mt 15:3-6, 7-9), and this is preferable because the charge of hypocrisy comes better after a concrete example of casuistry. The quotation of Is 29:13 follows the wording of the Septuagint—the Greek translation of the Old Testament. The key-phrase here, "teaching as doctrines the precepts of men" is not in the Hebrew. This fact would suggest that the argument is due to the evangelist or his source, in other words that it was shaped by Greek-speaking Christians. As it stands, the response of Jesus applies to the Pharisees a reproach which Isaiah had already addressed to God's people: they replace the true teaching of God with human teaching and precepts. The close of the pronouncement story (v.8) is a direct and resolute answer to the question of v.5. Mt 23 is an excellent commentary on this verse.

b) On Corban. 7:9-13 (Mt 15:3-6).

Mark, unlike Matthew (15:3-6), places the argument of Jesus in respect of Corban after the citation of Is 29:13. A concrete example of rabbinical casuistry effectively becomes a telling criticism of legalism. It is an extreme case where a preoccupation with the validity of vows leads to direct conflict with a commandment of God. The tone of v.9 is sarcastic: the contrast between "commandment of *God*" and "*your* tradition" is marked and the accusation is that the scribes did, in practice, prefer oral tradition and prescriptions to the written law (cf. Mt 23:16-24). The whole point of the argument in vv.10-13 hinges on the meaning of "Corban." *Korban,* a transliteration of an Aramaic word, means "an offering," "a gift devoted to God" (in Mt 27:6 it means "the temple treasury"). What is involved here is a vow of dedication. If a man had, for whatever reason, declared "Corban"—that is, destined for the temple treasury—what should go to the support of his parents, his vow would have been regarded as binding and could not be dispensed. In this way a solemn duty, enjoined by the Law, was set aside.

"Making void" is stronger than "rejecting" in v.9; it means, practically, invalidating or repealing a law of God. Nor is this an isolated example, for "many such things you do"—all matters of *"your* tradition." While Jesus came to "fulfil" the Law (cf. Mt 5:17), the Pharisees, by their tradition, "make void" God's word, emptying it of its spirit and of its binding force. Besides, Jesus, always gives priority to the needs of men (cf. 3:4).

c) On Defilement. 7:14-23 (Mt 15:10-11, 15-20).

This episode is closely connected with the foregoing. It serves as an explanation of the preceding discussion, for the benefit first of the crowd then of the disciples. While Jesus had not directly answered the question raised by the Pharisees, "Why do your disciples . . . eat with hands defiled?", he now explains to the crowd in the form of a "parable" (v.15) the reason for his followers' conduct. Then, for the benefit of his disciples, he explains the parable (vv.17-23)—this in keeping with the principle of 4:34. The message is clear and goes far beyond rejection of the oral law; it sets aside an important aspect of the written law (cf. Lev 11-15; Dt 14). The notion of "clean" and "unclean," he asserts, ought not to be sought outside of man but in his "heart," the source of moral action. The true notion of "cleanness" becomes apparent: man is "pure" and consecrated to God not by reason of a multiplicity of ritual ablutions, as the Pharisees seemed to believe, but by faithfulness to the divine law. The whole concept of cultic impurity is set aside. Holiness does not lie in the area of "clean" over against "unclean"; it is not in the realm of things but in the realm of ethics. It is to be found only in the human heart and is a matter of personal responsibility.

The introduction (v.14) is Marcan. In 6:34 Jesus' compassion for the crowd moved him to "teach them many things." Here, again, he gathered a crowd to him and began to teach. But he will speak to them only in parables (4:11,34). "Hear me, all of you, and understand" is a development of the "Listen" of 4:3; the admonition to understand implies that what follows is mysterious. The sweeping range of v.15 becomes apparent when we compare it with Mt 15:11—"Not what goes into the mouth defiles a man, but what comes out of the mouth, this defiles a man," and the apocryphal *Gospel of Thomas* —"For what enters into your mouth will not defile you, but what comes out of your mouth, it is that which will defile you." Both texts obviously are concerned with sins of the tongue. Mark's version is a principle of universal import: "there is nothing outside a man . . . the things which come out of a man . . ." Structured as antithetical parallelism, this saying is radical and strikes at the very distinction of clean and unclean, of sacred and secular. Not surprisingly, it has no parallel in Judaism for it denies a basic principle of Jewish religion and sets aside a large area of the Mosaic Torah. It is a flat denial that any external things or circumstances can separate a man from God (cf. Rom 8:38-39). We can be separated from God only by our own attitude and behavior.

Most manuscripts of Mark read as v.16—"If any man has ears to hear, let him hear." It may well be original, especially in view of the close structural similarity between 7:14-23 and 4:1-20 (the saying is found in 4:9,23). Here it would emphasise the mysterious character of Jesus' teaching to the crowds.

The setting (v.17) for the explanation is thoroughly Marcan. Jesus and his disciples withdraw from the people and enter a "house,"—the place where Jesus retires with his disciples and, apart from the crowd, instructs them (cf. 7:24; 9:33; 10:10). "His disciples asked him about the parable" (cf. 4:10,34). "Are you also without understanding" (v.18a) is much stronger than 4:13; the sterner tone is appropriate after 6:52. In substance v.18b repeats v.15a.

Food (even though *declared* unclean) cannot defile a
man. It enters his stomach only to be evacuated; it cannot
touch his heart. Verses 18b-19 represent a gentile-christian
explanation of the saying of Jesus (v.15). Mark introduces
it by means of his parable technique ("parable," as we
explained in commenting in chapter four, is conceived
by Mark as an enigmatic saying requiring explanation).
It was of special interest to gentile-christians that the
saying represented the abrogation of the whole Jewish
system of ritual purity and especially the abolition of
any distinction among foods. Mark's closing comment at
the end of v.19 makes this explicit (cf. a similar concept
in Acts 10:15: "What God has cleansed, you must not call
common," and the whole passage Acts 10:9-16).

Now (vv.20-23) the second part of v.15 is taken up and
explained. Such lists of vices were commonplace in hellenistic popular philosophy. For other similar lists in the
New Testament cf. Gal 5:19-21; Rom 1:29-31; 1 Pet 4:3.
In the Greek the first six nouns in Mark's list are in the
plural, indicating evil acts: acts of sexual vice, thefts,
murders, adulteries, acts of coveting or lust, and wickedness in general. The six following vices are: deceit, wanton-
ness, envy (literally, an "evil eye"), slander, pride (arro-
gance), and folly (stupidity of one who lacks moral judgment). Verse 23 simply explains the phrase, "what comes
out of a man" of v.20. "All these evil things" are found
within man himself; it is these and not anything external
to himself which defile him. That defilement can come
only from within is emphasised by the repeated phrases
"what defiles a man" (vv.20,23) which bracket the list of
sins and vices. Thus did a gentile-christian community
spell out the far-reaching implications of a revolutionary
saying of the Lord.

THE GENTILE WOMAN.
7:24-30 (Mt 15:21-28).

For Mark the presence of Jesus in the region of Tyre,
and his healing wrought for a gentile woman, carry great

weight. It signals Jesus' turning from the Jewish and toward the gentile world. The faith of this woman in the Jewish Messiah stands in contrast to the inhibiting inflexibility of Jewish legalism (7:1-23). Originally, the saying of Jesus in v.27, "It is not right to take the children's bread and throw it to the dogs" made clear that he accepts a sharp distinction between Jew and gentile as part of God's plan. In fact, Jesus did limit his preaching activity to Israel, while promising the gentiles a place in the kingdom, but only beyond the cross, and through God's eschatological act of power. From the vantage point of a successful gentile mission, Mark has modified the saying by prefacing, "let the children *first* be fed . . ."; in his day the turn of the gentiles had already come. He can find a trace of a "gentile mission" of Jesus but he does not dissemble how faint a trace it is.

The indications are that 7:24 - 8:26 was planned to meet the needs of gentile-christian readers. Mark wanted to show that the concern of Jesus was not limited to Jews but reached to non-Jewish peoples, beyond the confines of Galilee. But when we examine more closely the topographical references in 7:24 and 7:31 we find that it is Mark himself who has constructed this brief venture of Jesus beyond Jewish territory. Apart from this and the Gerasene demoniac episode (5:1-20), Mark has given only an intimation, expressed in terms of the journeys across the lake, of an active mission of Jesus to the gentiles. But it is enough for him to show that the door had been opened to them.

> [24]And from there he arose and went away to the region of Tyre and Sidon. And he entered a house, and would not have any one know it; yet he could not be hid. [25]But immediately a woman, whose little daughter was possessed by an unclean spirit, heard of him, and came and fell down at his feet. [26]Now the woman was a Greek, a Syrophoenician by birth. And she begged him to chase the demon out of her daughter. [27]And he said to her, "Let the children first be fed, for it is not right to take the

> children's bread and throw it to the dogs." [28]But she an-
> swered him, "Yes, Lord; yet even the dogs under the
> table eat the children's crumbs." [29]And he said to her,
> "For this saying you may go your way; the demon has left
> your daughter." [30]And she went home, and found the
> child lying in bed, and the demon gone.

In 7:24 there is a change of scene; the ministry in Galilee
has ended. "He arose and went"—the same statement in
1:35 and 10:1 indicates a new turn to the ministry. "The
region of Tyre" was not strictly gentile territory (though
Mark would have regarded it as such). It included Upper
Galilee which was gentile only in a very limited sense. The
"house" is where Jesus seeks retreat with his disciples (cf.
7:17; 9:33; 10:10). Reference in v.24b to Jesus' frustrated
desire for concealment makes the point that his presence
and authority could not go unnoticed (cf. 1:45; 7:36). The
glory of Jesus will shine out. The suppliant's little daughter
has an unclean spirit: Mark's predilection for exorcism
stories. The woman's prostration before him is both a mark
of deep respect and a recognition of Jesus' powers (cf.
1:40; 3:11; 5:22-23). "A Greek, a Syro-Phoenician by birth"
—Mark thereby asserts that the woman is gentile both by
religion and by birth. She is a representative of the gentile
world.

"Let the children first be fed." Paul had not only declared
that the gospel should be first preached to the Jews and then
only to the gentiles (e.g. Rom 1:16), but had followed the
principle through in practice (e.g. Acts 13:46; 18:6). It was
the conviction of earliest Christianity that the children
(Israel) must first be fed before the incorporation of the
gentiles into the people of God could be effected (Rom
1:16; 2:9-10; Acts 3:26; 13:46). Mark wants to insist that
the time for this had arrived in his day. The label "dog" was
in common use among Jews as a term of contempt applied
to gentiles. There really seems to be no way of softening
Jesus' saying, which is especially unexpected seeing that
he had ventured into gentile territory. Originally the story

must have been set in Galilee, a fact also suggested by the designation "Syro-Phoenician," which would have been unnecessary in a Tyrian setting. Jesus refuses the woman's request on the ground that he has been sent to Israel and not to the gentiles (cf. Mt 15:24). Yet, the story ends on a different note.

The woman took up Jesus' word and based her plea upon it. She does not question the truth of his statement but simply points out that when the "children" have been fed, then, indeed, the "dogs" can hope to receive their share too. She acknowledges the divinely ordained separation. In recognizing Jesus as the giver of Bread (v.28) she already acknowledges him as the "one loaf" (8:14) for gentile and Jew. Jesus bows to the woman's faith (cf. Lk 7:9) and assures her that her child is already healed. If Jesus had yielded to this cry of faith even while the division between Jew and gentile still stood, how much more, Mark seems to be saying, must the christian church go out to the gentiles now that Jesus had laid down his life as a ransom "for many" (10:45), had poured out his blood "for many" (14:24). Jesus had broken down the barrier between the two peoples (Eph 2:14).

HE HAS DONE ALL THINGS WELL.
7:31-37 (cf. Mt 15:29-31).

Mark has situated this miracle story in the region of the Decapolis. As in the previous episode he is concerned with Jesus' attitude to the gentiles. In the foregoing story, the casting out of the unclean spirit which possessed the gentile girl shows Jesus hearkening to the gentiles and setting them free. This time the spirit (cf. 9:17) not only departs but the man recovers his faculty of hearing and speaking. The healing has the symbolic intent of showing that the gentiles, once deaf and dumb towards God, are now capable of hearing God and paying him homage. They too have become heirs of the eschatological promise to Israel: "The ears of the deaf will be opened and the tongue of the dumb will cry for joy" (Is. 35:5-6).

³¹Then he returned from the region of Tyre, and went through Sidon to the Sea of Galilee, through the region of the Decapolis. ³²And they brought to him a man who was deaf and had an impediment in his speech; and they besought him to lay his hand upon him. ³³And taking him aside from the multitude privately, he put his fingers into his ears, and he spat and touched his tongue; ³⁴and looking up to heaven, he sighed, and said to him, "Ephphatha," that is, "Be opened." ³⁵And his ears were opened, his tongue was released, and he spoke plainly. ³⁶And he charged them to tell no one; but the more he charged them, the more zealously they proclaimed it. ³⁷And they were astonished beyond measure, saying, "He has done all things well; he even makes the deaf hear and the dumb speak."

The setting of the story (v.31) is manifestly Mark's own work and, at first sight, would suggest that his geography is very faulty. If we were to take his indications literally we would have to suppose that Jesus, starting out from the region of Tyre and wanting to go south-east to the lake, in fact set off north to Sidon and reached the lake from the east. This, in Irish terms, would be more or less the same as traveling from Killarney to Cork via Galway and Waterford. Or, in a New England setting, from Providence to Fall River via Boston and New Bedford. There is little doubt that we should put the bizarre geography down to theological intent (cf. 3:7-8). The "sea of Galilee" establishes a link between two places as different as Phoenicia and Decapolis and brings about the global unity "Galilee." This Galilee is a theological place: it is the "Galilee of the Gentiles" (cf. Is 9:1-2; Mt 4:12-16). It evokes the call of the gentiles to salvation. For Mark Galilee has become the place where the gospel of God is heard (1:14-15), where the first disciples are called to become fishers of men (1:17), where the crowds gather from all of ancient Israel (2:7-8), where unity is established between the divided territories (7:31) and where the disciples will be convened to see, again, him who had preached to them there (14:28; 16:7).

The deaf man had "an impediment in his speech" (v.32)—
a rare word (*mogilalos*) found only here in the New Testament, and once also in the Septuagint in Is 35:6 where it
translates the Hebrew "stammerer." The evangelist is
pointing to the Jewish hope that the Messiah would open
blind eyes and release dumb lips. Though the gesture of
taking the patient aside (v.33) is a feature of a hellenistic-
style miracle story such as this one, the phrase *kat' idian*
("privately") suggests something else and justifies a search
for a symbolic level. The actions of putting one's fingers
into the man's ears and touching his tongue with spittle are
common to the technique of Greek and Jewish healers.
Here the gestures have a certain "sacramental" quality
(cf. 8:23). "Looking up to heaven," as in 6:41, indicates
Jesus' intimacy with God. "Sigh" expresses his deep feeling
for the sufferer (cf. 1:41). "Be opened," characteristically,
Mark translates the Aramaic expression *ephphatha* (cf.
Ezek 24:26: "Your mouth shall be opened, and you shall
speak and shall no longer be dumb," where the same Greek
verb occurs). Both the word *ephphatha* and the use of
saliva passed at an early date into the baptismal rite.

The description of the cure (v.35) is given a solemn cast;
in 8:25 also the cure will be described in three clauses. The
fact that the injunction to preserve silence is disobeyed is
put very strongly (v.36). As in 1:45 the deed is "proclaimed":
the deeds of Jesus cannot but speak the good news. Astonishment is "beyond measure," the strongest statement of
astonishment in Mark. This miracle has exceptional significance. "He has done all things well" recalls Gen 1:31.
"He even makes the deaf hear and the dumb speak" is
certainly an allusion to Is 35:5-6. The Isaian reference to
the opening of the eyes of the blind will be developed by the
evangelist in the parallel miracle of 8:22-26, the cure of a
blind man. Recall of the Isaian text means that the age of
messianic salvation has arrived with Jesus (cf. Lk 7:22-23)—
and has arrived for the gentiles. We may also see in the
Greek chorus of the crowd the response in faith of the
christian community who perceive in the works of Jesus
the time of fulfillment announced by the prophet. It is

significant that the second miracle (8:22-26) is followed by the confession of Peter. In each case the christian community acknowledges its Messiah.

THE FEEDING OF THE FOUR THOUSAND.
8:1-10 (Mt 15:32-39).

The two Marcan feeding narratives have much in common but also carry some notable differences. Both are set in the desert, the second more explicitly so, and evoke the Exodus and the manna, bread from God. Both, in the description of the miracle, stress the great size of the crowd, and food so abundant that a large amount was left over. Both end with the dismissal of the crowd and a journey by boat. We are, beyond doubt, in the presence of a literary doublet. But Mark chooses to see two separate incidents and the indications are that he viewed the feeding of the five thousand as a sign to Jews and the feeding of the four thousand as a sign to gentiles. Already, in 7:27-28, there is a plea that the gentiles, too, be allowed to participate, to a limited extent at least, in God's goodness. But now it is no longer a question of their being permitted to gather crumbs: the disciples are to give them of the abundance of the table so that the crowds may be satisfied (8:8).

> **8** In those days, when again a great crowd had gathered, and they had nothing to eat, he called his disciples to him, and said to them, ²"I have compassion on the crowd, because they have been with me now three days, and have nothing to eat; ³and if I send them away hungry to their homes, they will faint on the way; and some of them have come a long way." ⁴And his disciples answered him, "How can one feed these men with bread here in the desert?" ⁵And he asked them, "How many loaves have you?" They said, "Seven," ⁶And he commanded the crowd to sit down on the ground; and he took the seven loaves, and having given thanks he broke them and gave them to his disciples to set before the people; and they set them before the crowd. ⁷And they had a few small fish;

and having blessed them, he commanded that these also should be set before them. [8]And they ate, and were satisfied; and they took up the broken pieces left over, seven baskets full. [9]And there were about four thousand people. [10]And he sent them away; and immediately he got into the boat with his disciples, and went to the district of Dalmanutha.

The vague introduction "in those days" (v.1) is enough for Mark to link this story with the foregoing. No place is mentioned but he evidently is still thinking of the "region of Decapolis" (7:31). Greater stress is laid on the people's physical hunger (8:1-4) than in 6:34-44; and here (unlike 6:35) Jesus takes the initiative. Here, too, compassion is occasioned by their physical need and not by the fact that they are as sheep without a shepherd who hunger for Jesus' teaching (cf. 6:34). The "three days" would seem to be a traditional detail; in the first feeding all took place on one day. "They will faint" (*ekluomai*)—apart from the parallel Mt 15:32 the verb occurs only in Gal 6:9 and Heb 12:3,5 where it means growing fainthearted in christian faith and practice. Is there a suggestion that Christians must take care to find sustenance in eucharistic food?

The surprised question of the disciples (v.4) rings strangely after 6:35-44; an indication that we have to do with a literary doublet. Their lack of understanding is again in evidence (cf. 6:52; 8:19). Here (cf. 6:35) the setting really is a desert, far from any habitation, a fact which accentuates the Exodus parallel. The form of the question focuses attention on Jesus as the only provider of bread. In v.6 we find the same eucharistic language as in 6:41 "took . . . gave thanks . . ." "broke . . . " "gave . . . " and the similar statement: "and gave them to the disciples to set before them" as in 6:41. "Having given thanks" (v.6): the verb "to give thanks" is found in Lk 22:19 and 1 Cor 11:24 as a synonym of "to bless" (cf. Mk 14:22; Mt 26:26). Here the disciples play a more active role and the eucharistic significance is heightened by the care to avoid any mention of the "few small fish" until after the distribution of the loaves.

In 6:43-44 five thousand had been fed and twelve baskets of the fragments of bread and fish were collected; in 8:8-9 four thousand are fed and seven baskets of fragments were collected. The differences are obvious but Mark has given us a clear pointer as to which are, for him, the significant variants: the baskets of fragments (cf. 8:19-20). In 6:43 the word for basket is *cophinos*, a wicker-work basket in which Jews carried food. The word and the significant number "twelve" evoke Israel. In 8:8 the word for basket *spyris*, an ordinary basket (distinct from the specifically Jewish *cophinos*) which might be large enough to hold a man (cf. Acts 9:25). The "seven," as opposed to the "twelve" has, too, a general, universalist import. There is no denying that Mark does (8:8-9) strikingly draw attention to the two feeding stories, deliberately repeating the numbers "twelve" and "seven" and using again the two different words for basket. By now we should have realized that Mark is no careless writer. These details for him are meaningful and in the setting of this section of his gospel we are justified in seeing in them deliberate pointers to the Jewish and gentile elements of the christian church.

In both stories all present "ate and were satisfied" and an abundance remained over: it is the abundance of the messianic age. "And he sent them away"—cf. 6:45: "while he dismissed the crowd"; in each case the dismissal is followed by a boat journey. Dalmanutha is unknown; Mt 15:39 has Magadan, also unknown. For Mark it would seem that Dalmanutha is on the western shore of the lake. There is no hint of the reaction of the crowd, usually astonishment and awe, that is a feature of the more developed miracle story. These stories are aimed at the disciples, that is, at christian readers. They, at least, should "understand about the loaves" (6:52).

NO SIGN SHALL BE GIVEN TO THIS GENERATION. 8:11-13 (Mt 16:1-4).

> [11]The Pharisees came and began to argue with him, seeking from him a sign from heaven, to test him. [12]And

he sighed deeply in his spirit, and said, "Why does this generation seek a sign? Truly, I say to you, no sign shall be given to this generation." [13]And he left them, and getting into the boat again he departed to the other side.

From 5:35 on we have had one wonder after another, culminating in the "second" great feeding miracle. For Mark's readers these signs were compelling, and demand for further signs could only reflect sheer perversity. But the scribes had already perversely attributed the exorcising power of Jesus to the prince of demons (3:22). Here the Pharisees play the role of the stubborn "generation" of Moses' time who so often "tempted" God by demanding further proofs of his power after he had worked so many signs (cf. Num 14:11,22; Dt 1:35). This passage is parallel to 4:10-12 because miracles, like parables, have a deeper level of meaning which can be missed. The Pharisees stand among "those outside" who will not see. The miracles of Jesus are sign enough—beyond them no sign will be given.

Mark shows that Jesus' signs are not intended to compel faith but to elicit it. To make his point, the evangelist has inserted the passage 8:11-13 and he has to "invent" a special boat journey to fit it in (cf. 8:10,13). A further reason for its presence here in the great sequence 6:35 - 8:26 is to balance the controversy with the Pharisees in 7:1-23. In contrast to the faith encountered in gentile territory (7:24-37) Jesus in Galilee is met by disbelief. The focus is on the saying of v. 12 and to this extent the passage is a pronouncement story.

The demand of "a sign from heaven" (v.11) presupposes that Jesus is allegedly a prophet and looks for him to legitimate himself as such; some apocalyptic portent is envisaged. "To test him" (cf. 10:2; 12:15)—their motivation is patent. They believe that their challenge creates a dilemma: if he tries to give a sign he will fail, and if he refuses he will lose popular support. For Jesus there is no such dilemma. "He sighed deeply" expresses deep emotion and indignation (cf. 3:5). It is a sign in which both anger and sorrow have a part; obstinate sin moved Jesus deeply.

"This generation" (cf. 8:38; 9:19; 13:30) reflects passages such as Dt 32:5; Ps 95:10; Num 14:11. As the generation which came up out of Egypt resisted Moses, so Jesus' generation resisted him, its deliverer. The Pharisees may have seen the miracles of Jesus, but they are "those outside" and so do not understand (4:11-12). "Truly (literally "amen") I say to you"—an introductory phrase, adding emphasis and solemnity to what follows, which is found exclusively in sayings of Jesus (cf. 3:28). "No sign shall be given." The Greek formula (*ei dothesetai*) is in fact a strong negation or an imprecation "May I die if God grants this generation a sign" (the passive points to God as the agent). The refusal could not be more absolute. The exceptive clause in Mt 12:40, "except the sign of Jonah," points to the resurrection of Jesus as the supreme sign. "He left them" (v. 13) because there was no scope for his ministry among them. He got into the boat again and crossed to "the other side;" for Mark this is to Bethsaida (v.22) and it means to the eastern shore of the lake. The crossing and recrossing of the lake, while hard to follow because of the imprecision of place-names, is certainly important for Mark as illustrating Jesus' bringing together of Jew and gentile.

THE ONE LOAF.
8:14-21 (Mt 16:5-12).

Mark has stressed the failure of the twelve to understand (4:13, 40-41; 6:52; 7:18; 8:4); in all cases they display lack of spiritual insight in failing to discern some hidden meaning in a word or deed of Jesus. The passage 8:14-21 is the climax of this theme in the first part of the gospel. Just as 8:11-13 is parallel to 4:10-12 with its theme of wilful obduracy, our passage in which Jesus strives to awaken the disciples to an understanding of the loaves is parallel to the explanation of the parable to them in 4:13-20. A series of seven questions conveys Jesus' bitter sorrow at their slowness. "Do you not yet understand?" is the burden of his censure. Where the Pharisees had been refused a sign (8:11-12), the disciples are shown up as those who had failed to see the signs given to them: they are like many Christians of the evangelist's own community. Mark writes with the special needs of his church in mind. Therefore he has exaggerated the obtuseness of the disciples. He has presupposed the eucharistic significance of the feeding stories. Where the mysterious feedings were meant to be a sign to the disciples, if they had eyes to see, the eucharistic mystery is still a sign to the christian faithful. More specifically, for him, Jesus as the "one loaf" is the bond between Jew and gentile.

> [14]Now they had forgotten to bring bread; and they had only one loaf with them in the boat. [15]And he cautioned them, saying, "Take heed, beware of the leaven of the Pharisees and the leaven of Herod." [16]And they discussed it with one another, saying, "We have no bread." [17]And being aware of it, Jesus said to them, "Why do you discuss the fact that you have no bread? Do you not yet perceive or understand? Are your hearts hardened? [18]Having eyes do you not see, and having ears do you not hear? And do you not remember? [19]When I broke the five loaves for the five thousand, how many baskets full of broken pieces did you take up?" They said to him, "Twelve." [20]"And the seven of the four thousand, how many basket full of broken pieces did you take up?" And they said to him, "Seven." [21]And he said to them, "Do you not yet understand?"

The drama of the episode is present from the first (v.14). The disciples, who had been so actively involved in two miraculous feedings, where Jesus had satisfied the needs of great crowds, are now concerned because they are short of bread! They "had only one loaf with them in the boat"—this is not just a vivid Marcan touch. The development of the passage will suggest that what the disciples fail to understand is that Jesus is the one loaf for Jews and gentiles—as the feeding miracles ought to have shown them. (Cf. 1 Cor 10:16-17; 12:12-13.)

The warning about leaven (v.15) manifestly breaks the natural sequence of vv. 14 and 16 and it is not taken up in the following dialogue. Yet the warning is not out of place. "Leaven" alludes to the leaven which had to be put away during Passover and the feast of Unleavened Bread (Ex 12:14-20); thus the Exodus theme of the feeding stories is being continued.   That a christian reader would also discern a reference to Jesus' death and resurrection is clear from the association of a warning against leaven and the idea of Christ as Passover lamb in 1 Cor 5:6-8. The disciples, and especially Mark's readers, are being warned to put aside the blindness that would hinder their recognition of Jesus. The evangelist had already noticed that the Pharisees and the Herodians had shown their ill-will by leaguing together against Jesus (3:6). Here he harks back, even more immediately, to 8:11-13 and 6:14-29 where the ill will of the Pharisees and Herod has been demonstrated. It is hinted that the disciples, too, are not free of such dispositions (cf. vv.17-21).

Following on v.14 the fact that the disciples have no bread becomes a point of contention (v.16) which underlines their incredible lack of undertstanding. We have something close to the Johannine technique where the hearers' literal understanding of a word leads to Jesus' exposition of its deeper meaning. The series of seven questions (vv.17-21) addressed primarily to the christian reader, bear on the meaning of the loaves. The first question simply echoes v.16; vv.19-20 bringing out the meaning of it—the feeding miracles *ought* to have opened their eyes. "Do you not yet perceive or understand?"   (cf. 7:18); they have become like "those outside" (4:11-12). "Are your hearts hardened?" (cf. 6:52). Their understanding is darkened; they have failed to discern the true dimension of the miracles. Mk 6:52 and 8:17 are the only passages in the New Testament which speak of the disciples' hardness of heart; Mark is couching his warning in the sharpest possible terms. "Having eyes do you not see, and having ears do you not hear?" (cf. Is 6:9-10; Jer 5:21; Ezek 12:2). In the light of 4:11-12 the question implies that the feeding miracles, like the parables, were meant to reveal to the disciples the "secret of the kingdom of heaven." "Do you not remember?"—this question leads to the following direct allusions to the miraculous feeding.

Bracketed by the repeated "do you not yet understand" (vv. 17,21) the specific recalling of the two feedings is marked as the key factor of the passage. The unexpected emphasis— on the baskets of fragments, is a further indication that this is just where we must look. We are meant to see that the number (twelve) and the *cophinos*, a basket commonly used by Jews, point to the Jewish world, while the number seven (universal) and the ordinary basket (*spyris*) indicate the gentile world. Those of gentile background as well as those of Jewish origin are both at home in the household of the faith. And their fellowship is achieved in the breaking of the bread. The Christian who cannot or will not see this merits the charge: is your heart hardened? It would seem that Mark has some Jewish-christian disciples primarily in view. Doubtless the kind of situation that Paul encountered in Jerusalem and Antioch (Gal 2) would also have cropped up again at a later date in other areas. It would not have been easy for pharisaic Jews, coming to Christianity, to shrug off their ingrained prejudice and enter into warm fellowship with gentiles.

THE CURE OF A BLIND MAN.
8:22-26.

This story rounds off the second "loaves section" (8:1-26) just as the healing of the deaf-mute (7:31-37) had rounded off the first (6:35 - 7:37). Both stories are found only in Mark and the close parallelism between them has long been remarked. We have to do with a single scheme used for two different incidents, a scheme proper to these two accounts.

> ²²And they came to Bethsaida. And some people brought to him a blind man, and begged him to touch

him. [23]And he took the blind man by the hand, and led him out of the village; and when he had spit on his eyes and laid his hands upon him, he asked him, "Do you see anything?" [24]And he looked up and said, "I see men; but they look like trees, walking." [25]Then again he laid his hands upon his eyes; and he looked intently and was restored, and saw everything clearly. [26]And he sent him away to his home, saying, "Do not even enter the village."

The position of the story of the blind man in the evangelist's plan is calculated, and its symbolic intent is unmistakable. It comes, dramatically, just after the castigation of the sheer hardness of heart, the total blindness, of the disciples. It thereby symbolizes the gradual opening of their eyes leading, at last, to a profession of faith (8:27-29). Indeed, the parallelism between vv.22-26 and 27-30 is remarkable and obviously intended. Jesus leads the disciples away from an inhabited area, 27a (23a), and in two stages, at first imperfectly, 27b-28 (23-24), then fully, 29(25) the truth about him is made plain. Jesus then commands secrecy, 30(26). The story is a sign of coming to faith. It tells us that Jesus alone can cure the blindness of the disciples; and it shows, too, that their lack of understanding is so serious that it can be penetrated only gradually. The second part of the gospel will show how imperfect that first glimmer of understanding is and how Jesus will have to struggle with their persistent obtuseness. The readers of the gospel are reminded that only the Lord can grant understanding. Already we have here, in embryo, the Johannine theme of the Light of the World (cf. Jn 9).

Bethsaida is a town on the north shore of the lake, just east of the Jordan mouth. For Mark (6:45) this is "the other side." "And they brought to him . . . and begged him to . . ." —verbally the same as 7:32. Again in v.23 there is much in common with 7:33—the taking of the man aside, the use of spittle, and the laying on of hands. "Do you see anything?"—the question of Jesus is unusual. This is the only cure in the gospels that is described as taking place gradually, in two stages. This factor may well have been a traditional device to bring out more graphically the difficulty of the healing and so add to the impressiveness of the miracle. But Mark saw it as a picture of the growth of faith (cf. vv.27-29). "I see men; but they look like trees walking" is a good rendering of an awkward Greek sentence. The idea is clear: the man is beginning to recover his sight, but as yet cannot distinguish objects clearly. In v.25 the gradual nature of the cure is emphasized. As in 7:35 the cure itself is vividly described in three co-ordinated phrases. "Do not even enter the village"—another, and preferable, reading is: "Tell no one in the village." This alternative reading would constitute a further link with the cure of the deaf mute: "And he charged them to tell no one" (7:36).

There is another healing of a blind man, Bartimaeus, at 10:46-52. These two stories (8:22-26; 10:46-52) should be seen as a frame for the intervening section. They stand at the beginning and the end of the way to Jerusalem and draw our attention to what Jesus has been doing: on the way he has been striving to open the eyes of his disciples.

Mark has brought us to the turning-point of his gospel. He has striven to achieve the unity of his mixed community. It is the manifest will of the Lord that gentiles should be called to salvation. Yet, the Lord, too, respected the divinely ordained division between the two peoples. Israel did have the right to hear the good news first. Still, the new way brought by Jesus is not a patching of the old nor a wine that can be poured into old wineskins. The new way of Jesus is just that: new. And in this new age not only do the traditions of men have no place but distinctions of clean and unclean have no meaning. Salvation is for all. Jesus is the one loaf for Jew and gentile alike. Differences must be resolved in the unity of eucharistic fellowship. But the community has still much, everything indeed, to learn. Mark will teach them, in the words and example of Jesus, what it means to be a Christian.

YOU ARE THE CHRIST.
8:27-30 (Lk 9:18-21; Mt 16:13-20).

In the evangelist's eyes the unique significance of Peter's confession rests upon the fact that here, for the *first* time, the disciples tell Jesus who, in their estimation, he is. Jesus takes the initiative and asks the disciples about the opinion of "men" ("those outside" (4:11)) and learns that they would not regard him as a messianic figure but, at most, as a forerunner of the Messiah. It is very clear that not only was his teaching riddlesome to the outsiders but that they had missed, too, the import of his works. Peter, however, has at last begun to see: "*You* are the Messiah." The sequel will show that this is but the first stage of his enlightenment; it is the risen Lord who will open their eyes fully. The disciples are bidden to keep silence; the prohibition is related to Jesus' own person. Mark, indeed, looks beyond Peter and the disciples to the christian community of his concern and bids his Christians take care that they really understand who their Christ is. There has been a studied preparation of the reader. From the start Mark has shown Jesus acting in an extraordinary manner which called forth the astonishment of the witnesses and led to a series of questions about him (1:27; 2:7; 6:2). Jesus himself heightens the effect (2:10,28). Who, then, is this Son of Man? Who is this Physician (3:16-17)? Who is this Bridegroom (2:19)? The themes of the amazement of the crowd and the incomprehension of the disciples stand as a constant question-mark over the first eight chapters of the gospel. And now, for the Christians who read Mark, the confession, "You are the Christ" is *their* profession of faith. And it is precisely because it is a profession of christian faith that Jesus is depicted as accepting it without comment. But we shall see how inadequate that confession might turn out to be.

[27]And Jesus went on with his disciples, to the villages of Caesarea Philippi; and on the way he asked his disciples, "Who do men say that I am?" [28]And they told him,

"John the Baptist; and others say, Elijah; and others one of the prophets." ²⁹And he asked them, "But who do you say that I am?" Peter answered him, "You are the Christ." ³⁰And he charged them to tell no one about him.

The modern town of Banias preserves the ancient name of Caesarea Philippi, Paneas (named from a grotto sacred to Pan) at a source of the Jordan on the slopes of Mount Hermon. The town had been rebuilt by the tetrarch Herod Philip who named it after Caesar Augustus. As Caesarea Philippi it was distinguished from Caesarea on the Mediterranean coast. Jesus and his disciples are "on the way" to Jerusalem (v.27), the way of the cross. The question of Jesus (v.27) prepares for the more personal and vital question of v.29. "Men," that is those outside the circle of his disciples (cf. 4:11). For Mark, these "outsiders" represent Israel. For a belief in a return of Elijah see Mal 3:1; 4:5; Mk 1:6; 9:9-13. As Elijah was thought to have reappeared in John the Baptist, some felt that John had returned to life in his successor, Jesus. "One of the prophets" reflects the expectation of "the prophet like Moses" who was supposed to appear in the final days (Dt 18:15,18; cf. Jn 1:21). The obvious parallel between 8:28 and 6:14-16 is due to Mark who had perceived that the conjectures of the people and the superstitious fears of Herod (6:14-16) would serve to convey popular speculation about Jesus.

"You are the Christ" (v.29). Peter's reply is emphatic: "*You* are the Messiah." The title "the Christ" occurs only seven times in Mark: 1:1; 8:29; 9:41; 12:35; 13:21; 14:61; 15:32. In 12:35, 13:21, and 15:32 it refers to the "anointed one" of Jewish expectation. The same might be said of 14:61 but since it is used in a solemn question of the high priest at the climactic moment of the trial of Jesus, it has a further resonance. The instance in 9:41 is a way of saying "Christians," while 1:1 is the title of the gospel. In three cases the title is qualified, as if the evangelist wished to remind his readers of the significance of a title that was well on the way to becoming a proper name: "Jesus Christ, the Son of God" (1:1), "the Christ, the Son of the Blessed" (14:61), "the Christ, the King of Israel" (15:32). Yet, it is evident that among all the occurrences of the title, 8:29 stands in high relief. Here Jesus is formally acknowledged as the Messiah of Jewish expectation and as the Christ of christian worship because the narrative is concerned with Christology.

"He charged them" (v.30). The Greek verb *epitimao* ordinarily means "to rebuke" or "to censure." If it is used in the sense of "charging strictly" as in 1:25, the idea of censure which the word implies must also be given place. Jesus is aware that the disciples do not yet understand the true nature of his messiahship. It is noteworthy that the prohibition to speak openly is for the first time explicitly related to Jesus' own person (cf. 1:44; 5:43; 7:36; 8:26).

CONCLUSION AND TRANSITION.
Who is Jesus?
8:27-33.

THROUGHOUT THE FIRST HALF of the gospel the question of Jesus' identity had been repeatedly raised and had met with various answers. Some, the religious leaders, had rejected the evidence of his works and his teaching; others have been impressed and have been prepared to acknowledge him as a prophet or as an Elijah-figure (6:14-15). The chosen disciples reacted with fear and wonder but had failed to understand him. Only the evil spirits had acknowledged Jesus for who he is. But now we have come to the point where the disciples do, at last, proclaim him as Messiah. The passage is the hinge of Mark's work, at once the climax of the first part, the secret of the Messiah (the identity of Jesus), and the transition to the second part, the mystery of the Son of Man (his destiny of death and resurrection). The second half of the gospel provides the answer to the question raised in the first half, Who is Jesus? But this answer is not understood by the disciples who cannot grasp his suffering messiahship.

The central importance of Peter's confession in Mark's editorial structure is indicated by the brusque change of tone and of orientation after Peter has acknowledged the messiahship of Jesus. In the actual structure of the gospel the prediction of the passion (8:31-32a) is Jesus' response to the confession of Peter. The following section of the gospel (8:31 - 11:10) is dominated by the prophecies of the passion (8:31; 9:31; 10:33-34), each of which is placed in a different geographical locale: Caesarea Philippi (8:27), Galilee (9:30), and on the way to Jerusalem (10:32). The violent protestation of Peter in 8:32 shows clearly that this is a new and unexpected teaching. "And he said this plainly"—it is indeed a turning point in the self-revelation of Jesus: until now he has said nothing explicitly about his messiahship. If he still charges his disciples not to reveal his messianic identity (v.30)—because their understanding of him is still so imperfect—he now speaks to them quite plainly of his destiny of suffering and death. For, in Mark's intention, 8:31 becomes the starting-point of the way of Jesus which ends in Jerusalem with the women at the tomb.

"And Peter took him and began to rebuke him" (v.32b). The idea of a suffering Messiah was entirely foreign to Peter. Despite his confession he had not grasped the essential meaning of messiahship. In his surprise and his upset at the unexpected prospect he dares to "rebuke" Jesus. His acknowledgement of Jesus as Messiah had set him and the disciples apart from "men" (v.27); but now Peter is rebuked for thinking as men think. Peter, and all like him who stand "on the side of men," stand opposed to God's saving purpose and align themselves with Satan.

The passage, in truth, is concerned not primarily with the historical situation of the ministry of Jesus, but with the historical situation of the church for which Mark is writing. The reply to Jesus' first question refers to opinions available in the Palestinian situation of the ministry (v.28). But, in the reply to the second question, the title "Christ" has christian overtones, and the prediction of the passion is cast in language of the early Church (vv.29,31). Peter's reaction and the sharp correction of it (vv.32-33) have much to do with an understanding of christology. Historically, Jesus and Peter engage in dialogue. At a deeper level, "Jesus" is the Lord addressing his church and "Peter" represents fallible believers who confess correctly, but then interpret their confession mistakenly. Similarly, the "multitude" (v.34) is the people of God for whom the general teaching (8:34 - 9:1) is meant. Thus, a story about Jesus and his disciples has a further purpose in terms of the risen Lord and his church.

Here, more obviously than elsewhere, Mark is writing for his community. Here, above all, he is concerned with christology. The confession of Peter is the facile profession of too many of Mark's contemporaries: You are the Christ. Everything depends on what they mean by that profession and its influence on their lives. They cannot have a risen Lord without a suffering Messiah. They cannot be his disciples without walking his road of suffering. Mark's admonition here is quite like that of Paul in Rom 8:15-17.

The specific details about place (v.27), and the rejection of Peter as Satan (v.33), which cannot conceivably have been invented, show that a historical nucleus lies within 8:27-33. But the end product is Marcan. On the basis of traditional data the evangelist has carefully composed the whole central part, the hinge of his gospel. And in it he has shown that the messianic story is no uninterrupted success story: it is a story of suffering, rejection, failure. This fact must influence and color all we say about life and salvation. Jesus immediately runs into opposition: "Peter . . . began to rebuke him." Quite obviously, Peter has spoken for all of us. Jesus confirms this: "You are on the side of men"—you think the thoughts of men. Not the thoughts of the proud, the arrogant, but the natural reaction of those who shrink from a way of suffering. Have we, at bottom, any different idea of salvation from that of Peter? Can we really conceive of salvation other than in categories of victory? We experience the saying of Jesus again and again as contradiction, we cannot reconcile ourselves to it. The rebuke of Jesus did not change Peter: he will deny the suffering Messiah. The other disciples will sleep and will abandon him.

And the church, which began with the twelve who failed to understand will, time and again, like them fail to understand.

The church must resist the temptation to re-interpret the scene, to turn it, somehow, into one of triumph. The church must never forget that it owes its existence not to a conqueror but to one vanquished, not to one who overcame but to one who was overcome. It owes its life to one who was judged by the standards of men: it is expedient that this man should die. And he was condemned to death, and crucified.

What is the meaning of the word that follows the prediction of suffering and death: ". . . and after three days rise again?" These words are not meant to allay our fears, not meant to soften the stark reality of suffering and death. That word of the victory of the Son of Man over death is a promise of victory for the oppressed, the vanquished, the silent in death—the forgotten. It is a word of warning against our human way of exalting the victorious and triumphant. Through the suffering Messiah victory is possessed by the vanquished; through the dead Messiah life is possessed by the dead. He and his way are the sole guarantee of our victory and of our life.

Part II
The Mystery of the Son of Man:
Revelation of Jesus' Suffering.
8:31 - 16:8.

THE WAY OF THE SON OF MAN.
8:31 - 10:52.

THIS, the first section of the second part of his gospel, is the unit in which Mark's *theologia crucis*, his central theological preoccupation, is most evident. We can discern in it a precise pattern, signposted by three announcements of the fate of the Son of Man. Each time a passion prediction is followed by the theme of the incomprehension of the disciples. Then Jesus stresses the demands of discipleship— Mark makes the point that discipleship involves following the Crucified One, that it is an *imitatio Christi*.

To imitate Jesus is to follow his way; the phrase "on the way" runs as a refrain through this section. At the outset, Jesus and his disciples are "on the way" (8:27) and at the end, when they draw near to Jerusalem, Bartimaeus, restored to sight, followed Jesus "on the way" (10:52). In between, we are repeatedly reminded. "On the way" the disciples had engaged in discussion on the issue of greatness (9:33-34). Jesus continued "along the way" (10:17), and resolutely led the disciples "on the way" to Jerusalem (10:52). The summons of 8:34 is given dramatic shape and content.

I. The First Prediction of the Passion and Its Sequel. 8:31 - 9:29.

THE SON OF MAN MUST SUFFER MANY THINGS. 8:31-33 (Lk 9:22; Mt 16:21-23).

> [31]And he began to teach them that the Son of man must suffer many things, and be rejected by the elders and the chief priests and the scribes, and be killed, and after three days rise again. [32]And he said this plainly. And Peter took him, and began to rebuke him. [33]But turning and seeing his disciples, he rebuked Peter, and said, "Get behind me, Satan! For you are not on the side of God, but of men."

The prediction of the passion (v.31), closely attached to Peter's confession by the editorial injunction to silence (v.30) is, in some sort, the title of the second part of the gospel which begins at this point and will reach a climax on Calvary (15:39). "And he began to teach" (v.31)—the words suggest a new orientation in the teaching of Jesus. Peter had just acknowledged Jesus to be the Messiah. Jesus employs the title of Son of Man to expound his understanding of what Messiah means (cf. 14:61-62). From now on the title will appear in connection with the passion and death of the Son of Man (9:9,31; 10:23,45; 12:31; 14:21) or with his glorious coming (8:38; 13:26; 14:62). "Must" (*dei*) expresses a conviction that the sufferings of the Messiah are in accordance with the will of God revealed in Scripture (cf. 9:12). Luke (24:26-27) states clearly: "Was it not necessary (*edei*) that the Christ should suffer these things and enter into his glory . . . He interpreted to them in the scriptures the things concerning himself." The passion of Jesus is not a quirk of fate.

The opening words, "the Son of man must suffer many things" (cf. 9:12) give the prediction in its simplest form; the formulation of the rest of the verse has been colored by the events, and the details have been conformed to the story of the Passion. To this extent the prediction is a *vaticinium ex eventu*. "Be rejected . . . be killed . . . rise again"—a remarkably complete outline of the Passion in its three stages: official rejection of the Messiah, his violent death, his victory over death. According to Mark, Jesus did refer to his death several times (cf. 8:31; 9:9,31; 10:34; 14:28), but certainly in less explicit terms than these texts suggest.

"And he said this plainly" (v.32) might be rendered: "and openly he proclaimed the word." This is the turning-point in the self-revelation of Jesus. If he still charges his disciples not to reveal his messianic identity (v.30), he now speaks to them quite plainly of his messianic destiny of suffering and death. This emphatic affirmation that Jesus spoke "openly" (*parrēsia*, cf. Jn 7:13,26; 10:24) of his passion shows the unusual character of the fact. Even when he had spoken "privately" to his disciples he had never spoken so clearly. Here it is impossible to miss the meaning of his words, and Peter's attitude (v.32b) shows that he had at once understood what Jesus had said, even though the divine necessity for the suffering escaped him altogether.

"And Peter took him": we can picture him, in his earnestness taking hold of Jesus and "rebuking" him. The idea of a suffering Messiah was entirely foreign to Peter. He realizes too that his own position will be affected: a disciple of a suffering Messiah is not a role that would appeal to him. The phrase "seeing his disciples" is proper to Mark: the rebuke is addressed to them too. "Get behind me, Satan" (*hypage opisō mou, Satana*)—the words recall Mt 4:10, "Begone, Satan" (*hypage, Satana*). This would suggest that Mark knew a form of the Matthew/Luke temptation story. The temptation in the wilderness (Mt 4:1-11; Lk 4:1-13) aimed at getting Jesus himself to conform to the popularly accepted messianic role; to become a political messiah. It was an attempt to undermine his full acceptance of the will of God and here Peter plays Satan's role. Peter's acknowledgment of Jesus as Messiah had set him and the disciples apart from "men" (v.27); but now Peter is rebuked for thinking as men think. Peter, and all like him, who stand "on the side of men," stand opposed to God's saving purpose and align themselves with Satan.

CONDITIONS OF TRUE DISCIPLESHIP.
8:34 - 9:1 (Lk 9:23-27; Mt 16:24-28).

After the first prophecy of the passion the three synoptists group a number of sayings to show that the followers of the suffering Messiah must be ready for suffering; their common theme is loyalty. These sayings fit this context because, after the confession of Peter and the first prediction of the passion, Jesus can ask for attachment to his person and not only for the acceptance of his message. Since the sayings are to be found, in a different form, in Q and even in John, it is probable that they originally circulated in isolation from one another. In Mark the passage is introduced by the statement: "And he called to him the multitude with his disciples, and said to them" (v.34)—a Marcan construction (cf. 4:10). The first five sayings are loosely linked by the particle "for" (*gar*) repeated in vv.35,36,37,38. There is no doubt that the last saying (9:1) has been added by the evangelist: his telltale formula, "And he said to them," makes that evident.

The passage asserts, unequivocally, that the disciples of the Son of man (v.31) must necessarily walk in his path. Only one who is willing to be called as a disciple and truly answers that call really understands Jesus. The loyal disciple cannot be preoccupied with his personal interests but will be faithful unto death in a sustained faithfulness to Jesus (v.34). This way of discipleship is not easy and one may be tempted to shirk from what it entails. But to seek thus to evade the risk and save one's life is to suffer the loss of one's true self. Only one who is prepared and willing to risk all for Jesus and for his gospel will attain to authentic selfhood (v.35). If man's life is so much more precious than anything else in creation, if no one can put a price on it, how much more precious is the eternal life that is won by the faithful disciple? (vv.36-37). A warning sounds for one who will not follow, the one who draws back and is ashamed of the Way, the one

who seeks to save his life. Christ, too, will be ashamed of
such a one, will disown him, when he returns in glory at the
end of time (v.38). And his return will not be long delayed;
already, in this generation, God's reign will be manifest in
power (9:1).

Mark undoubtedly looks beyond the ministry of Jesus.
Like the author of the Apocalypse, his concern is for a
persecuted community of his day. He reminds those Christians of a rejected and crucified Messiah that they ought
not be surprised that they, too, are called upon to suffer.
The cross has turned the values of this world upside down—
it is indeed "scandal" and "foolishness" (cf. 1 Cor 1:23). They
must be steadfast in face of persecution. They must not be
ashamed of Jesus' way of humiliation and suffering and
death if they do not want the glorious Son of Man to be
ashamed of them at his coming. And they hear his comforting assurance: "Surely, I am coming soon" (Rev 22:20;
cf. Mk 9:1).

> [34]And he called to him the multitude with his disciples,
> and said to them, "If any man would come after me, let
> him deny himself and take up his cross and follow me.
> [35]For whoever would save his life will lose it; and whoever
> loses his life for my sake and the gospel's will save it. [36]For
> what does it profit a man, to gain the whole world and
> forfeit his life? [37]For what can a man give in return for
> his life? [38]For whoever is ashamed of me and of my words
> in this adulterous and sinful generation, of him will the
> Son of man also be ashamed, when he come in the glory of
> 9   his Father with the holy angels." [1]And he said to
> them, "Truly, I say to you, there are some standing here
> who will not taste death before they see the kingdom of
> God come with power."

The first half of v.34 is an editorial link. "The multitude"
appears abruptly because, in Mark's intent, this is public
teaching. Significantly, even though Jesus is addressing
the people, ostensibly "those outside," he does not here
speak in parables (cf. 4:11,34). This is because he has spoken

of the suffering of the Son of Man and now goes on to state that all who follow him must share in his sufferings; already the veil over the messianic secret is being lifted. The necessity of suffering involves all who would follow Christ, that is, all Christians, and especially the particular community that is Mark's concern. In v.34b three conditions for loyal discipleship are laid down. "Let him deny himself"—not to be preoccupied with oneself and one's personal interests, but to have in mind only him whose disciple one would be. "Take up his cross"—this is unlikely to be an original feature of the saying of Jesus. A reference to the familiar Roman method of execution in Palestine, especially of those who were convicted of sedition, would most naturally be understood as an invitation to risk one's life in rebellion against the occupying power—certainly not the intention of Jesus. In its gospel context the saying evidently evokes the crucifixion of Jesus: the faithful disciple will be prepared to follow his Master even in his death. But this presupposes that Jesus' own passion and death had already set the pattern for his disciples. Explicit reference to the cross, in a saying of Jesus that always demanded readiness for the supreme sacrifice, emerged in the post-Easter tradition. Luke (9:23) adds "daily": taking up one's cross daily by patiently bearing trials and so dying to the world (cf. 1 Cor 15:31). "And follow me"—the first two conditions prepare the way for the third: continuous and sustained fidelity to Jesus, a following of him by acceptance of his way of life. Coming after mention of the cross, the demand means that the disciple must follow Jesus to the point of laying down life itself, the ultimate degree of self-denial. But, as the prediction of the suffering and death of Jesus also points to his resurrection (v.31), so, too, v.35 points to the attainment of true life.

"Life" (*psyche*, rendering the Semitic *nefesh*) means both "life" and "self." To save one's life is the opposite of denying oneself (v.34), while losing one's life means just that—the renunciation demanded of a disciple. Arrival at "selfhood" comes only through "giving up" oneself! "And the gospel's (sake)" (v.35); this phrase is proper to Mark and certainly reflects a time when Christians were in fact being persecuted for the sake of the gospel (cf. 13:9-13). The meaning of the paradoxical saying is this: one who, through fear of losing his (earthly) life, denies Jesus and thus thinks to save himself, in reality loses his eschatological life (his "eternal life," Jn 12:25) in God. By contrast, the one who does not hesitate to risk his earthly life in confessing Jesus gains eternal life in God. Even if death ensues (v.34) the disciple has gained eternal life: death is gain, not loss.

Verse 34 has shown the condition of discipleship and thereby has sketched a portrait of the loyal disciple: one who is committed to the following of Jesus, one who is not ashamed of that following. Now we are shown the contrast: one who will not follow, one who is ashamed of Jesus and of his way of humiliation and suffering (v.38). In the light of v.35 it would seem that the inconstant disciple will be "ashamed" of Jesus by denying him in time of persecution— he will seek to "save his life." The addition of "and my words" shows that Mark has the post-Easter situation in mind. Just as the disciples should not have been ashamed of the earthly Jesus, Christians must not be ashamed of the word of the Lord whom they encounter in the proclamation. This solemn pronouncement is of major importance for the Marcan community. But it is a word of warning, not a judgment saying. The Son of Man will come not to execute judgment but to gather his elect (13:17). The warning is that one may not be recognizable as belonging to Christ.

Threat is never the last christian word—the passage 8:27 - 9:1 ends on a note of promise. The saying of 9:1 is not only added by Mark (as his typical link-phrase, "and he said to them" suggests), but, very likely, was constructed by him on the basis of 13:30 and 8:38. It proclaims a visible manifestation of the kingdom, the reign of God, which will come "in power": not through any human effort, but by divine power. Furthermore, it will come soon, so soon that at least some of Mark's community will be alive to welcome it. That such was the evangelist's conviction will emerge even more clearly in 13:30-32. Here the saying provides an apt transition to the transfiguration, regarded as an anticipation of the glorious coming of the exalted Son of Man (cf. 13:24-27).

THE TRANSFIGURATION—LISTEN TO HIM.
9:2-8 (Lk 9:28-36; Mt 17:1-8).

The transfiguration episode ranks with the baptism (1:9-11) and Gethsemane (14:32-42) narratives and shows similarities with both. Rudolf Bultmann is representative of a goodly number of scholars who argue that it was originally a resurrection-story. The heavenly voice proclaims that the risen Jesus is indeed the Messiah. The "mountain" of Mk 9:2 is the same "mountain" of Mt 28:16 where the disciples met the risen Lord. The story serves Mark here as a heavenly ratification of Peter's confession and as a prophecy of the resurrection. Though much may be said for this view, it leaves some features of the story unexplained. Mention of "six days" is noteworthy considering that there are few references to time in the synoptic gospels. It is all the more remarkable that Luke (9:28), though he qualifies the statement ("about eight days"), is careful to preserve the reference. Obviously, in the tradition, there was a close connection between the event of Caesarea Philippi and the episode of the transfiguration.

While it is no longer possible to say what it was that transpired upon the mountain—was it vision? was it deep religious experience?—we must seek to understand what the episode means for Mark. It certainly is important for him. Perhaps his pointer, immediately before (9:1), to an imminent parousia, and the presence of Elijah and Moses, may help us to understand his purpose. We shall see in chapter 13 that Mark has to contend with some who, having pinned their parousia-hope on the traumatic event of the destruction of the temple in 70 A.D., were now disillusioned because that hope had been dashed. Was Jesus after all no greater than Elijah and Moses who, too, had been rapt to heaven? He was not really the Messiah, then, and that is why their expectation had been disappointed. For somewhat the same reason as the authors of Colossians and Hebrews (Col 1:15-20; 2:8-23; Heb 1:1 - 3:6), but in his own manner, Mark defends the uniqueness of Christ.

> [2]And after six days Jesus took with him Peter and James and John, and led them up a high mountain apart by themselves; and he was transfigured before them, [3]and his garments became glistening, intensely white, as no fuller on earth could bleach them. [4]And there appeared to them Elijah with Moses; and they were talking to Jesus. [5]And Peter said to Jesus, "Master, it is well that we are here; let us make three booths, one for you and one for Moses and one for Elijah." [6]For he did not know what to say, for they were exceedingly afraid. [7]And a cloud overshadowed them, and a voice came out of the cloud, "This is my beloved Son, listen to him." [8]And suddenly looking around they no longer saw any one with them but Jesus only.

"After six days"—outside of the passion narrative no other temporal statement in Mark is so precise. The presence of the three disciples, Peter, James, and John, underlines unmistakably the importance of the episode for Mark (cf. 5:37; 13:3; 14:33). A "high mountain" is the setting of a theophany. The geographical situation (Thabor, quite unlikely, or, more suitably, Hermon) has no relevance for Mark apart from the fact, perhaps, that the setting, still presumably in the general region of Caesarea Philippi, is vaguely gentile territory. The phrase "apart by themselves" emphasizes the revelatory character of the event; it is closely connected with the strict imposition of silence in v.9. In Rom 12:2 and 2 Cor 3:18 the verb "to be transfigured" is used of the "transformation" of the believer into the spiritual likeness of Christ. A transfiguration of the just in the world to come is an apocalyptic theme (Dan 12:3; 2 Baruch 51:3-10; cf. 1 Cor 15:40-44; 2 Cor 3:18). Thus, the transfiguration is an anticipation of the resurrection glory of Jesus. The garments of Jesus are described as glistening with heavenly light—this, too, has eschatological connotation (cf. Dan 7:9; Mt 28:3). "As no fuller on earth could bleach them"; this vivid and homely touch is proper to Mark, underlining the fact that the brightness is of heavenly origin.

"Elijah and Moses"—both Luke and Matthew have the normal order, Moses and Elijah. Mark may have put Elijah first because he will go on immediately to speak of the second Elijah (vv.11-13) or, more likely, because the tradition of Elijah being rapt to heaven is the better known (2 Kgs 2:11-12). "Talking to Jesus"— Luke gives the theme of the conversation: the "departure" (literally the *exodos* or death; cf. Wis 3:2; 7:6; 2 Pet 1:15) of Jesus at Jerusalem. In this and other respects Luke gives the impression that his version of the transfiguration story reflects an earlier form which is no longer discernible in Mark.

In the entire first part of Luke's narrative (9:28-32) Jesus holds the center stage. He goes up on a mountain, the place of divine manifestation. He becomes absorbed in prayer, and in the immediacy of God's presence, his countenance is altered and his raiment shines with heavenly whiteness. Two angels ("two men," Lk 9:30), the biblical mediators of revelation, appear to him and speak of his "departure,' that is, his death. In other words, Jesus, in an ineffable mystical experience, receives a revelation that his fate is to suffer and die. However, Jesus is not alone on the mountain: he has with him Peter and James and John. They do not share in the revelation but, as witnesses of his anticipated glory, they will be stronger to support the humiliation of the cross.

In Mark (perhaps already in his source) the aspect of revelation made to Jesus yields wholly to the theme of revelation granted to the disciples. And now the entire first part of the narrative prepares for this. Jesus leads the three disciples "up a high mountain" where he was transfigured "before them" (Mk 9:2). Moses and Elijah appear "to them" and it was for the disciples benefit that a heavenly voice was heard, speaking of Jesus in the third person (Mk 9:7;

Lk 9:35). In Luke Jesus is being presented as the new Moses who will reveal to the new people of God the secrets of the divine will. In order to be saved, one must listen to him. He had come to perfect the Old Testament revelation made in the Law (Moses) and the Prophets (Elijah). They disappear to leave "Jesus only" (Lk 9:36). Mark has given a different turn to the story and has adapted it to suit his purpose.

"It is well that we are here" (v.5)—that is to say, this is a happy moment which ought to be prolonged. "Booths" suggest the booths made of interlaced branches at the joyous feast of Tabernacles. But since Tabernacles had taken on an eschatological significance (Hos 12:9; Zech 14:16-19; Apoc 21:1-3) these "booths" evoke the heavenly dwelling-places of the blessed. The three booths, one each for Jesus, Elijah, and Moses, would have put all three on an equal footing. Peter really "did not know what to say;" he has, yet again, totally misunderstood. The voice from heaven will set the matter straight. The cloud which now over-shadows them is the cloud of God's *Shekinah* (the "presence" or "dwelling" of God) and the medium of his manifestation. "This is my Beloved Son"—in contrast to 1:11 the words are here addressed to the disciples: they hear the divine approbation of Jesus as the messianic Son. Elijah and Moses have disappeared and he stands alone. "Listen to him"—the Beloved Son is also the prophet-like-Moses whose teaching must be heeded (cf. Dt 18:15-19).

Mark intends us to see in the transfigured Jesus an anticipated glimpse of the risen Lord. As such the episode would be representative of that stage of christology which looked upon the resurrection as the decisive christological moment (cf. Rom 1:3-4; Acts 2:32-36; 5:30-31; 13:32-33). Jesus is not the mere equal of Elijah and Moses. He is supremely greater than they because by his victory over death he has been designated Son of God in power. Through the technique of Peter's misunderstanding Mark has again (8:31-33) corrected a christological error of some in his church. He can now resume his narrative. All is normal again. The disciples see before them, quite alone, their Master, no longer transfigured but in his familiar guise of everyday.

ELIJAH HAS COME.
9:9-13 (Mt 17:9-13; Lk 9:36).

> [9]And as they were coming down the mountain, he charged them to tell no one what they had seen, until the Son of man should have risen from the dead. [10]So they kept the matter to themselves, questioning what the rising from the dead meant. [11]And they asked him, "Why do the scribes say that first Elijah must come?" [12]And he said to them, "Elijah does come first to restore all things; and how is it written of the Son of man, that he should suffer many things and be treated with contempt? [13]But I tell you that Elijah has come, and they did to him whatever they pleased, as it is written of him."

The transfiguration had manifested the "Son of God"; the privileged disciples are strictly charged not to divulge this secret. Here the term or limit of the Secret, vaguely indicated in 4:21-22, is made explicit: it is the Easter resurrection. But, at the same time, we are told the need for secrecy. The disciples will not understand the mystery of his suffering and glory until the crucified Jesus will have risen from the dead. Not until then can he be proclaimed with understanding and in truth. And the Christian is reminded that the risen Christ is to be understood in the light of his cross and suffering. Typically, the disciples had not grasped his teaching, not even what "resurrection" meant (v.10). It is a signal to the Christian: he or she must strive to understand the mighty, transforming import of Resurrection.

The Elijah-passage (vv.11-13) is the answer to a difficulty that faced the early church. Christians maintained that Jesus was the Messiah. But Jewish tradition firmly held that Elijah would appear before the Messiah could come, a conviction based on Mal 3:2-3; 4:5-6. Implied in our text (v.11) is a denial that Elijah had come. Jesus answers the question of the disciples by first affirming the truth of Malachi's oracle and thus acknowledging that the scribes are, to that extent, right (v.12a). "To restore all things"— Elijah was to come before the Day of Yahweh to prepare the people and turn them to repentance (Mal 3:23); Jesus simply means that the tradition about Elijah is based on Scripture.

The second part of the reply (vv.12b-13) faces up to another objection: the christian claim that John the Baptist was the promised Elijah-figure is disproved by the well-known fate of the Baptist. The reply is in terms of the Baptist-Jesus typology. Elijah had indeed come, but men maltreated him and killed him (and so, of course, are disposed to maltreat the Son of man also). The Baptist's fate is prophetic of the fate of the Messiah. "As it is written of him"—the reference may be to such texts as 1 Kgs 19:2,10. The fate intended for Elijah had overtaken John: as Swete notes in his commentary, "he had found his Jezebel in Herodias" (cf. 6:14-29). In the long run, the phrase is meant to point to a divine purpose. It is fitting that the precursor should, beforehand, walk the way that the Son of man must walk—a point made explicitly in Mt 17:12. The christian retort to the Jewish objection is that John is the perfect Elijah to the Messiah who had come.

THIS KIND CANNOT BE DRIVEN OUT BY ANYTHING BUT PRAYER.
9:14-29 (Lk 9:37-43; Mt 17:14-20).

Many scholars discover inconsistencies in the narrative at this point due (they explain) to the conflation of two stories. But if we acknowledge that Mark's editorial activity has been extensive, we may reasonably maintain that there is here a single basic and coherent story. Mark has purposely set the narrative of the epileptic demoniac immediately after the transfiguration. As the heavenly acknowledgment at the baptism was followed by the temptation in the desert (1:12-13), so, too, the acknowledgment at the transfiguration is followed by an encounter with a demon. Mark has made the connection in the editorial passage 9:14-16. And he has introduced into the narrative the theme of the powerlessness of the disciples (vv.18b-19, 28-29). The story, which would have begun in v.17 ("One said to him, Teacher, I brought my son to you . . .") is found in vv.17-18a, 20-27, with vv.14-16, 18b-19, 28-29 as editorial additions of the evangelist.

This is the final exorcism story in Mark and the only one in the second part of the gospel. The motif of faith is strongly stressed. Jesus upbraids the faithless generation: all—scribes and Pharisees, the people, and the very disciples—have been without understanding and hardhearted. And now, the boy's father had doubted the power of Jesus: "if you can . . . ." He is told that faith does not put limits to the power of God. His cry is the heart of the story: he acknowledges his lack of faith and looks to Jesus for help. At this moment he stands in sharp contrast to the disciples who displayed their lack of trust. Jesus lifted up one who looked like a corpse, who was thought to be dead: now the disciples learn what rising from the dead meant (9:10)—Christ's victory over the forces of evil. Now they recognize the power and authority of Jesus. Only through union with their Master in prayer will they participate in that same power. Bereft of his presence, stripped of union with him, Christians are powerless and helpless.

> [14]And when they came to the disciples, they saw a great crowd about them, and scribes arguing with them. [15]And immediately all the crowd, when they saw him, were greatly amazed, and ran up to him and greeted him. [16]And he asked them, "What are you discussing with them?" [17]And one of the crowd answered him, "Teacher, I brought my son to you, for he has a dumb spirit; [18]and wherever it seizes him, it dashes him down; and he foams and grinds his teeth and becomes rigid; and I asked your disciples to cast it out, and they were not

able." [19]And he answered them, "O faithless generation, how long am I to be with you? How long am I to bear with you? Bring him to me." [20]And they brought the boy to him; and when the spirit saw him, immediately it convulsed the boy, and he fell on the ground and rolled about, foaming at the mouth. [21]And Jesus asked his father, "How long has he had this?" And he said, "From childhood. [22]And it has often cast him into the fire and into the water, to destroy him; but if you can do anything, have pity on us and help us." [23]And Jesus said to him, "If you can? All things are possible to him who believes." [24]Immediately the father of the child cried out and said, "I believe; help my unbelief!" [25]And when Jesus saw that a crowd came running together, he rebuked the unclean spirit, saying to it, "You dumb and deaf spirit, I command you, come out of him, and never enter him again." [26]And after crying out and convulsing him terribly, it came out, and the boy was like a corpse; so that most of them said, "He is dead." [27]But Jesus took him by the hand and lifted him up, and he arose.

[28]And when he had entered the house, his disciples asked him privately, "Why could we not cast it out?" [29]And he said to them, "This kind cannot be driven out by anything but prayer."

The redactional verses 14-16 form a transition from the transfiguration to the healing of the epileptic. "Scribes" are not mentioned again, by name, in the narrative, but are most likely addressed in v.16. The central theme is the powerlessness of the disciples. Jesus is absent and nothing goes right for them. They are unable to cope with an evil spirit and certainly would have been out of their depth in theological discussion with scribes.

In v.18a the distressing symptoms of epilepsy are described in detail (cf. v.20). In accordance with the ideas of the time, the recurrent convulsions and fits are ascribed to the periodical assaults of an evil spirit. "They were not able"—Mark underlines the disciples' inability: not only the man, but they themselves (v.28), were surprised to find that they were powerless in this case. After all, they had been given authority over unclean spirits (6:7,13). "O faithless generation"—an echo of Dt 32:5 (cf. Mk 8:12). The reproof is general and expresses the weariness of Jesus in face of the lack of faith manifested by his contemporaries—including the disciples.

The question of Jesus (v.21a) serves to bring out the gravity of the malady (vv.21b-22). The seizure could have come upon the boy at any time, so he could have toppled into fire or water; but the father attributes this to the malevolent design of the evil spirit. "But if you can do anything"—the man had been discouraged by the failure of the disciples. "Us"—his identification of himself with the boy is lifelike. "If you can!"—Jesus fixes upon the lack of faith. "All things are possible to him who believes": not that faith can do anything, but that faith will set no limits to the power of God. "I believe; help my unbelief": the man acknowledges that his faith is defective. For its strengthening and growth it needs the help of the Master—the christian overtones are obvious. With this cry from the heart the man emerges in a favorable light and stands in contrast to the disciples.

The spirit is not only cast out but is bidden, "never enter him again" (v.25). Since the affliction was not continuous but recurrent the demon must not only leave but must not return. "Like a corpse" (v.26), the boy lay motionless and pallid; most of the crowd took him for dead. "Took him by the hand"(1:31; 5:41); "lifted him up" (1:31); "he arose" (5:42); the parallels with the healing of Peter's mother-in-law and the raising of the daughter of Jairus are evident and deliberate. Even more markedly here we find the technical language of the early church's preaching of the death and resurrection of Christ. This kerygmatic intent, already present in the story of the daughter of Jairus, is more obvious here, coming in the middle of a section dominated by the predictions of the passion and resurrection. The cure, worked by Jesus, is a symbol and a presage of resurrection from the dead; the messianic power of Jesus is manifest. The theme comes dramatically here after the disciples' questioning about the meaning of rising from the dead (9:10).

In vv.28-29 Jesus is alone with the disciples "in a house" and they question him "privately," the Greek phrase *kat' idian* being an unmistakable Marcan label. This esoteric message to the disciples is addressed to the christian community. Jesus explains why the disciples had been unable to cope with the unclean spirit: prayer is vitally necessary, for the exorcist must rely on the power of God. The majority of manuscripts add "and fasting." But this is wanting in the most important manuscripts; and it is noteworthy that a similar gloss is found in some manuscripts of Acts 10:30 and 1 Cor 7:5. Its addition here is understandable but wrongheaded. Fasting would introduce something of one's own efforts while the point precisely made is reliance on the Lord. The theme of the powerlessness of the disciples, introduced into the narrative by Mark and stressed in this esoteric teaching, is a pastoral instruction to the church. The evangelist makes clear that, without Jesus, the disciples are helpless. Christians must seek to find union with him in prayer if they are to share in his power and have part in his work.

II. The Second Prediction of the Passion and Its Sequel. 9:30-10:31.

THE SON OF MAN WILL BE DELIVERED INTO THE HANDS OF MEN.
9:30-32. (Lk 9:43-45; Mt 17:22-23).

> [30]They went on from there and passed through Galilee. And he would not have any one know it; [31]for he was

teaching his disciples, saying to them, "The Son of man will be delivered into the hands of men, and they will kill him; and when he is killed, after three days he will rise." [32]But they did not understand the saying, and they were afraid to ask him.

The events of Caesarea Philippi and of the mount of transfiguration marked a new turn. Now the fateful journey to Jerusalem gets underway and, fittingly, the disciples are warned of the fate that awaits their Master there. It is a revelation granted to them alone, but they do not understand and are afraid. This second time Jesus' passion and resurrection are proclaimed in Galilee and in the context of a journey. In 9:9 we were shown that the need for secrecy about Jesus as Son of God was connected with the passion and resurrection of Jesus as Son of Man. Now the very presence of Jesus is marked with secrecy as he teaches his disciples about that mystery of death and life. This is the last reference because the stage is now set for the giving up of the secret in 14:62.

"The Son of man will be delivered into the hands of men." This is likely to be close to the form of the original passion-saying which underlies the existing greatly developed versions of the three passion-predictions (8:31; 9:31; 10:33-34). In Aramaic it might run something like: "God will (soon) deliver up the son of man to the sons of men." Mark's description, "Into the hands of men" is less precise but also of wider import than 8:31. In Dan 7:25 the "saints of the Most High" (= the Son of man) are "delivered into the hand" of Antiochus IV. Perhaps the betrayal by Judas is also in view as the manner in which God's saving design was set on foot. But the disciples do not yet understand the need for the suffering (v.32). Their thoughts are still the thoughts of men (cf. 8:33) and they cannot understand this teaching which is the revelation of God. Their fear (v.32) was a religious fear, like that of 4:41; 6:50; 10:32; they are always afraid when they are confronted with some manifestations of Jesus' person or mission. While Matthew

(17:23) simply has "they were greatly distressed," Luke (9:45) emphasizes further the disciples' lack of understanding and their fear.

THE COMMUNITY DISCOURSE.
9:33-50 (Lk 9:46-50; Mt 18:1-35).

A feature of this passage in all three synoptic gospels is that behind it one may still discern what must have been an elaborate unit skilfully articulated by a series of catch-words. This is most evident in Mark. But though the evangelist has used the source, he has not stuck slavishly to it (if indeed he had ever known it in its complete form). Here the passage is a pendant to his passion prediction, developing the theme of the incomprehension of the twelve and introducing that of the demands of discipleship. Our commentary, then, will not tackle the long passage (vv.33-50) as a whole but will regard it, as Mark seems to have done, as a grouping of shorter passages.

TRUE GREATNESS: LAST OF ALL AND SERVANT OF ALL.
9:33-37 (Lk 9:46-48; Mt 18:1-5).

> [33]And they came to Capernaum; and when he was in the house he asked them, "What were you discussing on the way?" [34]But they were silent; for on the way they had discussed with one another who was the greatest. [35]And he sat down and called the twelve; and he said to them, "If any one would be first, he must be last of all and servant of all." [36]And he took a child, and put him in the midst of them; and taking him in his arms, he said to them, [37]"Whoever receives one such child in my name receives me; and whoever receives me, receives not me but him who sent me."

On the journey through Galilee (v.30) Jesus and his disciples reached Capernaum and there, "in the house,"

he proceeded to teach them. They had been bewildered
by Jesus' further reference to his suffering (v.32); now
their profound lack of understanding appears at its most
blatant. They, disciples of a Master so soon to suffer bitter
humiliation and death—they are "on the way" to the
Jerusalem where it will take place—are all too humanly
involved in petty squabbling over precedence. The teacher
takes his seat and calls the twelve to him. The original
community discourse would have been a development
on the word *greatest* as in Lk 9:48: "He that is last among
you is the greatest." Mark sees here a lesson on the dignity
of service (cf. Jn 13:14-16); Matthew (18:2-3) transforms
it into a lesson on spiritual childlikeness.

The Aramaic word *"talya"* means "servant" or "child";
a word-play establishes a link between the "servant" of
v.35 and the "child" of vv.36-37. "Taking him in his arms"
(cf. 10:16)—proper to Mark—a vivid touch in his style.
This taking of the child is a symbolic action in the manner
of the prophets. "Receives" is to be taken in the sense of
"welcomes" (cf. 6:11); it means the loving service of the
weaker members of the community, those who stand in
greatest need of being served. "In my name," that is,
because of his connection with me, because he belongs
to me. A Christian is one baptized "into the name of"
Jesus (Mt 28:19; 1 Cor 1:13,15), so becoming his. That is
why one meets (serves) Christ himself in the disciple,
and the Father in Christ. This, then, is the dignity of
christian service.

Mark has made the point that the revelation of Jesus
cannot be received by one who is not ready to enter into
the spirit of discipleship and thereby become "last" and
"servant." As it stands, the passage is a pronouncement
story: the point of it lies in the sayings of vv.35b and 37
(with the symbolic gesture of v.36 underlining the message).
Jesus acknowledges that there is greatness in discipleship:
the dignity, the greatness, of service. And this is so because
the loving service of the least member of the community
is service of Jesus and of the Father. At the start (v.33)

Mark had drawn the special attention of his readers to this teaching, and to all that will be said until v.50. Perhaps the reader of today is once again attuned to the unambiguous message of this word of Jesus: greatness in his church is found in *diakonia,* service, and only there. Our first step is to have relearned this. It is high time for us to act accordingly, at all times, and at all levels.

HE THAT IS NOT AGAINST US IS FOR US.
9:38-41 (Lk 9:49-50; 11:23; Mt 12:30; 10:42).

> [38] John said to him, "Teacher, we saw a man casting out demons in your name, and we forbade him, because he was not following us." [39] But Jesus said, "Do not forbid him; for no one who does a mighty work in my name will be able soon after to speak evil of me. [40] For he that is not against us is for us. [41] For truly, I say to you, whoever gives you a cup of water to drink because you bear the name of Christ, will by no means lose his reward.

As a correlative of a belief in demons, the practice of exorcism was widespread in the hellenistic period among both Jews and gentiles. The apostolic church found itself faced with the problem of its attitude to non-christian exorcists who invoked the name of Jesus (cf. Acts 19:13-16).

This episode of the exorcist who was not a disciple is linked to the foregoing by the catchword "in my name"; here meaning an exorcism worked by invoking the name of Jesus. This is the only remark attributed by the synoptists specifically to John, and it is the only occasion in Mark where he appears alone. In the Lucan tradition he and his brother James manifest a similar spirit of intolerance, wanting to call down fire from heaven on a Samaritan village which had refused hospitality to Jesus and his disciples (Lk 9:54-55). "Not following us"—that is, not a disciple. The fact of casting out demons "in the name of Jesus" shows that the exorcist recognized the power of Jesus; he is thus not against Jesus and his disciples even if he is not joined to them. The saying of Jesus (v.39) offers his disciples a directive: they are not to forbid one who acts so. In the context it is a question of successful exorcism: the man was "casting out demons" (v.38), and Jesus speaks of a "mighty work" done by invocation of his name. By contrast, the sons of Sceva invoked the name of Jesus unsuccessfully (Acts 19:13-16). The presumption is that one who does a good deed in the name of Jesus cannot be an enemy of his; the saying of v.40 suits the context perfectly. In a christian setting the statement means that one is a member of Jesus' church as long as one does not categorically separate oneself from him.

In v.41 the catchword is again "in the name of," this time meaning "because"—because you are a christian. The smallest act of kindness shown to a disciple on the ground of his connection with Christ will not fail to have its reward. What is presupposed is God's kindness which will not overlook the slightest deed of generosity. "Reward" is not something we win for ourselves: it is always the free gift of a generous God. For Mark, of course, in its present context, the saying still applies to an outsider who is not hostile to Christ and who shows some kindness to a follower of his. "Because you bear the name of Christ" is certainly a later christian formulation. The title *Christos,* without the article, is frequent in Paul, but occurs nowhere else in this form in the synoptics and Acts. *Christou einai* ("to belong to Christ") is a Pauline phrase; cf. Rom 8:9; 1 Cor 1:12; 3:23; 2 Cor 10:7. Matthew and Luke omit the saying; the former, however, has a close parallel in 10:42.

These sayings of Jesus have an import beyond their Marcan setting. Christians of any age must take seriously the admonition, "He that is not against us is for us." Again, in our day, we are better conditioned to listen and to attend. We have Vatican II's "Constitution on the Church in the Modern World" and its "Declaration on the Relationship of the Church to Non-Christian Religions." And as for the disciples of Christ, in their relationship with one another, the "Decree on Ecumenism" bids them set aside petty jealousy and strive for true brotherhood.

SCANDAL.
9:42-48 (Mt 18:6-9; 5:29-30; Lk 17:1-2).

Jesus had come to seek out and save the lost. He came preaching good news to the poor: to all the needy, helpless, defenceless ones. Now he utters a grim warning against any who would hurt these "little ones," who would shake their faith in him. Deliberately to lead others astray, to snatch from them the hope that he has given them, is seen by Jesus as the blackest sin: the very denial of his demand of love. But a man's own enemy, his stumbling-block, may lie within himself (cf. 7:20-23). Occasions of sin are to be ruthlessly cut off. With the compelling emphasis of startling metaphor and threefold repetition the Lord urges men to make the costliest sacrifices in order to avoid sin and enter into life.

> [42]"Whoever causes one of these little ones who believe in me to sin, it would be better for him if a great millstone were hung round his neck and he were thrown into the sea. [43]And if your hand causes you to sin, cut it off; it is better for you to enter life maimed than with two hands to go to hell, to the unquenchable fire. [45]And if your foot causes you to sin, cut it off; it is better for you to enter life lame than with two feet to be thrown into hell. [47]And if your eye causes you to sin, pluck it out; it is better for you to enter the kingdom of God with one eye than with two eyes to be thrown into hell, [48]where their worm does not die, and the fire is not quenched.

"These little ones who believe in me": the humblest members of the christian community. "Causes to sin," literally "scandalizes" (cf. 4:17; 6:3)—a warning on the grievousness of the sin of those who lead simple Christians astray by voluntarily shaking their faith. "A great millstone," literally, "a donkey millstone," that is, a millstone turned by a donkey in contrast to the smaller handmill worked by a woman (cf. Mt 24:41). Death by drowning was a Roman punishment and was particularly repugnant to Jews; the warning, then, is very sharp.

The three logia (vv.43, 45, 47), linked by the catchword *skandalizō,* also treat of scandal, not, however, in terms of those who place a stumbling block before others, but in reference to whatever in oneself can cause one to stumble and fall into sin. There is no question, obviously, of actual mutilation, but the vivid Semitic mode of expression enjoins, in the strongest possible terms, the costliest sacrifice. "To enter life" (v.43) is the same as "to enter the kingdom of God" in v.47: both refer to the life of the world to come. "Hell," literally, "Gehenna." Originally, Gehenna—the Valley of the Son of Hinnom—was a ravine south of Jerusalem, where infants were offered in sacrifice to Moloch (Jer 7:31; 19:5-6; 39:35). It was desecrated by Josiah (2 Kgs 23:10) and was henceforth used as a dump for offal and refuse. Jeremiah warned that there the faithless ones of Israel would be destroyed by fire. As a site of ill-omen, it came to symbolize the place of future punishment (cf. 2 Esdras 7:36; Enoch 27:2). "To the unquenchable fire," omitted by many important manuscripts, is most likely a resume of the citation (Is 66:24) of v.48. If authentic, it simply makes explicit what is already implied by the term "Gehenna." Only crass literalism could have led to the later notion of hell as a place of fiery torment. Vv.44 and 46 (which are identical with v.48) are omitted by the best manuscripts. The conclusion of v.45 is uncertain; some manuscripts read "into the gehenna of fire" (cf. Mt 5:22; 18:9). "Where their worm does not die, and the fire is not quenched"—a quotation from Is 66:24

(LXX). This Isaian text, with its suggestion of maggots preying on offal, and refuse-burning fires perpetually smouldering, is aptly applied to Gehenna when one recalls the ill-omened refuse-dump that gave rise to the image. It is intriguing that in speculation on the fiery torments of hell this undying worm was conveniently lost to sight!

HAVE SALT IN YOURSELVES.
9:49-50 (Lk 14:34-35; Mt 5:13).

Mark still keeps in mind the need for renunciation and insists on it in face of the disciples' failure to grasp the necessity of suffering. And so, for him, the obscure sayings on salt refer to the spirit of discipleship. The disciple must be prepared for the test of the severest sufferings even unto death: he is not greater than his Master. There is no substitute for the true quality of discipleship. Christ's followers are meant to be a purifying and seasoning element in the world. If they fail they cannot draw their power from the world to which they are sent and which they serve. It is imperative, then, to find within oneself, and foster, the spirit of discipleship: a spirit of readiness for sacrifice, a spirit of true christian charity. This will bring about and sustain an atmosphere of peace in the community, and disputes about precedence, or any quarreling at all, will have no place. Thus, the discourse is fittingly rounded off (cf. vv.33-34).

> ⁴⁹For every one will be salted with fire. ⁵⁰Salt is good; but if the salt has lost its saltness, how will you season it? Have salt in yourselves, and be at peace with one another."

The saying of v.49 is found only in Mark. It is obscure and seems to be an allusion to Lev 2:13. Many important manuscripts add: "and every sacrifice will be salted with salt." It must be remarked that the saying has a merely verbal connection with v.48 (the catchword "fire"). Because we do not know its original context, we can only guess at its meaning. It may, perhaps, mean that, as the holocaust victim was salted before being consumed by fire, so, in the eschatological situation introduced by Jesus, the Christian will be purified by the salt and fire of suffering and persecution. He had been called upon to carry his cross (8:34) and to lose his life for Jesus' sake (8:35). He will show whether he has the "salt" of true discipleship.

V.50b is paralleled in Mt 5:13 and Lk 14:34 where the metaphor of savourless salt describes the uselessness of a disciple who has lost the spirit of devotion; he is fit only to be cast out, rejected. In Mark "salt" is a quality of the disciple: when it is lost there is no way of restoring it. The saying of v.50b might be understood in the sense of Col 4:5-6. Salt symbolizes wisdom which ought to "season" the words we speak to one another and so maintain peace in the christian community (cf. Job 6:6). In its present context the logion would seem to say more than that. The meaning probably is: "Have salt in yourselves, then you will be at peace among yourselves." "Be at peace with one another"—this constitutes a characteristic *inclusion:* the occasion of the discourse was a quarrel among the disciples (9:33-34); it is terminated by a recommendation to live at peace with one another (cf. 1 Thess 5:13).

WHAT GOD HAS JOINED TOGETHER.
10:1-12 (Mt 19:1-9; cf. Lk 17:18; Mt 5:32).

New Testament teaching on divorce has come under special scrutiny in recent times and Mk 10:1-12 figures prominently in all studies of the subject. Almost all contemporary exegetes and theologians perceive that Jesus seeks to restore marriage to the original form God intended it to have. Husband and wife are "two in one flesh," implying a covenant bond between persons far transcending physical union. Love, seeking only the good of the beloved, is the true marriage bond; love is, or should be, the call impelling a man to leave his father and his mother and to cleave in life-long union to his wife. Jesus prohibited divorce under the assumption that the marriage involved is a real marriage.

Implicity, then, the current trend is centred not so much on divorce as on marriage, and what marriage should ideally be. The measure of this is the perfect spousal love that is taught in Ephesians 5. This love is but one vital aspect of the entire "one commandment" of love which Jesus has given to us—the same love which should guide the pronouncements of a christian church. For those who are believers the solution to marriage difficulties is not desertion but forgiveness and a rekindling of love. The fact remains that Christians, no less than others, are human and frail. The entire question of divorce seems to call for great realism in looking at individual persons and the concrete situations in which they find themselves. It calls for an awareness of the greatest "realism" of all, a reality surpassing the ideal of irrevocable unity in marriage. And this is the real love which Jesus himself has for each of us. He understands our humanness (Heb 4:15-16), and he desires to give us the freedom in which to share his love. He is the truth who sets us free (Jn 8:32): in him rests the ultimate union of "two in one flesh."

10 And he left there and went to the region of Judea and beyond the Jordan, and crowds gathered to him again; and again, as his custom was, he taught them.

²And Pharisees came up and in order to test him asked, "Is it lawful for a man to divorce his wife?" ³He answered them, "What did Moses command you?" ⁴They said, "Moses allowed a man to write a certificate of divorce, and to put her away." ⁵But Jesus said to them, "For your hardness of heart he wrote you this commandment. ⁶But from the beginning of creation, 'God made them male and female.' ⁷'For this reason a man shall leave his father and mother and be joined to his wife,

> [8]and the two shall become one.' So they are no longer two but one. [9]What therefore God has joined together, let not man put asunder."
>
> [10]And in the house the disciples asked him again about this matter. [11]And he said to them, "Whoever divorces his wife and marries another, commits adultery against her; [12]and if she divorces her husband and marries another, she commits adultery."

"Beyond the Jordan," that is to say, Perea, a territory on the opposite side of the Jordan from Judea which, with Galilee, formed the domain of Herod Antipas. It is Mark's intent to indicate a decisive turning-point in Jesus' career: he goes forth to confront his enemies in Jerusalem. As he passes into Judea, Jesus can no longer remain incognito (cf. 9:30) and crowds flock to him again. He does not seek to withdraw but resumes his teaching activity— Mark emphasises this by his repetition of "again."

In Mark's formulation (vv.2-4 unlike Mt 19:3 with the addition "for any cause") the Pharisees' question is not related to the Shammai - Hillel controversy on the interpretation of the phrase "something shameful" in the text of Dt 24:1. It concerns simply divorce as such. In rabbinical style, question (v.2) is matched by counter-question (v.3). Nowhere in the written Torah is the permission of divorce explicitly spelled out; rather it seems to have been a custom taken for granted, a right given only to the husband to repudiate his wife without her having any redress. In the primary text of divorce legislation which we do have (Dt 24:1-4), while the issue is the prohibition of the re-marriage (to each other) of a divorced couple, it is admitted that a husband could divorce his wife for "something indecent," a "disgraceful" or "scandalous" thing—some fault which he had found to impute to her. However, he was required to produce a "writ of divorce" for her, a document setting her free from further obligations to him and allowing her to remarry (cf. Is 50:1; Jer 3:8). The Pharisees are justified in claiming (v.4) that the text of Deuteronomy ("Moses") does assume the practice of divorce.

Jesus (v.5) does not question their interpretation of the Law; but he does declare that Moses had written the "commandment" on divorce on account of man's *sklerokardia*, "hardness of heart"—his unteachableness, his failure to acknowledge God's moral demands and to obey the higher law contained in Genesis. The deuteronomic text referred not to a law but to a dispensation in view of Israel's stubbornness (cf. Dt 10:16; Ezek 3:17). Jesus carries his argument further (vv.6-9) by asserting that, from the beginning (the phrase, "from the beginning of creation" is used again in 13:19) God had no divorce in mind: by creating male and female God intended marriage to be for one man and one woman bound together in the indissoluble union implied by "one flesh" (Gen 1:27; 2:24). This monogamous union, moreover, was indeed indissoluble and unbreakable not only by reason of the two being one, but also because God himself brings the partners together and is the author of the marriage union: "What, therefore, God has joined together, let not man put asunder" (v.9). Jesus' prohibition of divorce is absolute.

An appendix (vv.10-12) to the pronouncement story is presented as an exposition which Jesus gives his disciples in private ("the house," appearing here abruptly in v.10, has its Marcan significance as a place of private instruction of the disciples, cf. 7:17; 9:29). Though looking beyond the Palestinian situation, the pronouncement is authoritatively placed on the lips of Jesus and confirms his prohibition of divorce. Jesus declares (v.11) that not only is divorce forbidden but also that marriage following divorce constitutes adultery because the first marriage bond has never been broken. The words "against her," referring to a man's first wife, go beyond Jewish law which did not consider that a man could commit adultery against his own wife. In Jewish law "adultery" (basically a sin of injustice) always signified sexual intercourse between a *married* woman and a man other than her husband. Thus, whereas a woman could commit adultery against her husband, a man could not commit adultery against his own wife but only against another married man.

The statement of v.12 goes quite beyond Jewish law since a woman was not allowed to divorce her husband. (In a very few, clearly defined, exceptions a woman might obtain, through the courts, the dissolution of her marriage—but this hardly affected the general principle). Mark has expanded the teaching of Jesus so as to meet the needs of gentile Christians living under Greco-Roman law. The teaching of the whole passage, pronouncement story and appendix, is unequivocal. It is a decisive, positive statement which must be taken with the utmost seriousness in any christian consideration of divorce.

LET THE CHILDREN COME TO ME.
10:13-16 (Lk 18:15-17; Mt 19:13-15).

This is a pronouncement story showing Jesus' attitude to children; its place here is on topical grounds, due, very likely, to the preceding teaching on marriage. Mark has delightfully brought the little scene to life: mothers anxious to present their children to the renowned Rabbi and wonder-worker; the disciples officiously intervening; Jesus indignant at their rebuff to children; his taking them into his arms. The point of the narrative lies in the sayings: children, better than any other are suited for the kingdom since the kingdom is a gift which must be received with simplicity. Jesus himself, in a true sense, is the kingdom; that is why children have a right of access to him. No one can enter upon the blessings of the kingdom who is not open and willing to receive the kingdom as a gift. It is probable that the story may have been influential in determining the early church's attitude to the practice of infant baptism.

> [13]And they were bringing children to him, that he might touch them; and the disciples rebuked them. [14]But when Jesus saw it he was indignant, and said to them, "Let the children come to me, do not hinder them; for to such belongs the kingdom of God. [15]Truly, I say to you,

whoever does not receive the kingdom of God like a child shall not enter it." [16]And he took them in his arms and blessed them, laying his hands upon them.

Children were brought to Jesus "that he might touch them": that they might receive the blessing of the great rabbi or, as he may have been regarded, of the prophet from Galilee. The disciples "rebuked" those who presented the children (evidently the mothers): their impatient attitude reflects that of the ancient world in which children were neither to be seen nor heard. Jesus' reaction was one of "indignation": here only in the gospels is this emotion ascribed to him—Luke and Matthew omit any reference to his indignation. In the clearest possible terms he shows that he desires and welcomes the coming to him of these little ones (cf. v.16). We, in a culture that is often sentimental in regard to children, can miss the revolutionary aspect of Jesus' conduct here, as we can fail to appreciate the import of his attitude to women.

"For to such belongs the kingdom of God"—the disposition of a child (receptivity, a willingness to accept what is freely given) is necessary for all who could enter the kingdom. This recalls the beatitudes (Mt 5:3,5). Consequently, to seek to prevent children from coming to him would be to seek to keep from the kingdom those who are naturally the least unfitted to enter. The solemn "Amen" confirms the seriousness of the pronouncement of v.15. One must receive the kingdom as a child receives it: with trustful simplicity and without laying any claim to it. Here the kingdom is presented both as a gift which men receive and a sphere into which they enter: one must be willing to receive the kingdom as gift before one can enter upon the blessings and responsibilities of it. "He took them in his arms"—proper to Mark (as in 9:36). He does so much more than had been sought (v.13). "And blessed them"—a strengthened form of the verb; that, with his laying of hands upon them, indicates a fervent blessing. In this sense the church is shown how it is to treat children.

It is not unlikely that this passage might have some connection with the question of infant baptism in the first century. The ascription of indignation to Jesus, for the only time in the gospels, would suggest that an important matter of principle was involved. We learn from Tertullian that those who practised infant baptism used this story to support their practice. A similar concern could account for the presence of the incident in our gospels: an occurrence which might have led to the solution of the question of infant baptism. The verb *koluo*, "hinder," is used, in a baptismal context, in Acts 8:36; 10:47; Mt 3:13-14, seemingly reflecting the enquiry whether anything hindered a candidate from being baptized. It may be that the same verb in Mk 10:14 is a gleam of a baptismal formula.

AND HE WENT AWAY SORROWFUL.
10:17-22 (Lk 18:18-23; Mt 19:16-26).

Though rather detailed, this narrative is a pronouncement story. Entry into the kingdom is still the subject as Jesus is asked what one must do to inherit eternal life. Jesus begins to answer the question by pointing to the duties towards one's neighbor prescribed in the decalogue; but he knows that observance of the law is not the whole answer. He was drawn to the man and invited him to become his disciple. But this aspiring disciple is to learn that discipleship is costly: he, a wealthy man, is asked to surrender the former basis of his security and to find his security in Jesus' word. He cannot see that the following of Jesus is the true treasure, the one pearl of great price (Mt 13:44,46) beyond all his great possessions. He cannot face the stern challenge of loving in deed and in truth by opening his heart to his brother in need (cf. 1 Jn 3:17-18). It is the saddest story in the gospel, this refusal of one whom Jesus loved to follow him. With this story Mark has returned to the theme of renunciation which is continued through vv.23-27 and 28-31.

¹⁷And as he was setting out on his journey, a man ran up and knelt before him, and asked him, "Good Teacher, what must I do to inherit eternal life?" ¹⁸And Jesus said to him, "Why do you call me good? No one is good but God alone. ¹⁹You know the commandments: 'Do not kill, Do not commit adultery, Do not steal, Do not bear false witness, Do not defraud, Honor your father and mother.'" ²⁰And he said to him, "Teacher, all these I have observed from my youth." ²¹And Jesus looking upon him loved him, and said to him, "You lack one thing; go, sell what you have, and give to the poor, and you will have treasure in heaven; and come, follow me." ²²At that saying his countenance fell, and he went away sorrowful; for he had great possessions.

Again (v. 17) we are reminded that Jesus is on his way to Jerusalem (cf. 10:1). Mark vividly describes the man running forward and falling upon his knees before Jesus; already we can gather that he is an impetuous character who may become readily discouraged. "Good Teacher" (here a fulsome compliment) is an address very rare in Jewish literature, and not surprisingly so because of the Jewish view that God alone is good (cf. Rom 7:18)—as Jesus speedily reminds the suppliant. "To inherit eternal life" means to gain entrance into the kingdom of God; to have existence with God beyond death (cf. Dan 12:2; 2 Mac 7:9). The man's question is unexpected from a Jew who would have taken for granted that observance of the law was the way to the kingdom; the implication is that the way of the law had left him unsatisfied. In view of Jewish reticence in ascribing goodness to any but God, Jesus rightly demands why and with what intent the man has spoken of him as "good." He ought to have recognized that all goodness derives from God. Rawlinson puts it well: "The Lord therefore refuses the ascription to himself personally of merit, as it were, in independence of God: as a christian saint in the like case might say 'Not I, but Christ,' so the Lord says virtually 'Not I, but my Father' (cf. Jn 5:19-24)." Matthew has smoothed out the difficulty of the saying: "Why do you ask me about what is good? One there is who is good" (Mt 19:17).

V.19 is the first part of Jesus' answer to the question about gaining eternal life. He points to those commandments of the decalogue which concern duties towards one's neighbor. This man is a typical representative of Judaism: he faithfully observes the law and seeks wisdom, and he is attracted to Jesus. It is not clear whether the impulsive reply (v.20) means that the man is expressing his relief: if the condition was the keeping of the decalogue, then eternal life was his already; or whether he implies that, despite his observance of the law, he remains inwardly dissatisfied and feels that there is some higher demand which he believes himself ready to meet. His question in v.17 would suggest that this latter is the burden of his reply. "And Jesus looking upon him loved him"—proper to Mark; it may mean that Jesus not only admired this man but showed him some gesture of affection. He wanted the man to become a disciple; but there is one condition: the renunciation of his riches. He is being asked to sacrifice the ground of his security and of his social status. Called to discipleship ("follow me"), he is being taught that christian discipleship is costly. "You will have treasure in heaven"—cf. Mt 13:14; Rev 3:17-18.

What a contrast (v.22) to the initial enthusiasm (v.17)! This is one of the saddest verses in the gospel, and one of the most human. No Christian, not even those who have "left everything and followed Jesus" (v.28) can afford to cast a stone at the unhappy man. Our "renunciation" is always so far short of what Jesus really asks. Nowhere else in the gospels, except in this story, do we read that a call of Jesus to follow him was refused.

The better to understand the scene, it must be put into its theological context. The theme of life (v.17) and the enumeration of the clauses of the decalogue (v.19) evoke the Jewish doctrine of the Two Ways. According to this the "path of life"—the indispensable condition of entry into life—is to love God (Dt 6:5) and to love one's neighbor (cf. Lev 19:18). This commandment of love for the neighbor, because of its positive formulation, transcends the negative prescriptions of the decalogue. In effect, Jesus is saying that, in order to gain eternal life, it is not enough to be guided by prohibitions; we must also positively love our neighbor and share our goods with him. Jesus does not propose two states of life, the one (observation of the decalogue) common to all Christians, and the other peculiar to an elite called to a more perfect life. The relinquishing of riches is demanded of *all* the disciples of Jesus, but this must be understood in the light of its guiding principle. What is involved is not the giving up of something regarded as evil in itself (riches), nor an asceticism that would make us worthy of the kingdom. Rather, what is in question is the concrete expression of our love for one another, and especially of our loving concern for our poorer brethren to whom we must give without counting the cost. This ideal of love goes beyond the demand of not killing, not stealing, and so on, as the decalogue is content to prescribe (M.-E. Boismard).

HOW HARD IT IS TO ENTER THE KINGDOM OF GOD.
10:23-27 (Lk 18:24-27; Mt 19:23-26).

The rich man's departure was dramatic witness that riches could come between a man and the following of Jesus; the words of Jesus drive the message home. For that matter, entry into the kingdom can never be an achievement of human resources and effort: it is always the work of God alone. And Mark has, yet again, stressed the disciples' slowness to understand (vv.24,26). This fitting appendix to the story of the rich man is, significantly, addressed to "the disciples": the usual Marcan device of introducing supplementary teaching aimed with particular sharpness at the readers.

> [23]And Jesus looked around and said to his disciples, "How hard it will be for those who have riches to enter the kingdom of God!" [24]And the disciples were amazed at his words. But Jesus said to them again, "Children, how hard it is to enter the kingdom of God! [25]It is easier for a camel to go through the eye of a needle than for a rich man to enter the kingdom of God." [26]And they were exceedingly astonished, and said to him, "Then who can be saved?" [27]Jesus looked at them and said, "With men it is impossible, but not with God; for all things are possible with God."

Jesus proceeds to turn the unhappy episode of the rich man to advantage in order to forestall any complacency on the part of his disciples; his words, specifically addressed to them, are reinforced by his challenging "look" (v.23; cf. 3:5). If he begins by stressing the difficulty of access to the kingdom for the wealthy, he passes quickly to the difficulty of entering the kingdom at all. The repeated "how hard . . . to enter the kingdom of God" (vv.23b,24b) frames the amazement of the disciples (v.24a). That amazement grows to astonishment (v.26) when they realize that the warning had been aimed at them (v.24b). Jesus' affectionate "Children" (found elsewhere only in John) expresses his awareness that this is a hard saying. He insists that it is exceedingly hard for anyone to enter the kingdom; indeed, it is impossible (v.27) on the basis of human achievement alone. The vivid figure of the impossible (v.25)—the contrast of the largest beast of burden known in Palestine with the smallest of domestic apertures—though applied to the rich, is taken by the disciples in a universal sense. They had perceived that he was warning them; but they cannot understand and can only helplessly exclaim: "Then who can be saved?" He "looked at them" (cf. 8:25; 10:21)—this is Mark's way of stressing a statement or reply of Jesus. The thought echoes Gen 18:14 (Septuagint): "nothing is impossible with God" (cf. Lk 1:37). Salvation is God's achievement, not man's: this is the miracle which makes possible the impossible.

LO, WE HAVE LEFT EVERYTHING.
10:28-31 (Lk 18:28-30; Mt 19:27-30).

Unlike the rich man, Peter and his companions had left their "all" (though so much less than his) and had answered Jesus' call. They are assured that they will not go unrewarded. Nor do they need to wait for recompense in the afterlife: they have their compensation here and now in the warm fellowship of authentic christian life. In their poverty they are the least of all but in the age to come they will outrank the great ones of the earth. V.30 probably reflects the experience of the early Christians, including their experience of persecution. Mark balances the sayings on the need for renunciation (vv.21,23-25) with the promise of its reward. The saying of vv.29-30 is a further appendix to the story of the rich man, with v.28 linking it to the previous passage.

> 28 Peter began to say to him, "Lo, we have left everything and followed you." 29 Jesus said, "Truly, I say to you, there is no one who has left house or brothers or sisters or mother or father or children or lands, for my sake and for the gospel, 30 who will not receive a hundredfold now in this time, houses and brothers and sisters and mothers and children and lands, with persecutions, and in the age to come eternal life. 31 But many that are first will be last, and the last first."

The verse 28 is editorial: it is a cross reference to 1:17-18 and 2:14 and is prompted by 10:21, Jesus' invitation to the rich man. Peter's question sums up the significance of that episode for the disciples. The rich man refused to follow Jesus: the rich who trust in their riches cannot enter the kingdom except through God's miraculous intervention. The disciples, however, have left all; Peter states the fact with some complacency. His implicit question is made explicit in Mt 19:27—"What then shall we have?" The items announced (v.29), given disjunctively, include all material possessions listed under the heads of home, relatives and property. "For my sake and for the gospel"—the same phrase occurs in 8:35. It is the present of Mark; sacrifice and reward are verified in the evangelist's own time.

The promised rewards (v.30), listed cumulatively, are omitted by Matthew and Luke. It is likely that the saying of Jesus in v.30 would have run: ". . . who will not receive a hundredfold, and in the age to come eternal life," with the rest of the present verse reflecting the experience of the early Christians. Mark has introduced the contrast "in this time/in the age to come" and has taken up again the enumeration of v.29 to specify that it is in the here and now the followers of Jesus receive a hundredfold for what they have left in order to follow him. "With persecutions"—this may be meant to give an ironical twist to the hundredfold "reward" for total renunciation. More simply, it reflects the harsh reality of christian experience. Yet, despite the afflictions which assailed them, the early Christians found abundant compensation in their new brotherhood (cf. Rom 16:13). With the same expression in v.17, "eternal life" forms an inclusion which brackets this passage. The saying of v.31 occurs also, in a wholly different context in Mt 20:16; Lk 13:30. We have no way of knowing, with certainty, the original import of the saying. Mark, seemingly, understands it to mean that while the rich and prosperous are first in this world, those who have left all things (and consequently are the last here below) will be first in the world to come.

The Third Prediction of the Passion and Its Sequel. 10:32-52.

GOING UP TO JERUSALEM.
10:32-34 (Lk 18:31-34; Mt 20:17-19).

The setting and the developed form of this final prediction of the passion make it the most solemn of all. Jerusalem, the goal of the journey, is explicitly named, and Jesus is depicted as marching resolutely to his destiny. Its precision and detail turn this prophecy into a synopsis of the passion narrative. Thus the stage is set for the entry into Jerusalem (11:1-10) and for all that follows.

> ³²And they were on the road, going up to Jerusalem, and Jesus was walking ahead of them; and they were amazed, and those who followed were afraid. And taking the twelve again, he began to tell them what was to happen to him, ³³saying, "Behold, we are going up to Jerusalem; and the Son of man will be delivered to the chief priests and the scribes, and they will condemn him to death, and deliver him to the Gentiles; ³⁴and they will mock him, and spit upon him, and scourge him, and kill him; and after three days he will rise."

The journey had begun in the far north (Caesarea Philippi, 8:27) and had continued on its slow way southward (9:30,33-34; 10:1,17). Its goal was Jerusalem (11:11); here that goal is explicitly mentioned. "Going up to Jerusalem" is a stereotyped formula to describe a journey, especially a pilgrimage, to the holy city. This ascent is the only journey to Jerusalem narrated in the gospel. Undoubtedly, Jesus did visit the city many times, but only once did he do so "messianically," and Mark has deliberately presented this single description of the "going up" to convey this messianic purpose. Just as Peter's confession was centrally important in Mark by the fact that it occurred but once, so too, the uniqueness of this ascent to Jerusalem gives it a special value. Jesus tells the twelve explicitly that he goes to Jerusalem to be "delivered up" and "condemned to death" (v.33), but a preliminary stage will be his messianic entry into the city (11:1-10). In Mark's plan, then, Jesus must go to Jerusalem only on this one occasion—in order to fulfill his messianic destiny there.

Mark has already presented Jerusalem as the center of hostility to Jesus. Twice he has mentioned that hostile scribes, come from Jerusalem, had engaged in controversy with him (3:22; 7:1). This journey is leading to further conflict in Jerusalem with "the chief priests and the scribes" (11:15-18), with "the chief priests and the scribes and the elders" (11:27-33). "Jesus was walking ahead of them"—he knew where he was going and what fate awaited him in that city. Luke (9:51) has put it aptly: "When the days drew near for him to be received up, he set his face to go to Jerusalem." The resolute bearing of Jesus as he led the way stirred the disciples with "amazement" and "fear," a feeling of foreboding. They sensed that something was in the air. Their distress is highlighted by the repeated "going up to Jerusalem" (vv.32,33). We are being prepared for their failure at the testing time.

"And taking the twelve again"—the teaching is for them alone (8:31; 9:9,12,31). "He began to tell them what was to happen to him"—a general statement like this, followed by direct discourse (vv.33-34) is typical of Mark (cf. 1:14-15; 4:2). This (vv.33-34), the most developed of the passion predictions, is manifestly, in form, a *vaticinium ex eventu*. It corresponds very closely with the stages of the passion narrative. The Son of man will be delivered to the chief priests and the scribes (14:53), who will condemn him to death (14:64) and deliver him to the gentiles (15:1). They will mock him (15:15), and kill him (15:24,37). But, after three days, he will rise (16:1-8).

IT SHALL NOT BE SO AMONG YOU.
10:35-45 (Mt 20:20-28).

The stark words of vv.33-34 fall on ears deafened by selfish ambition. Jesus asks of one who would follow him a readiness to face and share his sufferings. The power of the risen Lord will break through their self-seeking and give backbone to the facile enthusiasm of James and John who will indeed walk manfully in the way of their Master. As it is, their request for the first places in the kingdom is one which Jesus not only will not but cannot grant: these are at the disposition of the Father who is no respecter of persons. Lack of understanding persists in the resentment of the other disciples who feel that the brothers have tried to "pull a quick one" on them. This leads to Jesus' earnest repetition (cf. 9:35) of his teaching on true greatness. He had come as the servant of all, as one who would lay down his life to rescue men from the oppression and slavery of sin. Authority in his church must wear the unmistakable livery of *diakonia*, service. Any suggestion of dominance, any vestige of oppression, must stand as a denial of him and all he represents. In this regard the church has much to learn and very much more to unlearn.

> [35]And James and John, the sons of Zebedee, came forward to him, and said to him, "Teacher, we want you to do for us whatever we ask of you." [36]And he said to them, "What do you want me to do for you?" [37]And they said to him, "Grant us to sit, one at your right hand and one at your left, in your glory." [38]But Jesus said to them, "You do not know what you are asking. Are you able to drink the cup that I drink, or to be baptized with the baptism with which I am baptized?" [39]And they said to him, "We are able." And Jesus said to them, "The cup that I drink you will drink; and with the baptism with which I am baptized, you will be baptized; [40]but to sit at my right hand or at my left hand is not mine to grant, but it is for those for whom it has been prepared." [41]And when the ten heard it, they began to be indignant at James and John. [42]And Jesus called them to him and said to them, "You know that those who are supposed to rule over the Gentiles lord it over them, and their great men exercise authority over them. [43]But it shall not be so among you; but whoever would be great among you must be your servant, [44]and whoever would be first among you must be slave of all. [45]For the Son of man also came not to be served but to serve, and to give his life as a ransom for many."

The episode of the two brothers (vv.35-40) originally had no connection with the prophecy of the passion; it finds its place here as an illustration of the incomprehension motive. Matthew spares the two disciples by attributing this ambitious request to their mother (Mt 20:20-21), while Luke omits the story altogether. The brothers approach the Messiah (8:29) and quite firmly put their request, but in general terms. Jesus receives them graciously and asks what they have in mind. They demand nothing less than the first places in Jesus' triumph. "In your glory"—glory (*doxa*) as at 8:38 and 13:26 is the eschatological glory of Jesus at the parousia; so, at least, Mark understands it. The original setting of the verse is uncertain and the brothers are motivated more by selfish ambition than by any clear idea of what they want. They were disciples of one whom they had acknowledged as Messiah: they were on to a "good thing" and they were determined to make the most of their good fortune. The episode admirably suits Mark's purpose of emphasizing the chronic incomprehension of the disciples and, with its sequel (vv.41-45), carries a barbed message for his readers.

The disciples have been naive, not realizing what it was they asked and what might be the implications of their request. "The cup that I drink"—in the Old Testament "cup" is the symbol both of joy (Pss 22:5; 115:4) and of suffering (Ps 74:9; Is 51:17-22; Jer 32:1; Ezek 33:31-34); our context demands the latter sense and, specifically, the idea of redemptive messianic suffering (cf. Mk 8:31; 9:31; 14:36; Jn 18:11). "The baptism with which I am baptized"—immersion in waters ("baptism") is a metaphor for overwhelming calamity and suffering (Ps 42:7; Is 43:2; Job 9:31). Matthew (20:23) has omitted the clause, but Luke (12:50) has an important parallel: "I have a baptism to be baptized with; and how am I constrained until it is accomplished!" The "baptism" is the passion which will "plunge" Jesus into a sea of suffering. The two brothers are being told: you do not know the price that must be paid to share my glory. Here indeed it is like Master like servant—and Jesus must suffer these things before entering into his glory (Lk 24:26). They must be prepared to accept the full implication of following Jesus.

The brothers are unabashed and answer with the same confidence (v.39) that Peter will display (14:29,31). And he and they will find, to their comfort, that they can indeed bear all things—when Jesus supports them. Yes, James and John will indeed, Jesus promises, drink his cup and partake in his baptism. On the whole, this first part of the answer (vv.38-39) to the brothers' request has been affirmative. They do not appreciate what they really ask nor have any idea of the heavy cost, but Jesus does promise them that, having suffered like himself, they will also enter into his glory.

The second part of Jesus' answer (v.40) concerns, more directly, their demand for the first places in the kingdom. But it is an evasive answer. Jesus is not empowered to grant these places to whom he pleases; they have already been allotted (by God). The appointment of places in the kingdom is at the Father's disposition only; discipleship does not entitle one to receive a special reward nor to make any demand. As in 13:32 Jesus' words imply a subordination to the Father.

Jesus' answer is in two parts and it would seem that the practical refusal of the request (v.40) is answer enough. Though it is widely maintained that vv.38-39 are secondary, they do point the brothers a way of having what they really seek: fellowship with Jesus and a share in his glory. Jesus promises to give them all that he can grant. Almost despite themselves they will become true disciples. Whatever about their provenance, the sayings are primary in Mark's purpose.

The other ten are not less incomprehending than John and James; they are indignant at being circumvented by the shrewd pair (v.41). This is an appropriate occasion for another telling lesson in discipleship (vv.42-45). Jesus solemnly asserts that, in the community of his disciples, there is no place for ambition. His church is a human society: there is need for authority, there must be leaders. But those who lead will serve their brethren, and the spirit of authority is *diakonia*. Surely, Jesus has intended the paradox and asks for it to be taken seriously. There is the shining light of his own example: he served God's purpose, the salvation of men, by laying down his life in the service of men. There really can be no justification at all for styles and trappings and exercise of authority inspired by the powers and princes of this world. Centuries of tradition cannot weigh against the stark words of the Lord. *It shall not be so among you*—we have no right to urge the burden of history against a demand as stark as that. Sooner or later we must find courage to admit, not only in word but in deed, that we have not hearkened to this word of the Lord.

Mark, with his reference to the indignation of the ten (vv.41-42a), again highlights the pettiness of the disciples (cf. 9:34-35) while Jesus' words on his imminent suffering and death still ring in their ears. Their incomprehension is glaring. And v.42a gathers them for esoteric teaching: the reader's attention has been firmly drawn to this passage. In vv.42b-45 we are no longer concerned with the kingdom of God (vv.37-40) but with the christian community. A saying (v.42b) in synonymous parallelism, illustrates the principle and the exercize of authority in the world. "Lord it over them"—have complete dominion over; "exercise authority over," in parallelism, would have the same sense of despotism and absolute power. "Those who are supposed to rule over" is sarcastic: they are arrogantly unaware of the ultimate source of all authority (cf. Jn 19:11). The sarcasm is heavy in Luke's "those in authority over them are called benefactors" (22:25). By and large the saying depicts a notion of authority that goes with the principle of absolute monarchy (or its equivalent). And the history of christendom has shown that, once the same principle of authority found a footing within the church, authoritarianism inevitably flourished.

"But it shall not be so among you." One has often thought that these words are, in their way, the saddest in the gospels. They are so unambiguous, so stark; they represent not only what Jesus had said more than once, but reflect his own way. And yet...the form and exercise of authority in the church have been, almost from the first, and still remain in large measure, the antithesis of Jesus' clear demand. He tells us that his church is not an earthly kingdom. He demands that those who hold authority in the church must be the servants of those whom they lead: the principle of authority is admitted, but the manner of its exercise is bluntly characterized as service. No, not only the "servant" Jesus boldly demands, but the *slave of all*! The great Paul was unashamed not only to call himself but to *make* himself "a slave to all" (1 Cor 9:19; cf. 2 Cor 4:5). Thus he could, with so much greater authority, urge his brethren to be servants of one another in the freedom of love (Gal 5:13). This service ennobles because it is a service of disinterested love and is consistent with true freedom. For it is the service of setting others free to achieve their full potential in Christ. Yes, the words of Jesus are clear: unlike worldly rulers, concerned with power and glory, his disciples are to serve, without pomp or display.

The ground of the paradoxical behavior required of disciples is to be found in the example of the Son of Man himself (v.45). The close of the logion specifies in what sense Jesus is to "serve" men: he will give his life as a ransom for them. *Lytron* ("ransom") was originally a commercial term: the ransom is the price that must be paid to redeem a pledge, to recover a pawned object, or to free a slave. In the Septuagint the term is predicated metaphorically of God, who is frequently said to have bought, acquired, purchased, ransomed his people (e.g. Ps 49:8; Is 63:4). In its Marcan form the saying is related to Is 53:10-11, and "ransom" (*lytron*) is to be understood in the sense of the Hebrew word "*āshām*" of Is 53:10, "an offering for sin," an atonement offering. By laying down his life for a mankind enslaved to sin, Jesus fulfills the saying about the Servant in Isaiah 53:10-11. Jesus has paid the universal debt: he has given his life to redeem all others. But this is metaphor, not crude commerce.

It has been customary to compare 10:45 with Lk 22:27 and to argue that the former is a development, under Pauline influence, of the latter. It is at least as likely that both the Marcan and the Lucan texts derive independently from

Palestinian tradition. The really Greek form of the Marcan saying is found in 1 Tim 2:6—"the man Christ Jesus, who gave himself as a ransom (*antilytron*) for all" (*hyper pantōn*). Compare Mk 10:45—"The Son of man came . . . to give his life (*tēn psychēn autou*) for many" (*anti pollōn*). The idea is certainly present in Paul (e.g. Gal 3:13; Rom 3:24; 1 Cor 7:23) but nowhere is there any close parallel to Mk 10:45. It is far more likely that Paul has developed a theme introduced by Jesus than that Mark has here condensed the thought of Paul and attributed it to Jesus. Taylor comments finely: "It is wise never to forget that *lytron* is used metaphorically, but it is equally wise to remember that a metaphor is used to convey an arresting thought. Jesus died to fulfill the Servant's destiny and his service is that of vicarious and representative suffering. We are ill-advised if we seek to erect a theory upon 10:45 alone, but equally so if we dismiss it as a product of later theological construction."

HE FOLLOWED HIM ON THE WAY.
10:46-52.

This narrative focuses on the blind man who is thereby presented as a model of faith in Jesus in spite of discouragement, and as one who eagerly answers the call of the Master and follows him in the way of discipleship. For Mark the story sounds a new departure in the self-manifestation of Jesus. He finds himself acclaimed, repeatedly, as "Son of David," a title for the Messiah; far from imposing silence, he calls the man to his presence and openly restores his sight. The way is being prepared for the manifestation of the humble Messiah (11:1-10). The days are near for him to be delivered up and he set his face to go to Jerusalem (10:32; cf. Lk 9:51). God's purpose is already working itself out. Very soon the true nature of his messiahship will be clearly seen. The need for secrecy no longer urges.

We have seen that the story of the healing of a blind man in 8:22-26 has a manifestly symbolical meaning in reference to the opening of the disciples' eyes. We can reasonably assume that Mark has a purpose in placing a healing miracle at this point too. That other healing came immediately before Jesus and his disciples had set out "on the way" (8:27); and, at the close of the section 8:27 - 10:52 Bartimaeus will follow him on the way. That journey was meant to heal the blindness of the disciples—here it is this blind man who sees. It takes faith to recognize the mercy and pity of the Son of David and follow him in the way of humble discipleship (11:1-10). Like the blind man in Jn 9, Bartimaeus emerges as a forthright and attractive character. The story focuses on him to an unusual extent. He would seem to be held up as an encouragement to believers.

> [46]And they came to Jericho; and as he was leaving Jericho with his disciples and a great multitude, Bartimaeus, a blind begger, the son of Timaeus, was sitting by the roadside. [47]And when he heard that it was Jesus of Nazareth, he began to cry out and say, "Jesus, Son of David, have mercy on me!" [48]And many rebuked him, telling him to be silent; but he cried out all the more, "Son of David, have mercy on me!" [49]And Jesus stopped and said, "Call him." And they called the blind man, saying to him, "Take heart; rise, he is calling you." [50]And throwing off his mantle he sprang up and came to Jesus. [51]And Jesus said to him, "What do you want me to do for you?" And the blind man said to him, "Master, let me receive my sight." [52]And Jesus said to him, "Go your way; your faith has made you well." And immediately he received his sight and followed him on the way.

Jesus and his disciples are now (v.46) well on the road to Jerusalem (v.32); Jericho is situated only fifteen miles northeast of the city. "A great multitude"—a concourse of pilgrims on the way to the holy city for Passover. A blind beggar was not an unusual sight; his position outside the town gate on the road to Jerusalem was an advantageous pitch. Apart from the disciples, Jairus (5:22), and now this beggar, Mark has named no one else earlier than the passion narrative; this would suggest that Bartimaeus was known in a christian circle as one whose sight Jesus had restored. Matthew has two blind men. Luke (18:35-43), for purely literary reasons, has put the miracle at the entry of the town because he wants to fit in the episode of Zacchaeus (19:1-10), which takes place at Jericho, and the parable of the pounds (19:11-27) which he sets in the context of departure for Jerusalem (19:11).

The blind man senses that something unusual is afoot and his enquiry reveals that Jesus of Nazareth is present (vv.47-48). "Son of David" is a manifestly messianic title: Jesus is the Davidic king, the heir of the promise made to David (2 Sam 7:12-16; 1 Chr 17:11-14; Ps 89:29-38). Bartimaeus asks Jesus to show mercy to him, to have pity on him. It is an implicit request to heal his blindness. He would have accepted that the opening of the eyes of the blind was a work of the Messiah (Is 29:18; 32:3; 35:5). "And many rebuked him"—their motivation is not clear; perhaps they resented his importunity. The real significance here is that whereas, hitherto, Jesus had commanded silence when his messiahship was acknowledged (cf. 3:12; 8:30), it is the onlookers who now seek to silence the man while Jesus calls him to himself and heals him. The man's repeated cry intensifies the contrast. We cannot doubt that Mark has engineered this situation. Jesus is openly, and repeatedly, acclaimed as "Son of David" and he shows implicit approval. But, as in the case of Peter's acknowledgment of him as Messiah (8:29,31), so here, too, he will give his own distinctive understanding of messiahship (11:1-10). This time there is no need for secrecy (cf. 8:30): emphasis on suffering ever since Caesarea Philippi has ruled out a triumphalist flavor to the title.

Jesus challenges the man to make his request (v.51). His question is the same as that to James and John (v.36). The simple and humble request of Bartimaeus is so different from their selfish demands; he understands so much better than they the authority of Jesus who does not dominate but has come to serve (vv.42-45). Unlike them (v.39) he is aware of his need and of his helplessness and finds his only hope in Jesus' nearness. And Jesus responds to his need: "your faith has made you well." "Faith" is confident trust in God and in the healing power of Jesus (cf. 5:34). "Made you well," literally "saved you" has the same overtones of salvation as in 5:28,34. "Followed him on the way" could mean that the man joined the crowd on the way to Jerusalem. There can be no doubt that Mark means: he followed Jesus on the way [of christian discipleship]. The phrase "on the way" and the following of Jesus form an inclusion with v.32. Only one of faith, enlightened by Jesus, can walk his way without consternation and without fear.

JESUS IN JERUSALEM.
11:1 - 13:37

LO, YOUR KING COMES TO YOU.
11:1-11 (Lk 19:29-40; Mt 21:1-11).

FOR MARK'S READERS this coming to Jerusalem had an obvious messianic significance, but for Jesus' contemporaries it was not clear (cf. Jn 12:16). It is likely that the episode really took place not at Passover but at a feast of Dedication, and Mark's narrative would suggest that it was a modest affair: the immediate disciples and Jesus riding in their midst. Nothing would have seemed more commonplace than a man riding on a donkey; and a group of pilgrims, waving branches and shouting acclamations from Ps 118, would not have occasioned a second glance at the feast of Dedication. Yet, whatever others might have thought, Christians knew that the last entry of Jesus into Jerusalem (as it is here presented), however unassuming it may have been in fact, was the solemn entry of the Savior-King into his city. Jesus himself took the initiative: he would enter as the humble Messiah-King of Zechariah. But, even here, there is a studied reticence. The text of Zech 9:9 is not quoted (cf. Mt 21:5); there are no "crowds" (Mt 21:9), no "multitude" (Lk 19:37,39); the people had *not* actually acclaimed Jesus as "Son of David" (cf. Mt 21:9) though they had spread their cloaks and leafy branches for his passage. This reticence on the part of Mark is, however, matched by a forward step in the unveiling of the messianic secret. It is being revealed in terms of what Mark understood Jesus' messiahship to mean. In this entry to Jerusalem Jesus himself, for the first time in the gospel, is making a messianic gesture—but in a special way, wholly in keeping with his destiny of one who had come to serve and to lay down his life.

> **11** And when they drew near to Jerusalem, to Beth-phage and Bethany, at the Mount of Olives, he sent two of his disciples, [2]and-said to them, "Go into the village opposite you, and immediately as you enter it you will find a colt tied, on which no one has ever sat; untie it and bring it. [3]If any one says to you, 'Why are you doing this?' say, 'The Lord has need of it and will send it back here immediately.'" [4]And they went away, and found a colt tied at the door out in the open street; and they untied it. [5]And those who stood there said to them, "What are you doing, untying the colt?" [6]And they told them what Jesus had said; and they let them go. [7]And they brought the colt to Jesus, and threw their garments on it; and he sat upon it. [8]And many spread their garments on the road, and others spread leafy branches which they had cut from the fields. [9]And those who went before and those who followed cried out, "Hosanna! Blessed is he who comes in the name of the Lord! [10]Blessed is the kingdom of our father David that is coming! Hosanna in the highest!"
>
> [11]And he entered Jerusalem, and went into the temple; and when he had looked round at everything, as it was already late, he went out to Bethany with the twelve.

The fateful journey nears its close. Bethphage and Bethany are the villages nearest Jerusalem on the road from Jericho. Both villages lay on the east slope of the Mount of Olives. The Mount of Olives was, in Jewish expectation, associated with the coming of the Messiah (cf. Zech 14:4).

It is idle to speculate whether the precise directions of Jesus (vv.2-3) indicate a previous arrangement with the owner of the colt. Mark, quite clearly, presents Jesus as displaying supernatural knowledge in making these arrangements (cf. 14:13-15). When we accept the intent of the passage to describe Jesus' approach to Jerusalem as a messianic king, we may see in the phrase, "a colt tied," an evocation of Gen 49:8-12 ("Binding his foal to the vine and his ass's colt to the choice vine," 49:11) which proclaims the advent of a king from Judah. "On which no one has ever sat" is a common requirement in a beast used for religious purposes. "The Lord" has need of the colt: the only place in Mark where Jesus is so designated; the title underlines the dominant role of Jesus here.

The garments (v.7) provide an improvised saddle; the spreading of garments on the road (v.8) was a form of royal homage (cf. 2 Kgs 9:13). "Leafy branches" recall the procession on the feast of Tabernacles (or Dedication). The description evokes the triumphal entry of Simon Maccabeus and his followers into Jerusalem, "with praise and palm branches ... and with hymns and songs" (1 Mac 13:51)—and this became a feature of the annual feast of Dedication.

Despite the "many" of v.8, Mark does not give the impression that the accompanying crowd is very large; yet they walk before and behind Jesus, forming a procession. "Hosanna" is a transliteration of a Hebrew word meaning "Save now"; it became an acclamation (like Hallelujah). "Blessed be the kingdom of our father David that is coming" —the acclamation is directed to the kingdom and not to Jesus. Contrast Matthew (21:9): "Hosanna to the Son of David." The entry as depicted here meant the coming of a Messiah who was poor, an advent in humility, not in glory. What is at stake, for Jesus, is the nature and manner of his messiahship. At this moment, come to the city that will so soon see the passion and death, he can manifest himself. But he does not come as a temporal ruler or with worldly pomp. He comes as a religious figure, a prince of peace, "humble and riding on a donkey" (Zech 9:9). Mark's narrative in 11:11 is consistent with his modest presentation in

11:1-10 and must reflect what really took place, or something very like it. Jesus entered the temple by himself, unobserved and unapplauded; the procession seems to have petered out before the actual entry. His "looking around" involves a critical examination which sets the stage for the next episode.

"IT WAS NOT THE SEASON FOR FIGS": THE END OF THE TEMPLE.
11:12-25 (Lk 19:45-46; Mt 21:12-22).

Here we have an example of Mark's sandwich technique: the account of the cleansing of the temple is inserted between two phases of the other narrative of the fig tree. He thereby signals that the stories should be understood in relation to each other. The cursing (v. 21) becomes a judgment on the temple. On the way from Bethany to Jerusalem a leafy tree seemed to promise fruit; but a typically Marcan explanatory phrase explains that "it was not the season (literally, "time," *kairos*) for figs." This jarring note alerts us: we must look to a symbolic meaning. It is an eschatological crisis: the temple tree is barren at the "time" of visitation. The Messiah "went to see" and found it fruitless. It is thereby cursed: "There will not be left here one stone upon another, that will not be thrown down" (13:2). Matthew has enhanced the miraculous aspect of the episode: "And the fig tree withered at once" (Mt 21:19).

But what lies behind this strange story? We may take our choice. Jesus did sentence the fruit tree to death; or a parable of his (something like that of Lk 13:6-9) had been turned into a miracle story; or a conspicuous withered tree by the road from Bethany to Jerusalem had given rise to the legend that Jesus had cursed it. For Mark, at any rate, it is a prophetic gesture symbolizing the end of the temple and its worship.

> [12]On the following day, when they came from Bethany, he was hungry. [13]And seeing in the distance a fig tree in leaf, he went to see if he could find anything on it. When

he came to it, he found nothing but leaves, for it was not the season for figs. [14]And he said to it, "May no one ever eat fruit from you again." And his disciples heard it.

[15]And they came to Jerusalem. And he entered the temple and began to drive out those who sold and those who bought in the temple, and he overturned the tables of the money-changers and the seats of those who sold pigeons; [16]and he would not allow any one to carry anything through the temple. [17]And he taught, and said to them, "Is it not written, 'My house shall be called a house of prayer for all the nations'? But you have made it a den of robbers." [18]And the chief priests and the scribes heard it and sought a way to destroy him; for they feared him, because all the multitude was astonished at his teaching. [19]And when evening came they went out of the city.

[20]As they passed by in the morning, they saw the fig tree withered away to its roots. [21]And Peter remembered and said to him, "Master, look! The fig tree which you cursed has withered." [22]And Jesus answered them, "Have faith in God. [23]Truly, I say to you, whoever says to this mountain, 'Be taken up and cast into the sea,' and does not doubt in his heart, but believes that what he says will come to pass, it will be done for him. [24]Therefore I tell you, whatever you ask in prayer, believe that you receive it, and you will. [25]And whenever you stand praying, forgive, if you have anything against any one; so that your Father also who is in heaven may forgive you your trespasses."

Jesus "cleansing" of the temple disrupted the temple's cultic life. He is depicted as driving out those who offered for sale animals and birds and other commodities required for the sacrifices, the pilgrims who bought from them, and the money-changers who changed the Greek and Roman money of the pilgrims into the Jewish and Tyrian coinage in which alone the temple dues could be paid. He prohibited the carrying of the sacred vessels. It is inconceivable, especially so near Passover with its influx of pilgrims, that

Jesus could really have cleared the crowded temple courts and brought the whole elaborate business to a standstill. His action, on a necessarily very limited scale,was a prophetic gesture, and would have been recognized as such (v. 18).

The motivation of his action is given in v.17. It begins with the Marcan emphasis on the teaching of Jesus and runs into a quotation of Is 56:7 with an echo of Jer 7:11. It was God's intention that the temple should be a house of prayer "for all nations"—of special interest to Mark. This had not been achieved, because the temple remained the jealously-guarded preserve of Israel. Worse, it had become a "den of robbers"—that is, a refuge of "robbers" as Jer 7:8-11 makes plain. The temple and its services have become an escape-hatch: the temple cult, it was felt, will automatically win forgiveness of ill behavior and bring about communion with God. Because it was so abused, the temple cult has no longer any *raison d'être*. Jesus' prophetic act signals its end. That gesture presaged what his death was to achieve (15:38; cf. 13:2; 14:58; 15:29).

As in Galilee (3:6), priests and scribes are determined to do away with Jesus (v.18). But now they fear; and the reason proferred by Mark is the astonishment of the multitude at Jesus' teaching (cf. 1:27). Coming after the episode of the cleansing of the temple, Peter's drawing of attention to the withered tree (vv.20-21) serves to highlight the temple crisis. It is an explanation of the destruction of the temple, preparing for chapter 13 and 14:58.

The verses 22-25 are found in various places in the other gospels. Here they become Mark's comment on the preceding narrative. The insistence on prayer is suggested by "house of prayer" (v.17). As for faith, like 1 Cor 13:2, which seems to echo this "mountain" saying, the point is that faith, rather than extraordinary miracles, is decisive. It is a strong way of saying that faith can achieve the seemingly impossible. Confident prayer is based on a faith that believes that God gives even before man asks. Faith and prayer, not temple cult, are now the way to God. Because Mark always understands "faith" in relation to Jesus, he is saying that Jesus has replaced the temple. It is quite the view of the fourth evangelist: "The hour is coming when neither on this mountain nor in Jerusalem will you worship the Father . . . the true worshipers will worship the Father in spirit and in truth" (Jn 4:21,23).

The saying on forgiveness, which reflects a knowledge of the Lord's Prayer (cf. Mt 6:12) has been loosely attached to the theme of prayer. Some manuscripts add v.26—an addition from Mt 6:15. For Mark these explanatory verses emphasize the transition from a reserved temple to a house of prayer for all nations. Jesus is now where God is to be found.

THE AUTHORITY OF JESUS.
11:27-33 (Lk 20:1-8; Mt 21:23-27; cf. Jn 2:18).

> ²⁷And they came again to Jerusalem. And as he was walking in the temple, the chief priests and the scribes and the elders came to him, ²⁸and they said to him, "By what authority are you doing these things, or who gave you this authority to do them?" ²⁹Jesus said to them, "I will ask you a question; answer me, and I will tell you by what authority I do these things. ³⁰Was the baptism of John from heaven or from men? Answer me." ³¹And they argued with one another, "If we say, 'From heaven,' he will say, 'Why then did you not believe him?' ³²But shall we say, 'From men'?"—they were afraid of the people, for all held that John was a real prophet. ³³So they answered Jesus, "We do not know." And Jesus said to them, "Neither will I tell you by what authority I do these things."

This section introduces a series of five controversy-stories akin to those in 2:1 - 3:6. This first one is a pronouncement story. It focuses on Jesus' conviction that his authority was from God. The three groups, chief priests, scribes, and elders are mentioned together as in 8:31; 14:43,53; 15:1. The point of the question in v.28 is to expose a lack of authority on Jesus' part. The matter of the authority of Jesus was also central in 1:27.

The authority (*exousia*) in question is not legal or political right but divine authority. Jesus responds with a counter question which implies that John's authority came from God. He asks his question with insistence. His opponents find themselves trapped. If they acknowledge the heavenly origin of John's authority they convict themselves of unbelief; furthermore, they would have to acknowledge that Jesus' authority, too, is from God. Because of John's standing with the people, they dare not brand him as a charlatan. They must reply evasively. Jesus has effectively rejected their right to challenge him. He has decisively won round one. But, also, he has shown his hand. He has claimed, as they cannot fail to observe, that his authority was from God.

THE WICKED TENANTS.
12:1-12 (Lk 20:9-19; Mt 21:33-43).

The allegorical features of this parable are evident: the vineyard is Israel, the maltreated servants are the prophets, the slain son is Jesus. The common view has been that these allegorical traits could not have been intended by Jesus. To the extent that the narrative goes back to him it can only have been in the form of a "pure" parable. Now we realize that authenticity cannot be gauged by the absence or presence of allegory. We must base our judgments on other considerations.

> **12** And he began to speak to them in parables. "A man planted a vineyard, and set a hedge around it, and dug a pit for the wine press, and built a tower, and let it out to tenants, and went into another country. ²When the time came, he sent a servant to the tenants, to get from them some of the fruit of the vineyard. ³And they took him and beat him, and sent him away empty-handed. ⁴Again he sent to them another servant, and they wounded him in the head, and treated him shamefully. ⁵And he sent

another, and him they killed; and so with many others, some they beat and some they killed. [6]He had still one other, a beloved son; finally he sent him to them, saying, 'They will respect my son.' [7]But those tenants said to one another, 'This is the heir; come, let us kill him, and the inheritance will be ours.' [8]And they took him and killed him, and cast him out of the vineyard. [9]What will the owner of the vineyard do? He will come and destroy the tenants, and give the vineyard to others. [10]Have you not read this scripture:

'The very stone which the builders rejected
has become the head of the corner;
[11]this was the Lord's doing,
and it is marvelous in our eyes'?"

[12]And they tried to arrest him, but feared the multitude, for they perceived that he had told the parable against them; so they left him and went away.

The introduction (v.1a), like the conclusion (v.12), was written by Mark. In his setting the parable forms part of the controversy between Jesus and the Jewish authorities. The "them" are the chief priests, scribes and elders of 11:27 (cf. 12:12). As "those outside" Jesus speaks to them in parables (4:11,34). The description and equipping of the vineyard is based on the allegory of Is 5:1-7 which represents Israel as the vineyard of the Lord. Mark's most notable modification is to make the vineyard the possession of an absentee landlord who has let it out to tenants. It follows that failure is not on the part of the vineyard (the people); the failure is of the stewards, the leaders of the people. The owner lives abroad, a foreigner or, at least, an absentee landlord. His rent would be an agreed proportion of the crop. By implication, these tenants are unproductive.

The landlord sends three servants in turn to collect his rent: the first was beaten, the second wounded and outraged, the third killed (vv.3-5). The "many servants," some of whom were beaten and others killed, are the prophets of Israel (e.g. 1 Kgs 18:13; 22:27; 2 Chr 24:20-22; 36:15-16;

Neh 9:26). So had God striven with an obdurate people, sending to them, time and again, his servants the prophets. And now, his supreme graciousness: he has sent his only Son. This is the ultimate test. But the tenants, the leaders, do away with him. The detail about casting the corpse out of the vineyard is meant to underline their malice: he was left unburied. Jesus' rhetorical question in v.9 gives punch to the parable; his reply points to judgment on faithless Israel. The stewards, the leaders of the covenant people, have brought upon themselves their own dismissal; they have rejected the Son of God. God looks to other servants; the Good News has passed to the gentiles. The parable is aptly in place after 11:12-21 and after the question about Jesus' authority (11:27-33). Matthew has provided a telling commentary: "Therefore, I tell you, the kingdom of God will be taken away from you and given to a nation producing the fruit of it" (Mt 21:43).

With the quotation of Ps 118:22-23 in vv.10-11, the figure passes from vineyard to that of building: God's rejected Son has become the cornerstone, the foundation, of the new community. Mark's readers can take heart; they are stones in a building raised by God himself with Jesus Christ as the chief corner-stone (cf. Eph 2:19-22). In his conclusion (v.12) Mark, typically, distinguishes between the hostile teachers of Israel and the common people who were sympathetic to Jesus (cf. 11:18). The leaders had perceived the deeper level of this parable only too well (v.12). But they remain "those outside" (4:11) because they reject its challenge. They cannot bring themselves to accept Jesus.

THE PHARISEES' QUESTION.
12:13-17 (Lk 20:20-26; Mt 22:15-22).

> [13] And they sent to him some of the Pharisees and some of the Herodians, to entrap him in his talk. [14] And they came and said to him, "Teacher, we know that you are true, and care for no man; for you do not regard the position of men, but truly teach the way of God. Is it

lawful to pay taxes to Caesar, or not? [15]Should we pay them, or should we not?" But knowing their hypocrisy, he said to them, "Why put me to the test? Bring me a coin, and let me look at it." [16]And they brought one. And he said to them, "Whose likeness and inscription is this?" They said to him, "Caesar's." [17]Jesus said to them, "Render to Caesar the things that are Caesar's, and to God the things that are God's." And they were amazed at him.

This is the finest example of a pronouncement story in the gospel—a narrative which climaxes on a notable saying of Jesus. Everything is subordinated to the pronouncement. In this case the question bears on the mutual rights of God and of Caesar. In Mark's setting the story continues the series of controversies.

As in 3:6, Pharisees and Herodians are hostile; here they are said to have been sent by "the chief priests and the scribes and the elders" ("they," v. 13; cf. 11:27) to set a trap for Jesus. It was a clever tactic, one which seemingly could not fail. Their flattery (v. 14)—Jesus is an upright teacher who, without any pandering to man's opinion, or any yielding to human standards, teaches the way of living that God demands—underlines their malicious intent. Ironically, their description of his character and his mission is wholly true. The question is cleverly framed: "should we . . . or should we not?" Though Mark speaks of "taxes," a specific tax is in question: a poll-tax imposed since 6 A.D. on all inhabitants of Judea, Samaria, and Idumea. Its introduction was bitterly resented, sparking off a revolt (cf. Act 5:37), and it was never accepted by the ultra-nationalist Zealots. It was tolerated by the Pharisees and, presumably, by the Herodians, since both groups were prepared to go along with the *status quo*. A positive answer by Jesus would be bitterly resented by all nationalists; a negative answer would offend the Pharisees and, besides, leave him open to being delated to the Romans, since non-payment of the tax was tantamount to rebellion.

This tax had to be paid in the silver coinage of Tiberius (A.D. 14-37), a coinage bearing the image of the Emperor and the inscription: "Tiberius, Caesar, son of the divine Augustus, the high priest." Jesus' request that a coin be produced, and his question, lay the basis of his answer. The supposition is that these coins are ultimately the property of the Emperor who had them minted. The validity of one's coinage was coterminous with the range of one's sovereignty. By using the coinage of Caesar, the Jews were, *de facto*, acknowledging Caesar's authority and were under obligation to pay taxes to him.

Jesus' answer implies that there need not be conflict between the demands of a state and those of God. However, it must be remembered that he holds that the claims of God are all-embracing (cf. 12:29-30). Therefore, obligations due to the state fall within the divine order. Jesus disassociates himself from an apocalyptic view according to which this world was wholly unimportant, and from a Zealot attitude that saw the world (in the power of the evil one) as something to be fought against. Christians could deduce from Jesus' principle that Christianity need involve no disloyalty to the state. But principle it remained and they had to work out for themselves the implications of it. It is not always easy to draw a clear line between a civil sphere where Caesar has his rights and a religious sphere where God rules. It is not always easy to discern what rightfully belongs to Caesar and where loyalty to the state makes unacceptable demands. Mark's readers, at least, will have learned from bitter experience that rendering to God the things that are God's had brought them into conflict with the state (13:8-11). Jesus taught no neat doctrine of the relations of church and state. The church must continue, in changing and fluctuating social conditions, to sort out its obligations, to discern as honestly as possible, what is due to God and what is due to Caesar.

THE SADDUCEES' QUESTION.
12:18-27 (Lk 20:27-38; Mt 22:23-33).

> [18]And Sadducees came to him, who say that there
> is no resurrection; and they asked him a question, saying,

19"Teacher, Moses wrote for us that if a man's brother dies and leaves a wife, but leaves no child, the man must take the wife, and raise up children for his brother. 20There were seven brothers; the first took a wife, and when he died left no children; 21and the second took her, and died, leaving no children; and the third likewise; 22and the seven left no children. Last of all the woman also died. 23In the resurrection whose wife will she be? For the seven had her as wife."

24Jesus said to them, "Is not this why you are wrong, that you know neither the scriptures nor the power of God? 25For when they rise from the dead, they neither marry nor are given in marriage, but are like angels in heaven. 26And as for the dead being raised, have you not read in the book of Moses, in the passage about the bush, how God said to him, 'I am the God of Abraham, and the God of Isaac, and the God of Jacob'? 27He is not God of the dead, but of the living; you are quite wrong."

Again a pronouncement story, with the punch-line coming in v.25. The Sadducees, mentioned here for the only time in the gospel, were a priestly and aristocratic party. Their theology was conservative and traditionalist. Taking their stand on the Pentateuch (without necessarily denying the validity of other Old Testament books) they rejected the later traditions and writings which the Pharisees accepted. And, of course, they rejected the new beliefs proposed in these later sources, especially belief in immortality, angels, and spirits (cf. Acts 23:6-8). The case they present to Jesus—designed to show that belief in the resurrection leads to absurdity—is based on the law of levirate marrage (Dt 25:5-10). At the time the law was in abeyance, but it could be invoked in argument and might even be urged to show that Moses had not believed in resurrection.

Jesus begins by pointing out that the Sadducees are mistaken on two grounds. He would have shared the Pharisees' acceptance of a wider canon. The Sadducees were in fact rejecting Scripture which held for resurrection. Secondly, they did not understand the power of God who is capable of achieving something beyond human imagining and, in particular, make resurrection life something different and higher than life in this world. This is the point Jesus stresses in his pronouncement (v.25). It represents the current more sophisticated (as opposed to the popular) notion of the resurrection: it worked a transformation so that the conditions of the resurrection life will be quite different from those of the present life. Paul's teaching in 1 Cor 15:35-50 is a good formulation of this view. Arguments against the possibility or reality of resurrection life based, like that of the Sadducees' story, on earthly conditions, are irrelevant. Jesus' firm declaration would have been particularly helpful to the gentile church. His more spiritual view of the resurrection would help to overcome the obstacle which the resurrection, more crudely conceived, presented to Greeks (1 Cor 15; Acts 17:32).

The manner of resurrection has been dealt with; now in vv.26-27 Jesus turns to the fact of resurrection. The process is typical of the rabbinical manner of argumentation. In Ex 3:6 Yahweh declared: "I am . . . the God of Abraham, the God of Isaac and the God of Jacob." But by the time of Moses the three patriarchs had been long dead. And yet, because their God is always God of the living, the patriarchs must, though dead, be destined for life; they will be raised to life. He had named himself their God, he had made promises to them which could not fail, promises which death could not annul. Their hopes of resurrection lay in their fellowship with God. By standards of modern exegesis this scriptural argument is hardly convincing. Yet the reason for life beyond death adduced here is congenial to modern man. "Proofs" of the immortality of the soul, presupposing a questionable dichotomy between "soul" and "body," do not seem to carry much weight any more. For the Christian the real ground of immortality lies in fellowship with the

risen Lord and with the living God. Paul has said it all—
"thanks be to God who gives us the victory [over death]
through our Lord Jesus Christ" (1 Cor 15:57).

A SCRIBE'S QUESTION.
12:28-34 (Lk 20:39-40; 10:25-28; Mt 22:34-40).

> ²⁸And one of the scribes came up and heard them
> disputing with one another, and seeing that he answered
> them well, asked him, "Which commandment is the first
> of all?" ²⁹Jesus answered, "The first is, 'Hear, O Israel:
> The Lord our God, the Lord is one; ³⁰and you shall love
> the Lord your God with all your heart, and with all
> your soul, and with all your mind, and with all your
> strength.' ³¹The second is this, 'You shall love your
> neighbor as yourself.' There is no other commandment
> greater than these." ³²And the scribe said to him, "You
> are right, Teacher; you have truly said that he is one, and
> there is no other but he; ³³and to love him with all the
> heart, and with all the understanding, and with all the
> strength, and to love one's neighbor as oneself, is much
> more than all whole burnt offerings and sacrifices."
> ³⁴And when Jesus saw that he answered wisely, he said
> to him, "You are not far from the kingdom of God." And
> after that no one dared to ask him any question.

In another pronouncement story, Jesus gives the answer
to the question, "Which commandment is the first of all?"
It was a question the rabbis sought to answer. They looked
for the commandment that outweighed all the others, one
that might be regarded as a basic principle on which the
whole Law was grounded. We find something of this in
Matthew's declaration: "On these two commandments
depend all the law and the prophets" (Mt 22:40). Because
it is an honest question by one well-disposed (vv.32-34)
Jesus answers directly. He begins by quoting the opening
formula (Dt 6:4) of the *Shema*, the "creed" which every

Israelite man recited morning and evening, and joins to it
Lev. 19:18 on the love of the neighbor. He had been asked
to name the first commandment; he responds by naming
two commandments. This is of great importance. It would
seem that Jesus was the first to bring together these two
commands of love of God and love of neighbor. That is
because, for him, the one flows directly, and necessarily
from the other. Love for neighbor arises out of love for
God. He had taken and welded the two precepts into one.

In the synoptic gospels, only here and in Lk 11:42, is
there word of man's love for God, and it appears sparingly
in the rest of the New Testament. Usually, the emphasis is on
God's love for man. And this is as it should be. It is because
God has first loved us that we love God (Rom 5:5,8; 1 Jn
4:11). Indeed, love for one another is the test of the reality
of our love of God (1 Jn 4:20-21). Jesus himself showed in
his life and death the quality of this twofold love. His love
for God motivated his total dedication to his mission; his
love for men marked him as one who had come to serve the
saving purpose of God, one who laid down his life as a ransom for mankind (10:45).

The scribe's reply (vv. 32-33) is proper to Mark. He agrees
fully with Jesus' answer and further specifies that the true
love of God and the loving service of others is more important than elaborate cult. His insistence on love with the
whole heart is a recognition that love cannot be measured.
Love is incompatible with a legalism that sets limits, that
specifies what one should do and should avoid. Jesus' assurance that this scribe is not far from the kingdom of God
is, in truth, an invitation. And we sense that this time the
invitation will not be in vain (cf. 10:17-23). Nowhere else
in the gospels does a scribe emerge in such a favorable light.

This is the end of the questioning of Jesus (v. 34b). One
does not long engage in debate with him. Meeting with
Jesus is too radical an experience: one must quickly come to
a decision, to accept or to reject. It is now Jesus' turn to
ask his question.

JESUS' QUESTION.
12:35-37a (Lk 20:41-44; Mt 22:41-46).

> ³⁵And as Jesus taught in the temple, he said, "How
> can the scribes say that the Christ is the son of David?
> ³⁶David himself, inspired by the Holy Spirit, declared,
> 'The Lord said to my Lord,
>
> Sit at my right hand,
>
> till I put thy enemies under thy feet.'
> ³⁷David himself calls him Lord: so how is he his son?'"

This series of controversies has ended. Jesus now takes
the initiative (as he had done in the last of the earlier series,
3:1-6). He is once again the teacher, but this time in the
temple (cf. 14:49). It might seem that his question (v.35) is
designed to contest the Davidic descent of the Messiah.
Rather, it is meant as a criticism of the scribes' understanding of Davidic messiahship—and so, of their refusal
to understand the real personality of Jesus. Ps 110, the
opening verse of which is quoted here, is a royal psalm,
addressed to the king—"my lord" refers to the king. Sitting
at the right hand of Yahweh means the king's adoption
as God's son, the acknowledged status of the Davidic king
(2 Sam 7:14). The argument here depends on the then
current acceptance of the psalm as a composition of David
(it is, in fact, later). On this supposition David presents an
oracle of Yahweh addressed to one whom he entitles "my
Lord." This solemn attestation of David is underlined by
the formula, unique in the synoptics, "inspired by the Holy
Spirit." This adds weight to the further question in v.37.
If the great David addresses the Messiah as "Lord" then the
Davidic sonship of the Messiah must be understood in a
sense that will acknowledge his superiority to David.

The use of Ps 110 is prevalent in the New Testament. Its
opening verse is employed in reference to the Easter victory
of Jesus in Mt 22:24; Acts 2:34-35 and Heb 1:13 and is
paraphrased in Jesus' reply to the high priest's question
(Mk 14:62). The christian view was that the oracle found

fulfillment in the elevation of the risen Lord to the right hand of God. Jesus is indeed son of David and his heir. But the true kingdom is Kingdom of God and the true heir is Son of God—"born of the seed of David according to the flesh; designated Son of God in power as of resurrection from the dead" (Rom 1:3-4). At Easter, Jesus as royal Son, was enthroned in the heavenly kingdom of God.

It is at this point in his gospel, the very end of the ministry, that Mark has raised directly the issue of the rightful meaning of the messianic title, Son of David. In 10:45-48 he had Jesus addressed as "Son of David" and had offered no comment, apart from Jesus' own brief appearance as the humble prince of Zechariah (11:1-10). But now he intimates that this title, like everything about Jesus, can be understood only when one acknowledges who Jesus is: the Son of God already on earth (1:11) destined to be exalted to the right hand of God (14:62).

A WARNING AGAINST THE SCRIBES.
12:37b-40 (Lk 20:46-47; Mt 23:5-7).

> [37b]And the great throng heard him gladly.
>
> [38]And in his teaching he said, "Beware of the scribes, who like to go about in long robes, and to have salutations in the market places [39]and the best seats in the synagogues and the places of honor at feasts, [40]who devour widows' houses and for a pretense make long prayers. They will receive the greater condemnation.

In 12:35-37a the teaching of the scribes (v.35) has been shown to have been inadequate; now their conduct is censured. Here, at the close of the ministry, it is shown that Jesus' break with the scribes, noted throughout the gospel (2:6-7,16; 3:22; 7:1-13; 9:14; 11:27-33; 12:35) is now total. There is the usual distinction (v.37b) between the enthusiastic crowd and the opponents. Mark is making the point that the break is with official Judaism, not with the Jewish people as such. And Jesus is cast in his role of teacher. The scribes prided themselves on their theological learning and—most of them being Pharisees—on their meticulous religious observance. On both scores they invited and received deference; to that end they took care to wear distinctive dress. The "best seats" in the synagogue: just in front of the ark containing the sacred scrolls of the Law and the Prophets and facing the people. The charge in v.40 is more serious. Not only do they make an ostentatious display of long-winded prayer; they are shown to be greedy and exploiters of the helpless. Judaism has some scathing condemnations of unscrupulous scribes. However, the sweeping character of the charges here reflects the animosity between the church and official Judaism, an animosity much more trenchantly expressed in Mt 23. This portrait of the scribes stands, and is meant to stand, in sharp contrast to the attitude and conduct of christian religious leaders (9:33-37; 10:42-45). But what has been, and continues to be, the reality in the church? Distinctive dress, signs of deference, places of honor at religious and civil functions! It is not easy to see wherein a difference lies between this and the conduct of the scribes outlined and censured here in vv.38-39.

THE WIDOW'S MITE.
12:41-44 (Lk 21:1-4)

> [41]And he sat down opposite the treasury, and watched the multitude putting money into the treasury. Many rich people put in large sums. [42]And a poor widow came, and put in two copper coins, which make a penny. [43]And he called his disciples to him, and said to them, "Truly, I say to you, this poor widow has put in more than all those who are contributing to the treasury. [44]For they all contributed out of their abundance; but she out of her poverty has put in everything she had, her whole living."

This charming vignette may have found its setting here partly because of the catchword *widow* (vv.40,42). More importantly, it is in place because, as an example of true Jewish piety, it contrasts with the counterfeit piety of the scribes. The poor widow who receives Jesus' approbation represents the common people. The break is not with them but with their leaders. The "treasury" here is, most likely, one of the thirteen trumpet-shaped receptacles which were placed in the court of the temple. The "copper coin" (*lepton*) was the smallest in circulation, equivalent to half a *quadrans* (penny) the smallest Roman coinage. It is an insignificant sum. Mention of two coins is important: the woman could have kept one for herself. With his technique of the summoning of the disciples to Jesus, Mark alerts the reader to the significance of the episode. Wealthy people had been generous (v.41); yet this poor widow's mite is an immeasurably greater gift than theirs for she has given of her all—her "whole living" (v.44). She had let go of every shred of security and had committed herself wholly to God. This word to the disciples is the final word on discipleship and fittingly closes the ministry. And it serves as a perfect transition to the story of how the one who had come to serve is going on to give "everything he had," not only his living, but his very life, for humanity (cf. 10:45).

THE FAREWELL DISCOURSE: WHAT I SAY TO YOU I SAY TO ALL: WATCH!
13:1-37 (Lk 21:5-36; Mt 24:1-51).

This chapter, which concludes the narrative of the ministry of Jesus and, in view of his departure from this world, prepares the disciples for events yet to come, falls into the literary form of farewell discourse. We find this form, the "last will and testament" of a great man, in the Old Testament, e.g. Moses (Dt 31-32), Joshua (Jos 23-24), Samuel (1 Sam 12), David (1 Chr 28-29) and, in the New Testament, Jn 13:31 - 16:33 (Jesus) and Acts 20:17-35 (Paul). The chapter falls, too, into the category of apocalypse. Some distinctive features mark it off from Jewish apocalypses to which it bears an evident resemblance. Such features are the positive value attached to persecution, which provides an opportunity of witnessing to Christ and spreading his gospel, and the central position of Christ in the ultimate vindication of the faithful.

While presented as the farewell discourse of Jesus the chapter is a thoroughly Marcan construct. Too often it has been seen as a maverick section with little relation to the rest of the material in this writing. Viewed with sharper discernment it is seen to have close contacts with what goes before and what is to come. Indeed, it may well be the key to a proper understanding of the gospel. Our commentary will proceed largely on the assumption that it is just that.

> **13**   And as he came out of the temple, one of his disciples said to him, "Look, Teacher, what wonderful stones and what wonderful buildings!" [2]And Jesus said to him, "Do you see these great buildings? There will not be left here one stone upon another, that will not be thrown down."
>
> [3]And as he sat on the Mount of Olives opposite the temple, Peter and James and John and Andrew asked him privately, [4]"Tell us, when will this be, and what will be the sign when these things are all to be accomplished?"
>
> [5]And Jesus began to say to them, "Take heed that no one leads you astray. [6]Many will come in my name, saying, 'I am he!' and they will lead many astray. [7]And when you hear of wars and rumors of wars, do not be alarmed; this must take place, but the end is not yet. [8]For nation will rise against nation, and kingdom against kingdom; there will be earthquakes in various places, there will be famines; this is but the beginning of the sufferings.
>
> [9]"But take heed to yourselves; for they will deliver you up to councils; and you will be beaten in synagogues; and you will stand before governors and kings for my sake, to bear testimony before them. [10]And the gospel

must first be preached to all nations. [11]And when they bring you to trial and deliver you up, do not be anxious beforehand what you are to say; but say whatever is given you in that hour, for it is not you who speak, but the Holy Spirit. [12]And brother will deliver up brother to death, and the father his child, and children will rise against parents and have them put to death; [13]and you will be hated by all for my name's sake. But he who endures to the end will be saved.

[14]"But when you see the desolating sacrilege set up where it ought not to be (let the reader understand), then let those who are in Judea flee to the mountains; [15]let him who is on the housetop not go down, nor enter his house, to take anything away; [16]and let him who is in the field not turn back to take his mantle. [17]And alas for those who are with child and for those who give suck in those days! [18]Pray that it may not happen in winter. [19]For in those days there will be such tribulation as has not been from the beginning of the creation which God created until now, and never will be. [20]And if the Lord had not shortened the days, no human being would be saved; but for the sake of the elect, whom he chose, he shortened the days. [21]And then if any one says to you, 'Look, here is the Christ!' or 'Look, there he is!' do not believe it. [22]False Christs and false prophets will arise and show signs and wonders, to lead astray, if possible, the elect. [23]But take heed; I have told you all things beforehand.

[24]"But in those days, after that tribulation, the sun will be darkened, and the moon will not give its light, [25]and the stars will be falling from heaven, and the powers in the heavens will be shaken. [26]And then they will see the Son of man coming in clouds with great power and glory. [27]And then he will send out the angels, and gather his elect from the four winds, from the ends of the earth to the ends of heaven.

[28]"From the fig tree learn its lesson: as soon as its branch becomes tender and puts forth its leaves, you know that summer is near. [29]So also, when you see these

things taking place, you know that he is near, at the very gates. ³⁰Truly, I say to you, this generation will not pass away before all these things take place. ³¹Heaven and earth will pass away, but my words will not pass away.

³²"But of that day or that hour no one knows, not even the angels in heaven, nor the Son, but only the Father. ³³Take heed, watch; for you do not know when the time will come. ³⁴It is like a man going on a journey, when he leaves home and puts his servants in charge, each with his work, and commands the doorkeeper to be on the watch. ³⁵Watch therefore—for you do not know when the master of the house will come, in the evening, or at midnight, or at cockcrow, or in the morning— ³⁶lest he come suddenly and find you asleep. ³⁷And what I say to you I say to all: Watch."

STRUCTURE

The structure of Mk 13 is readily discernible. After an introduction (13:1-4) depicting two separate scenes, the discourse falls into three main parts: vv.5-23, 24-27 and 28-37. The first and last of these parts are cast in chiastic form (A, B, A'). For that matter, the whole discourse might be said to have a broadly chiastic shape with vv.24-27 forming the center of it.

Introduction 13:1-4

Scene 1 (vv.1-2)   Jesus talks with one of his disciples outside the temple and forecasts the destruction of the temple.

Scene 2 (vv.3-4)   Jesus, seated on the Mount of Olives, opposite the temple, replies to a twofold question of his disciples: when will "this" (*tauta*) be—the destruction of the temple; what will be the "sign" when "all these things are to be accomplished"—the sign of the eschaton.

While the first scene looks to the basic issue for Christians, the destruction of the temple, the second scene prepares for an answer to a problem the disaster had raised for believers.

I. The Signs of the Parousia 13:5-23

   a. Take heed that no one leads you astray (5-6)
   b. When you hear of wars (7-8)
   c. Take heed . . . of persecutions (9-13)
   b'. When you see wars . . . destruction (14-20)
   a'. Take heed of false Christs and false prophets (21-23).

II. The Parousia of the Son of Man 13:24-27.

III. The Nearness of the Parousia 13:28-37.

   a. Parable: the fig tree (28-29)
   b. Saying: "within this generation" (30)
   c. Saying: solemn confirmation (31)
   b'. Saying: "of that day or that hour, no one knows" (32)
   a'. Parable: doorkeeper watches (33-36)

Conclusion: Take heed (37).

INTRODUCTION

Scene 1. 13:1-2.

Mark has been preoccupied with the temple since 11:11 when Jesus came to it in judgment and, with prophetic gestures (11:12-25), had heralded its end. If he now leaves the temple it is to forecast its destruction (vv.1-2); and Jerusalem is never again mentioned by name in this gospel (cf. 14:13). As he leaves the temple a disciple draws Jesus' attention to what was, in truth, the grandeur of the Herodian temple, for Herod's temple was one of the most remarkable buildings of its time. Jesus' response is a grim prediction of the total destruction of the magnificent building; it spells out in clear words what was implied in the fig-tree episode (11:12-14, 20-21). This "prediction" of Jesus is a *vaticinium ex eventu*; when Mark wrote, the destruction of the temple was an accomplished fact. Not only a fact, but a major problem. His discourse of ch. 13 is written to deal with the issue raised by the destruction of the temple and the dashing of the eschatological hope that had become attached to it. In the standard technique of apocalyptic an historical event is presented as though still lying in the future—while the writer then passes on to deal with the truly future repercussion of that epochal event. The end of the temple is such an epoch-making event. It is properly Mark's starting-point.

Scene 2. 13:3-4.

The carefully designated setting admirably lends to this discourse the solemnity and extraordinary importance that Mark wants it to have. The Mount of Olives, in Jewish tradition, was associated with the coming of the Messiah: Jesus is enthroned upon the eschatological mountain and looking down upon the doomed city. The discourse is not only "in private"; it is reserved for four of the twelve, the four whose call is described in 1:16-20—and who have been longest with Jesus. Mark has thus warned his reader that this reply to the disciples' question is of exceptional moment. And so indeed it was for Mark's community. Already the question (v.4) evokes the fuller significance of the end of the temple. It is a two-fold question regarding the *when* of these things (*tauta*)—the destruction of the temple (v.2), and the *sign* that will precede the accomplishment of all these things (*tauta panta*)—the eschaton. In this way, the end of the temple is associated with the end of all things. And this, indeed, would appear to be the problem involved. Christians, already convinced of an imminent parousia, would, very naturally, link that hope to the grim events of the Jewish war (66-70 A.D.), a fitting scenario for the End. Expectation would have heightened as the crisis sharpened. And then came their shock and bewilderment when the end of the city did not, after all, usher in the End (cf. 9:2-9). That is why the discourse focuses on the parousia (vv.24-27) and its nearness (vv.28-36), and fits the war, the end of the temple, and the contemporary trials of Christians into the category of preliminary signs (vv.5-23).

I. SIGNS AND WARNINGS.
13:5-23.

False Prophets (13:5-6, 21-23).

The discourse begins with a note of warning, "Take heed lest . . ." (v.5b) which corresponds to the conclusion of v.21: "Do not believe." The warning is about many who would lead others astray. They will come in Jesus' name declaring "I am he!"; the Greek formula *ego eimi* ("I am") affirms the presence of Jesus. These deceivers are more clearly designated in the corresponding v.22 as "false Christs and false prophets" who seduced the people with signs and wonders and who declared that they knew where the Christ would appear (v.21). These must be christian prophets who invoked the authority and even assumed the identity of Jesus. We know that in Judaism at the time there was intense messianic expectation, fomented by the events of the war, and more than one messianic claimant had won a following. It is not surprising that in the explosive atmosphere of the Jewish war some Christians, too, would have put themselves forward as the re-incarnation of the Christ to come, for the atmosphere was one of unbearable tension and fanaticism. Indeed, we find that Paul, earlier, far away from that grim historical situation, had had to take a stand against those who claimed that "the day of the Lord" had come (2 Thess 2:1-12). Elsewhere, we read of the "antichrists" who have come at the "last hour"—men from within the christian community (1 Jn 2:18-19), and the "wolves" within the fold (Acts 20:29-30). Mark, too, has to face the challenge of prophets who, themselves deluded, had led others astray. By his designation of them as "false," and by his reiterated warning, he refutes their claims. And then he goes on to give his explanation of the events. He does so with the serene conviction of the great prophets of Israel and their resounding "Thus says Yahweh." Mark, speaking in the name of the risen Lord, can confidently declare: "I have told you all things beforehand" (v.23).

Wars and Rumors of Wars. 13:7-8 [14-20]

In 2 Thess 2:2 the phrase "do not be alarmed" warns against a premature anticipation of the Lord's Day; here (v.7) it is linked to the assurance that "the End is not yet." "Wars and rumors of wars" had become commonplace in apocalyptic descriptions of the end of the world; they were regarded as a necessary feature of a divine purpose—"this must take place" (cf. Dn 2:28). World-wide conflict, earthquakes, famines point to an upheaval of apocalyptic dimensions. The grim experience of war conditions in Palestine would have been aggravated by rumors of war and disasters throughout the Empire. These rumors would feed the conviction of the fanatics that now indeed was the moment of the inbreaking of the kingdom, now was the time of the End. Mark challenges this interpretation and insists that the hour is but the beginning of the "birthpangs," a traditional term to express the view that the messianic age would come to birth through a period of woes. We shall see that the corresponding verses (14-20) describe these events in greater detail. Christians are assured that these upheavals are, after all, but the first pains of childbirth. However, they do know that they live in "the beginning of the sufferings," and the warning of v.9 is sounded.

Persecution 13:9-13.

The admonition to take heed (v.9) marks a transition to this central section of the chiasmus which deals with the hard lot of Christians. Noteworthy is the threefold repetition of "to deliver up" (vv.9b,11a,12a): persecution and suffering are their lot, as for their Master. They will be haled before Jewish tribunals (v.9a) and gentile authorities (v.9b). The Jewish historian Josephus informs us that shortly before the war of 66-70 A.D., Jews throughout Syria and Palestine were victims of violence and pogroms; Christians would have been caught up in these events. He also mentions that the Zealots, when they had won control of Jerusalem, held summary trials.

Paradoxically, these Christians, though in the guise of arraigned prisoners, will be bearing witness to the Name. Even more strangely—for God's ways are not the ways of man—persecution will be the occasion of the wider mission to the gentiles (v.10; cf. Acts 8:1-5). For that matter, one may say that christian suffering is itself that proclamation: by suffering as Jesus suffered, they are making him present to their world. For Mark, it is wholly fitting that the suffering and death of Christians should open the way to the gentiles. Already he had shown that the death of the precursor had coincided with the first sending of the twelve on their mission (6:7-30). He will show that the death of Jesus tears away the veil of division between Jew and gentile (15:38). Moreover, by asserting that the gospel must "first" be preached, Mark is asserting that the gathering in of the full number of the gentiles (cf. Rom 11:35) is part of God's plan. Hence this present suffering of Christians does not mark the End. In their trials Christians are assured of help (v.11). It is not said that the Spirit will speak up on behalf of the disciples. Rather, they are assured of the help of the Spirit; and the preparation of the defence is less the drafting of an apologia than a prayer. Here is a sign and a promise of God's help in time of trouble.

Most painful of all is the fact of family division (v.12). This, too, had become a commonplace of apocalyptic (e.g. 2 Esdras 5:9). However, here, denunciation from within, like hatred coming from all sides (v.13) would again suggest the troubled days of the war. We know that the Jews, especially in Jerusalem, were riddled with divisions—the pro-Roman priestly party, the Pharisees, the moderates, with the Zealots (split among themselves) against everybody.

The prophets who declared "Here is the Christ!" or "I am he" could only aggravate the plight of Christians. Yet, Mark is thinking, too, of a wider issue. He knows that Christians were, in fact, hated on account of the Name of Jesus (cf. 1 Pet 4:12-16). There is a call for constancy and a promise: whoever endures faithfully to the End will win salvation—one who has not sought to save his life and has not been ashamed of Jesus and his word (8:35,38). Suffering must be endured and the gentile mission urgently undertaken (v.10). These, and not the delusions or wonders of false prophets, are the signs. But they are not the End.

The Abomination of Desolation. 13:14-20.

The solemn setting of the discourse, we have seen (v.3), has alerted the reader to its exceptional importance. If, then, Mark still finds it necessary to further nudge the reader ("let the reader understand," v.14), it can only be because he wants to drop a dark hint, to point the christian reader to a hidden clue. In quite the same way the author of the Apocalypse of John introduces his revelation of the number of the Beast with the caution: "This calls for wisdom: let him who has understanding reckon . . ." (Rev 13:18; cf. also Rev 13:9). So, in Mark, we are to look to the meaning of "the desolating sacrilege set up where he ought not to be" (v.14). At first sight it does not seem to offer much of a riddle. The phrase, "the abomination of desolation" comes straight from Daniel (Dan 9:27; 11:31; 12:11) where it refers to the heathen altar which Antiochus Epiphanes built over the Temple altar of burnt offering in 168 B.C. (cf. 1 Macc 1:54). It would, then, be an apt expression to describe the destruction of Herod's temple in 70 A.D. And Matthew (24:15) makes explicit reference to the temple— "standing in the holy place." The puzzling feature is that Mark speaks of this "desolating sacrilege" in personal terms, the Greek word *hestēkota* ("standing") is masculine. This mysterious person is standing where he should not be, that is, in the temple. One thinks of "the lawless one," the Antichrist, of 2 Thess 2:1-12. But Mark may be thinking of a more sinister presence. The destruction of the temple, though misinterpreted by the false prophets, is, nevertheless, the great apocalyptic disaster. The "holy place" has become the seat of the powers of evil. It is the parousia of Satan: cf. Rev 20:7-9. This fits the widespread apocalyptic view that this present world is in the power of the Evil One. And the christian reader, with understanding, can "see," can perceive, this frightful feature of the great disaster. This marks the climax of the anti-temple theme and reflects at its sharpest the estrangement of the Marcan church from Judaism.

It is important to note that with v.14 there is a definite change in time references. Hitherto everything has been in the present: the end is not yet (v.7), this is but the beginning of the sufferings (v.8), the gospel must first be preached to all nations (v.10). But from v.14 on, everything is addressed to the reader's future: when you see the desolating sacrilege, then flee (v.14); then if anyone says, "Look, the Christ is here . . . there," do not believe it (v.21); in those days—after that tribulation (v.24),—then you will see (v.26)—then he will send (v.27). The fall of Jerusalem has brought about a drastic situation, and set off a train of events in which Mark's community had been caught up. They live in "those days" (v.17) between the parousia of Satan and the parousia of the Son of Man.

It is evident that vv.15-18 originally referred to the war situation and to flight before imminent siege-threat to the city. Patently, the description fits the destruction of Jerusalem and the Palestinian local color is obvious. But now, for Mark, "Judea" is where Satan is enthroned. It is the climax of the anti-Jerusalem bias that we have noted throughout. The future of the christian community is not with Judaism but lies in the wider "Galilee of the Gentiles" (7:31). Christians are to look to the parousia of the Son of Man in that "Galilee" (14:28; 16:7). That Mark is looking beyond the historical end of Jerusalem is clear in vv.19-20. The Jerusalem disaster is but the first moment of unparelleled tribulation that will involve the whole of creation (v.19)—"those days" mark that eschatological time of tribulation. The feature of the shortening of the days of tribulation (v.20) expresses the idea that God, in his mercy and for the sake of his elect, shortens the period of tribulation for mankind. Notice the comforting emphasis: "the chosen ones whom he chose" (v.20), that is the christian community.

The warning in v.21-22 is not merely a repetition of that in vv.5-6. Mark is alerting his readers to an ever-present danger. That fanaticism which surfaced during the days of the War is not dead. We have noticed his care to counter a facile confession of Christ with his insistence on the necessity of suffering (8:29-38). These false prophets had not learned that lesson; in the great tribulation they may make appeal to the Christ of their own desire and imagining. But there is the comfort that they will not succeed in leading astray the faithful Christian precisely because he is "the elect whom God has chosen" (v.20). (Cf. the sealing of the servants of God in Rev 7:3.) And there is the note of warning: *Take heed*, echoing the opening word of Jesus (v.5) and tying together this whole section. And by putting it all under the seal of Jesus' foreknowledge (v.23) Mark claims to be the true prophet.

II. THE PAROUSIA OF THE SON OF MAN. 13:24-27.

Though Mark has been at pains to correct a false parousia expectation, he himself firmly believes in a real parousia and in the imminence of it. "Those days," the days of the "tribulation" have already begun (vv.17,19). The parousia itself, of course, is not part of the present crisis, but follows hard upon it. Mark has expressed this key section of the apocalyptic drama in language almost entirely drawn from the Old Testament. The passage is properly a collage of prophetic texts. The cosmic signs which accompany the parousia (vv.24-25) are part and parcel of Jewish apocalyptic descriptions of the day of the Lord, for they, too, looked to Old Testament texts. The stage is set; now the Son of Man can appear.

The Son of Man has already manifested his authority on earth (2:10,28). In Mark's perspective he has, already, for the salvation of men (10:45), suffered and died, and risen from the dead (8:31; 9:31; 10:33-34; 9:9,12; 14:21,41). Yet, he is the same Son of Man who will be revealed at his parousia (8:38; 13:26; 14:62), for the parousia marks his definitive manifestation. Then he *will be seen*: seen in fulness instead of being dimly perceived. Only then will he be seen in power and in the glory of his Father (8:38; 13:26). This is the real message of hope for Christians. This promise and this hope they cling to while the Lord is absent (2:20; 13:34). It is this that enables them, no matter what their present situation, to endure to the end (13:9-13).

Already 8:38 had warned that only those who, here and now, in this vale of tears, are not "ashamed" of a suffering Son of Man will rejoice in his glorious coming. That is why Mark will go on, insistently, to urge watching and readiness for the coming (13:33-37). And, for the faithful ones, that coming will be joy indeed. The Son of Man will not come to execute judgment. The one purpose of his appearing will be to gather together the scattered people of God—a familiar Old Testament expectation. Here they are *his* elect, they belong to Christ (cf. 1 Thess 4:15-17; 2 Thess 2:1). This gathering will be the last task of those "ministering spirits sent forth to serve, for the sake of those who are to obtain salvation" (Heb 1:14).

III. THE NEARNESS OF THE PAROUSIA.
13:28-37.

After his comforting presentation of the parousia, Mark continues that encouragement by stressing its nearness. But he insists that the intervening time must be spent in watchfulness. True to his understanding of discipleship, outlined in chs. 8-10, there can never be room for complacency in the life of the Christian.

The fig tree emerges again (cf. 11:12-14, 20-21) but now as a parabolic promise of the nearness of the coming of the Son of Man. It helps to answer the question: How soon is the parousia? A fig tree is singled out because in Palestine, where most trees are evergreens, the appearance of buds or leaves on the fig tree is a sure sign of the end of winter and the beginning of summer. The "when" of v.28 echoes the "when" of vv.14,11,7, and implies the answer to the twofold question of v.4. The first part of that double question is answered in v.29; when Christians see the destruction of the temple and its possession by the abomination of desolation they will know that the prediction of Jesus had been true; and then, too, they will know that the coming of the Son of Man is near. As to when "all these things are to be accomplished" (v.4), the end will come in "this genera- tion," that of Mark himself; the Son of Man is "at the very door" indeed. This is fully consistent with 9:1. The evangelist has left us in no doubt as to his conviction. The parousia will occur in his own lifetime; or, at least, his generation will not have quite passed away before the End comes. His ultimate assurance is not founded on the end of the temple but is anchored in the authority of the words of Jesus (v.31), that is, the gospel itself (8:35,38). Mark is sure that in 9:1 and 13:30 he is being true to Jesus who regarded his death and vindication as marking the end, with nothing else to wait for (cf. 14:25). The End will be after the destruction of the temple and in this generation—of this Mark is sure. But he will not specify day or hour, because he cannot. For that matter, not even the members of the heavenly court (the angels), not even the Son himself, know the precise date of the End—the Son and the angels who are the protagonists of the parousia (13:26-27). It remains the secret of the Father. Nevertheless, the time of the parousia had been set. This generation is the last generation.

There can be no doubting that Mark earnestly expected an imminent parousia. Was he, then, mistaken? In one sense, obviously, yes; the parousia of the Son of Man did not happen in his generation, nor has it occurred nineteen centuries later. Yet, we can find a basic truth in Mark's conviction. The death and rising of Jesus did usher in the last age. In Jesus, God has spoken his final word (cf. Heb 1:2); there remains only the consummation (cf. 1 Cor 15:28). Besides, "parousia" is a symbol, an apocalyptic symbol (cf. Mk 13:24-27; 1 Thess 4:16-17); it gives dramatic expression to the belief that God's saving plan is perfectly rounded. And there is a fittingness about the symbol. God's definitive act was the sending of his Son. The re-appearance of that Son, against the backdrop of the cosmos (cf. 13:24-27), signaled the triumphant close of the drama of salvation. While we cannot share Mark's view that the End is very near, nor look for a coming of the Son of Man in clouds, we do share his faith in God's victory in Christ. And, for each of us, the "parousia" will be our meeting with the Son of Man when we pass out of this life into the life of God. It should be our christian hope that we stand among the elect to be fondly welcomed by him.

The exhortation of v.33 is Mark's own introduction to the parable of the Doorkeeper. "Take heed" (vv.5,9,23) is the keynote of the farewell discourse of ch. 13. "Watch" means do not permit yourselves to fall asleep! "Time" (cf. 1:15) is the appointed time fixed in an ordered divine plan. In its context the "time" refers to the incalculable "day or hour" of v.32. The call to watchfulness in v.33 brings out the exhortation latent in v.32.

The parable of the Doorkeeper, as Mark found it, had already gone through a process of reshaping. It certainly resembles the Watching Servants of Lk 12:35-38—indeed both should be regarded as widely variant forms of the same parable. We have noted that the evangelist gave v.33 its form and prefaced it to the parable; v.37 is wholly his. The substance of the parable itself (vv.34-36) he took from the tradition where, already, it was related to a changed situation. The main sentence of v.35, "Watch therefore . . . lest he come suddenly and find you asleep," is the application of the parable. Significantly, it is "the master of the house" who will come, not the "man" of v.34: it is Christ himself. The parable is now understood in christological terms. Christ is the departing Lord and the parousia will mark his return. The doorkeeper represents the waiting disciples, the community of believers, and the divisions of the night are a symbol for the lapse of time before the coming. This meaning is borne out by Mark's care to bracket the first part of the parable with the warning, "for you do not know when the time will come" (v.33b), "for you do not know when the master of the house will come" (v.35b).

Mark's most significant expansion of the application of the parable is in his phrase, "and he puts his servants in charge [literally, gave them authority (*exousia*)], each with his own work" (v.34). *Exousia* is a weighty term in Mark's vocabulary. In 1:22,27; 2:10; 11:28,29,33 it is the authority of Jesus with which he teaches and acts: in 3:15 and 6:7 it is the authority of the twelve, bestowed on them by Jesus. It is because they have received authority from Jesus that their only greatness is in service (9:35; 10:44). For Mark, an apostle is a *doulos* ("slave"), and nevertheless has *exousia*. But Mark is looking not to the past but to the present. The authority given by Jesus to the twelve is operative in the evangelist's community. And he looks, not only to the leaders, but beyond them to the whole community: "What I say to you, I say to *all*" (v.36).

Then there is the place of the parable in Mark's farewell discourse. The summit of the discourse is reached in 13:26— the Son of Man will come on the clouds of heaven. Mark knows that in and through Jesus' proclamation the kingdom of God has drawn near (1:15). He was aware that Jesus had spoken of the kingdom coming in the fullness of power within the span of his own generation (9:1). But now the christian community needs to have an explanation of why a long interval has elapsed despite Jesus' assurance of the imminence of that coming. Mark had already, in v.32, given the basic answer: despite the nearness of the coming, the day and hour are known to God alone. The detailing of the night-watches in v.35 acknowledges the delay and stresses that waiting means watchfulness at every hour. The opening "Take heed" (v.5) and the final "Watch" (v.37) emphasize that Mark's real interest in this passage is centered in the exhortation, and his lesson is for all Christians without exception: "I say to *all*." The repeated call to watchfulness indicates how he wanted, not only the parable but the whole discourse, to be understood: not as a guide in calculating a deadline, but as an inspiration and a warning, to live one's life at each moment in preparedness for the meeting with Christ.

Mark addresses his gospel to his own contemporaries. His Jesus speaks to them directly, especially in the passages of discipleship concern and in the farewell discourse. In chapter 13 Mark has a more positive purpose than that of correcting a false expectation, just as his use of Son of Man goes far beyond the aim of setting right a mistaken christology. He wants to lead his readers to the point at which they will firmly accept the tribulation and the testing of the present, to confirm them in the conviction that it will climax in the coming of Jesus as Son of Man. Buoyed up by that hope, they will endure these trials as Jesus endured his passion. They will be disciples of whom Jesus will not be ashamed (cf. 8:38).

PASSION AND RESURRECTION.
14:1 - 16:8.

AFTER THE FAREWELL discourse (ch. 13) the curtain goes up on the final act of the drama. We have been well prepared for the denouement, not only in the explicit predictions of the passion, but in hints, more or less veiled, right from the beginning. The Son of Man *must* suffer many things. In this divine necessity Mark finds his reply to the question: Who, then, is this? The precise answer is spoken by the centurion: "Truly, this man was Son of God!" (15:39). But the whole gospel has prepared for that solemn declaration.

It had been the scholarly view that Mark had at hand, when he wrote, a more or less complete passion-narrative. He had done little more, it was thought, than provide this narrative with an introduction, albeit an extensive introduction. More recent studies on the gospel, applying the methods of redaction and composition criticism, have shown that this passion narrative, no less than the rest, is Mark's work. Of course, here as before, Mark has used traditional material. But he has put his stamp upon the whole gospel. He has written a work, finely conceived and skillfully executed. From beginning to end this gospel is truly *kata Marcon*—according to Mark.

210

MARKED FOR DEATH.
14:1-11 (Lk 22:1-5; 7:36-38; Mt 26:1-16).

14 It was now two days before the Passover and the feast of Unleavened Bread. And the chief priests and the scribes were seeking how to arrest him by stealth, and kill him; [2]for they said, "Not during the feast, lest there be a tumult of the people."

[3]And while he was at Bethany in the house of Simon the leper, as he sat at table, a woman came with an alabaster jar of ointment of pure nard, very costly, and she broke the jar and poured it over his head. [4]But there were some who said to themselves indignantly, "Why was the ointment thus wasted? [5]For this ointment might have been sold for more than three hundred denarii, and given to the poor." And they reproached her. [6]But Jesus said, "Let her alone; why do you trouble her? She has done a beautiful thing to me. [7]For you always have the poor with you, and whenever you will, you can do good to them; but you will not always have me. [8]She has done what she could; she has anointed my body beforehand for burying. [9]And truly, I say to you, wherever the gospel is preached in the whole world, what she has done will be told in memory of her."

[10]Then Judas Iscariot, who was one of the twelve, went to the chief priests in order to betray him to them. [11]And when they heard it they were glad, and promised to give him money. And he sought an opportunity to betray him.

The Plot. 14:1-2
The feast of Passover, which could be celebrated only in Jerusalem, began at sundown. That moment marked the beginning of 15 Nisan by Jewish liturgical reckoning of the day (sundown to sundown). The lambs had been slaughtered and offered in the temple on the late afternoon (that is, 14 Nisan); the meal followed between sundown and midnight (15 Nisan). The Feast of Unleavened Bread, originally a feast of the barley harvest during which unleavened bread

was eaten, was celebrated from 15 to 21 Nisan. The two feasts had become combined and Mark's designation (Passover and Feast of Unleavened Bread) was not unusual. The precise "two days," a feature of Mark's concern with time division throughout the passion narrative, alerts one to a divine purpose in all that is to transpire. Hostile action against Jesus, so long before made explicit (3:6), now looks for its moment. Yet, even here God has his say. "Not during the feast"—so decreed human prudence. But Jesus did die during the feast!

She Has Done a Beautiful Thing to Me. 14:3-9.

The sequel to the priests' plot is obviously Judas' betrayal (14:10-11). The intercalated anointing scene is thereby highlighted by Mark and is meant to be understood in the context of that framework. This story of the anointing is located at Bethany (11:11) in the house of "Simon the leper," doubtless one known in the circle where the story originated. The woman is not named, nor are those who object to her action: interest falls on the sayings (vv.7-9). The "ointment" was a perfumed unction of some sort. Of primary importance are the woman's action and Jesus' words.

The woman has come to do "what she could." We do not know her motivation; very likely it is a display of love (cf. Lk 7:47). Her gesture is misunderstood. "Some" were indignant at this waste; it is not said who these are but, interestingly, Matthew says bluntly "the disciples" (Mt 26:8). On the surface, their viewpoint is very reasonable. The price of the ointment represents about a year's wages for a laborer; it would provide a square meal for a goodly number of poor. Jesus' reaction is verbally close to his admonishment of the disciples when they sought to turn away those who brought children to him (10:14)—"do not hinder them." At a deeper level it recalls 2:19—when the bridegroom is present it is not time for fasting. There will be all the time in the world for caring for the poor; but this is a privileged moment and the pouring of this ointment is no extravagance. The woman has made a lovely gesture, more significant than she knew. Anointing for burial was not her intent; that is how Jesus chose to see it. He thereby gives notice that he expected to die a violent death and suffer a rude burial.

The story fits smoothly into Mark's christological perspective. By pouring the ointment over Jesus' head (compare Jn 12:3—the feet of Jesus are anointed) the woman is symbolically proclaiming him to be the Messiah, the Anointed of God (cf. 2 Kgs 9:1-13; 1 Kgs 1:38-40). She, however vaguely, has recognized him as Israel's Messiah. Jesus graciously accepts anointing but relates it to his death—he is the Messiah who will suffer and die. It is Caesarea Philippi all over again: "You are the Christ"—"The Son of Man must suffer many things . . ." (8:29,31). The evangelist's assessment comes in verse 9. Her gracious deed has won her immortality. She has become a herald of the Good News. Her gesture, at the opening of the passion, points to the heart of the Good News: salvation through the death of the Savior. Poignantly, the lovely gesture of this unknown woman stands between the deadly intent of priests and scribes and the betrayal of Jesus by a disciple.

Betrayal. 14:10-11.

Priests and scribes were wondering how they might arrest Jesus "by stealth" (v.1); now, unexpectedly, an occasion is presented to them. But there is nothing fortuitous about it. The verb translated "betray" is, literally, "to deliver up," practically a technical term for a delivering up which is God's will; Judas is serving God's purpose (cf. 14:21). Mark's reticence is noteworthy. He offers no explanation of the treachery (cf. Lk 22:3; Jn 12:6; 13:27). Nor does Judas strike a bargain with the priests as in Mt 26:15; he receives no more than a promise of money for his pains. While it is true that Judas is consistently described in the gospel tradition as "one of the twelve," that designation has special urgency here. The bitterness of the fate of Jesus is beginning to emerge.

THE LAST SUPPER.
14:12-25 (Lk 22:7-23; Mt 25:17-29).

12And on the first day of Unleavened Bread, when they sacrificed the passover lamb, his disciples said to him, "Where will you have us go and prepare for you to eat the passover?" 13And he sent two of his disciples, and said to them, "Go into the city, and a man carrying a jar of water will meet you; follow him, 14and wherever he enters, say to the householder, 'The Teacher says, Where is my guest room, where I am to eat the passover with my disciples?' 15And he will show you a large upper room furnished and ready; there prepare for us." 16And the disciples set out and went to the city, and found it as he told them; and they prepared the passover.

17And when it was evening he came with the twelve. 18And as they were at table eating, Jesus said, "Truly, I say to you, one of you will betray me." 19They began to be sorrowful, and to say to him one after another, "Is it I?" 20He said to them, "It is one of the twelve, one who is dipping bread in the same dish with me. 21For the Son of man goes as it is written of him, but woe to that man by whom the Son of man is betrayed! It would have been better for that man if he had not been born."

22And as they were eating, he took bread, and blessed, and broke it, and gave it to them, and said, "Take; this is my body." 23And he took a cup, and when he had given thanks he gave it to them, and they all drank of it. 24And he said to them, "This is my blood of the covenant, which is poured out for many. 25Truly, I say to you, I shall not drink again of the fruit of the vine until that day when I drink it new in the kingdom of God."

Preparations for the Passover. 14:12-16.

Mark's precise dating (cf. 14:1) is not quite accurate: he has the first day of Unleavened Bread on 14 Nisan (when the lambs were sacrificed); properly it is 15 Nisan. His concern is to connect this meal of Jesus with the Passover and, in v.14, he clearly designates it as a passover meal. His other and chief purpose is to highlight Jesus' foreknowledge and authority. The construction of this passage is very like that of the preparation for the entry to Jerusalem in 11:1-6 where the intent is the same. Here, as there, two disciples are sent off with a precise description of the situation they will encounter and are told exactly what to say. And here, too, all turned out as the Teacher had assured them. The Jesus who had perceived the somber significance of the anointing knows that his hour has come. He goes to meet it.

Here only in Mark is the last supper designated as a passover meal; this means that, in his chronology, Jesus died on the feast of Passover. John states with equal clarity (Jn 18:28; 19:14) that Jesus died on 14 Nisan. We may find such discrepancy disconcerting. Yet the essential is that the synoptics and John firmly connect the death of Jesus with Passover: the synoptics by having him eat the passover meal and die on the Feast; John by having him die at the hour that the Passover lambs were being sacrificed. Surely a dramatic instance of their concern for theological significance rather than factual detail.

Betrayal—"Let a Man Examine Himself . . ." 14:17-21.

All had been prepared (v.16); one would expect an account of the Supper, with its new covenant rite (vv.22-25). But Mark has intercalated the announcement-of-betrayal passage (vv.18-21). For that matter he has done so by means of his "insertion technique"—the repetition of two nearly identical phrases: "as they were at table eating" (v.18) and "as they were eating" (v.22). He thereby calls attention to the verses framed by these phrases. The reader must take them especially to heart.

Quite often, Mark is judged guilty of careless writing when, in v. 17, he specifies "the twelve." We were told that "two of his disciples" had been sent to prepare the Passover meal; now we read that he came "with the twelve" — surely it ought to be "with the *ten*." The fact is that, neither in the synoptics nor in John is it specified that only "the twelve" were present at the Last Supper. All that Mk 14:17 declares is that Jesus, with the twelve, came to a previously prepared meal. And, surely, the two disciples who had made preparation (vv. 13-16), at least they, were with Jesus and the twelve. This observation is not unimportant. It could lend credence to the claim of the fourth evangelist that the "beloved disciple" — not one of the twelve — was present at the "Last Supper." It may come as a salutory warning that, in simple fact, we do not know who exactly took part in the farewell meal.

Jesus' opening words echo Ps 41:9—"Even my bosom friend in whom I trusted, who ate of my bread, has lifted his heel against me." One who "is eating with me ... dipping bread in the same dish with me": the horror of treachery in the sacred setting of tablefellowship. There is an added awfulness: it is one of the twelve. The disciples do not really grasp what is at issue; they are filld with consternation.

Shattering as it is, betrayal is in accordance with the divine necessity for the passion: "as it is written." But human responsibility is not thereby diminished. "The woe pronounced on him [Judas] is not a curse, but a cry of sorrow and of anguish. The expression 'Alas for that man,' and the saying 'It were better, etc.' are not threats but a sad recognition of facts" (Taylor). More importantly, what is written is that the Son of Man "goes": death is freely chosen and accepted by Jesus himself. And, behind it all, is the chastening admonishment to the reader. Mark has placed the betrayal episode in the setting of eucharistic tablefellowship. The Christian must ask: "Is it I?—am I a betrayer of the Lord Jesus?" One is reminded of Paul in 1 Cor 11:.8—"Let a man examine himself . . . ."

The Lord's Supper. 14:22-25.

The phrase, "And as they were eating," not only resumes the meal episode but, as a conscious echo of v.18a, emphasizes the betrayal warning. "The Son of man goes": the shadow of death is cast darkly over this meal. Jesus "took bread," "blessed," "broke," "gave": the same actions and the very same words as in both feeding stories (6:41; 8:6). There is no doubt that the correspondence is intentional; the vocabulary there was prompted by the eucharistic language here. Then the disciples "did not understand about the loaves" (6:52; cf. 8:17-21); now the mystery is being revealed. Jesus is the "one loaf" (cf. 8:14) for Jews and gentiles because, as he tells them, his body is being given and his blood poured out for Jew and gentile (vv.23-24).

"This is my body"; Paul (1 Cor 11:22) adds "which is for you." But this is already firmly implied in Mark both through the repeated references to Jesus' death since the beginning of the passion narrative and the explicit statement in the cup saying. "This is my blood of the covenant"—Ex 24:8 is certainly in mind: "Behold the blood of the covenant which the Lord has made with you." By the sprinkling of sacrificial blood the people of Israel shared in the blessings of the covenant given at Sinai. Likewise this blood of the cup "will be poured out" (a future nuance) "for many" (a semitism, meaning "all"): a new covenant is being forged and sealed whose blessings are offered to all. The death of Jesus founds the new community. The Last Supper helps us to understand the meaning of Jesus' death on Calvary.

The saying of v.25 is likely, in some form, to have been part of Mark's liturgical tradition. It is, in essence, quite like the declaration in 1 Cor 11:26—"For as often as you eat this bread and drink the cup, you proclaim the Lord's death until he comes." As it stands in the Supper narrative, Jesus looks forward, beyond death, to the kingdom. As in the predictions of the passion (8:31; 9:31; 10:33-34) death is not the last word. Here Jesus looks, with sure hope, to the eschatological banquet. His words also mark a break: the close association, supremely marked by tablefellowship, with his disciples is at an end. But by expressing to them his own serene expectation, he is assuring them of renewed communion in the kingdom; this point has been made explicitly by Matthew (26:29).

The whole of this Supper narrative (14:22-25) is based on the eucharistic liturgical tradition of Mark's church. While less explicit than the Pauline tradition (1 Cor 11:23-26) it has the same significance. In both, the body and blood are given: the context is sacrificial death. In both the blood seals a new covenant. In both the eucharistic meal anticipates the eschatological banquet of the kingdom. And if Mark does not have Paul's "Do this in remembrance of me" (1 Cor 11:24-25), the eucharistic liturgy of his church was the living fulfillment of that word.

PROPHECY OF DENIAL.
14:26-31.

> [26]And when they had sung a hymn, they went out to the Mount of Olives. [27]And Jesus said to them, "You will all fall away; for it is written, 'I will strike the shepherd, and the sheep will be scattered.' [28]But after I am raised up, I will go before you to Galilee." [29]Peter said to him, "Even though they all fall away, I will not." [30]And Jesus said to him, "Truly, I say to you, this very night, before the cock crows twice, you will deny me three times." [31]But he said vehemently, "If I must die with you, I will not deny you." And they all said the same.

Attention turns to Jesus and his disciples again and to something more serious than misunderstanding. Judas is not the only failure—all will fail in their measure. A hymn of praise concluded the Passover meal; the hymn here is in keeping with the presentation of the Last Supper as a Passover meal. Mark has used the journey towards the Mount of Olives as a peg for Jesus' warnings to his disciples. If one looks at the context of the quotation from Zechariah, one finds there the key to verses 27-28. After declaring, "Strike the shepherd, and the sheep will be scattered" (Zech 13:7) the oracle goes on to declare that two-thirds of the shepherd-king's people will perish (v.8). The remnant will be refined and tested to become truly God's people (v.9). Jesus promises that his community, too, though shattered by the fate of their shepherd, will be reconstituted by him. He looks beyond death and promises that the scattered flock will be gathered together again. The phrase, "I will go before" is capable of being taken as "I will lead you" or "I will go there first"; it is clear from 16:7 that Mark takes it in the second sense. Also, that reminder of the angel in 16:7 shows the importance of this saying for Mark.

Mark's "Galilee," we have seen, is not a precise region on a map but is the area of gentile mission. This promise of Jesus is not too far removed from the commission of the Lord in Mt 28:19 — "Go therefore and make disciples of all nations." A fuller discussion of this matter will be held over until our comment on 16:7. This procedure is in harmony with the thrust of the evangelist's own approach: he briefly introduces matters that will be taken up at a later point.

Peter at least is confident that if all the others fail, he certainly will not. Perhaps the most effective retort to a certain scholarly view that has found in Mark an anti-Peter polemic is this brash confidence. The attractiveness of Mark's Peter is that we can all identify with him. And the genius of Mark is that, if we are honest, we must acknowledge that the Peter-in-us has deserved the rebuke of the Lord here, and throughout the gospel. Peter had seen himself as an exception—he, at least, will not be "scattered." Now he is bluntly told that, in fact, he is being singled out for failure. Of course, true to character, and true to disciple hard-heartedness, he is totally deaf to the word of the Lord. He is quite sure that he would die rather than deny Jesus. The thorough humanness of Peter is his supreme redeeming quality. And one feels that this is precisely why the human Jesus set such store by him.

Peter is a leader and his example is infectious. Now all the others, a moment ago filled with consternation (v.19), find new courage. They, too, are quite ready to die for their Master. That is as it should be, for Mark has repeatedly emphasized that Jesus' suffering and the suffering of his disciples go hand in hand (8:31, 34-38,9:31; 10:32-34,39,52). Now they learn that this cannot be their doing but is a gift of grace. It can only be because Jesus had gone before.

GETHSEMANE.
14:32-42 (Lk 22:39-46; Mt 26:36-46; cf. Heb 5:7-8).

Mark's story takes a dramatic turn. We have become accustomed to the idea of Jesus' death. We have been given clues, particularly in 10:33-34, a few pages back. But we have come to expect that Jesus will go, unruffled, to meet his fate (cf. 10:32). We could not be quite prepared for what the evangelist has to tell us, beginning here and ending with the last breath of Jesus (15:37). When one reflects that this passion-story was penned by one whose faith was centred on a risen Lord, one must wonder at the perception of this man. Tradition can have a sound instinct. Tradition has made of Mark a disciple of Paul. While it is not likely that he was, literally, Paul's follower, the Apostle would have found in him a kindred spirit. And one might add that the christian church has never wholly accepted the gospel of Paul and of Mark. And understandably, for it is uncomfortable Good News. To preach Christ crucified can never be comfortable or popular.

[32]And they went to a place which was called Gethsemane; and he said to his disciples, "Sit here, while I pray." [33]And he took with him Peter and James and John, and began to be greatly distressed and troubled. [34]And he said to them, "My soul is very sorrowful, even to death; remain here, and watch." [35]And going a little farther, he fell on the ground and prayed that, if it were possible, the hour might pass from him. [36]And he said, "Abba, Father, all things are possible to thee; remove this cup from me; yet not what I will, but what thou wilt." [37]And he came and found them sleeping, and he said to Peter, "Simon, are you asleep? Could you not watch one hour? [38]Watch and pray that you may not enter into temptation; the spirit indeed is willing, but the flesh is weak." [39]And again he went away and prayed, saying the same words. [40]And again he came and found them sleeping, for their eyes were very heavy; and they did not know what to answer him. [41]And he came the third time, and said to them, "Are you still sleeping and taking your rest? It is enough; the hour has come; the Son of man is betrayed into the hands of sinners. [42]Rise, let us be going; see my betrayer is at hand."

The word Gethsemane means "oilpress." John (Jn 18:1-2) speaks of a garden, apparently situated at the foot of the Mount of Olives. The presence of Peter, James and John is of major significance. They were with Jesus at the raising of the daughter of Jairus (5:27), at the transfiguration (9:2-8), and (with Andrew) heard his apocalyptic discourse (13:3). The reader is alerted: here he must pay special attention. It is almost impossible to convey in English the import of the Greek words which depict Jesus' state of mind—he is horrified and shocked. Again we are fascinated by the brilliance of Mark's portrayal. The Jesus who had, up to now, almost casually contemplated his fate, is here brought rudely face to face with the harsh reality. Now he knows a sorrow that threatens life itself. He bids his disciples keep on the alert—they are to "keep awake" (cf. 13:37). In fact, they will soon fall fast asleep (v.37).

Mark shows a tendency to make a statement about Jesus, usually about his teaching activity, and follow it up immediately with direct discourse. Here we have a striking case in point. There is a progression from a first description of the content of the prayer to a more explicit expression of the prayer in direct speech: v.35 gives first, in indirect form, the substance of the prayer and prepares the reader for the full impact of v.36. "The hour" is specified in v.41: it is the hour of the delivering up of the Son of man—the divinely appointed hour. "Cup" is an Old Testament metaphor for punishment and divine retribution. It stands for the burden of human sin that Jesus has to bear in undergoing his redemptive death. His *Abba*, an intimate word for "father," indicates his awareness of a special, a unique, relationship to God. It is so dramatically right that, for the first time in the gospel, that name is uttered. The utterance of this trustful *Abba* already contains "thy will be done." The obedient Son cries out to the Father and puts himself wholly in the hand of the Father. Indeed, Jesus' distress mirrors the sentiment of the Father who so loves a sinful world that he delivers up his Son. Gethsemane brings us face to face with the reality of divine love.

Jesus prayed to be spared from the hour, prayed to have the cup removed. This was the moment of final, decisive temptation. His work had begun with an encounter with the tempter (1:12-13). He was never free of that insidious presence of evil. Even the hot-blooded, generous Peter could become a Satan for him (8:33). Now was the climax—the hour of the power of darkness (cf. Lk 22:53). Jesus is face to face with naked evil. He is being tempted to eliminate suffering from his messianic way. It is the supreme test, for evil is overcome not by violence but by loving obedience—"he was heard for his godly fear" (Heb 5:7). Jesus, in Gethsemane, had come to terms with the necessity of suffering.

Three times Jesus comes to the disciples and three times he finds them sleeping, another instance of the Marcan predilection for threes. The spotlight has turned from the praying Jesus to the sleeping disciples. They, too, are involved in this eschatological conflict. They are being asked to pray that they may not fall in the struggle that confronts them. Danger is from without—they must watch, and from within—they must pray. Instead, they sleep. "And they did not know what to answer him"; that had been the very situation of the three at the transfiguration (9:6). Now is the climax of their misunderstanding. This is the last time Jesus speaks to them. They cannot hear his word of warning "for their eyes were very heavy." They have closed their eyes to what has transpired at Gethsemane. Their misunderstanding has grown into failure; Peter has reverted to Simon again. The last suffering Son of Man saying (v.41) falls on their deaf ears.

For Jesus, all is now clear. It had seemed to him that the way of the cross was the path he was asked to walk. Now, through anguished prayer, it had become clear to him that what seemed to be asked really was asked of him. In that certainty he has found peace. It is no longer a stricken Jesus (vv.34,35) but a serene Jesus, victor in temptation, who can call to his disciples, "Rise, let us be going" and walk resolutely to meet his betrayer and his fate. He has spoken for the last time of his suffering role. Now he undergoes that suffering.

It is important that Mark has so closely woven the theme of discipleship misunderstanding with that of Jesus' temptation. It is his most dramatic answer to any objection to a suffering Messiah. Jesus himself has been brought to the brink of rejecting it. The evangelist leaves no doubt that suffering messiahship is not easily accepted; he knows, as fully as Paul, that the cross is foolishness and scandal. The three disciples do not understand. The reader is duly warned. One must watch and pray. Good intentions are not enough. Discipleship is a way of life. And the course of that way has been plotted by Jesus: "Rise, let us be going . . ."

THE ARREST.
14:43-52 (Lk 22:47-57; Mt 26:47-56; Jn 18:2-11).

> [43]And immediately, while he was still speaking, Judas came, one of the twelve, and with him a crowd with swords and clubs, from the chief priests and the scribes and the elders. [44]Now the betrayer had given them a sign, saying, "The one I shall kiss is the man; seize him and lead him away safely." [45]And when he came, he went up to him at once, and said, "Master!" And he kissed him. [46]And they laid hands on him and seized him. [47]But one of those who stood by drew his sword, and struck the slave of the high priest and cut off his ear. [48]And Jesus said to them, "Have you come out as against a robber, with swords and clubs to capture me? [49]Day after day I was with you in the temple teaching, and you did not seize me. But let the scriptures be fulfilled." [50]And they all forsook him and fled.
>
> [51]And a young man followed him, with nothing but a linen cloth about his body; and they seized him, [52]but he left the linen cloth and ran away naked.

Jesus is ready and the drama opens without delay. The Son of Man goes to his fate in obedience to a divine purpose (cf. 14:21). His lot is indeed bitter: "One of the twelve" is hastening to betray him. Judas is accompanied by an armed rabble, one despatched by the religious authorities; their plot was bearing fruit (14:1-2). There is no mention of temple police (Lk 22:52) or Roman troops (Jn 18:3,12). The "betrayer" is, literally, "the one who delivered him up"—Judas is serving a divine purpose. Judas greeted Jesus in the manner in which a disciple would salute his rabbi; yet betrayal with a kiss is singularly distasteful and Luke underlines the fact (Lk 22:48). In the Marcan narrative Jesus does not speak to Judas. The person who wounded the high priest's slave is not named in contrast to Jn 18:10 where the wielder of the sword is Peter and the slave is named Malchus; while Luke notes that Jesus healed the wound. Mark gives the impression of a clumsy attempt to defend Jesus by someone other than a disciple. Jesus protests at the manner of the arrest: it characterizes him as a man of violence. But he is a man of peace, a teacher who does not need to disguise his teaching. The phrase "day by day in the temple" implies a longer Jerusalem ministry than the few days allowed by Mark. Reference to the fulfillment of the scriptures does not point to specific texts but asserts that here God's will is being done: the Son of Man is being delivered up. The "all" who fled are the disciples. They forsook him. Even one who still "followed" Jesus after the disciples had deserted quickly loses heart. Jesus is left all alone.

The "young man" (v.51) remains a riddle. Traditionally, this young man has been taken to be the evangelist. It is felt however that the passage is too compressed and enigmatic to be a reference to a factual occurrence. But what if Mark has painted himself into the scene somewhat in the manner in which medieval artists had slipped themselves into their paintings? This young man (*neaniskos*) is "seized" as Jesus had been "seized" (vv.44,46). He escapes by leaving his linen cloth (*sindōn*—mentioned twice) behind. The dead Jesus is wrapped in a linen cloth (*sindōn*—mentioned twice, 15:46). The *neaniskos* reappears in 16:5, now clad in "a white robe." Is Mark the mysterious *neaniskos*, the proclaimer of the death and of the resurrection? It is scarcely to be doubted that the "young man" carries symbolic import. We are left to guess at Mark's precise intent.

TRIAL AND DENIAL.
14:53-72 (Lk 22:54-71; Mt 26:57-75; Jn 18:12-27)

Recognition of extensive Marcan redaction in this passage not only helps our understanding of it but enables us to come to terms with serious objections to the legal procedures of the trial, notably a night sitting of the Sanhedrin. It seems now that it is Mark who has shaped individual traditions into the form of a trial. His purpose is firmly christological; he is not concerned with Jewish law and customs. In a similar way, John has built up the appearance of Jesus before Pilate into a moving drama (Jn 18:28-19:16). We have to take Mark on his own terms and not read into his narrative considerations which are not his concern. We observe, too, that the evangelist has intercalated his trial scene into the story of Peter's denial (14:53-54, 66-72). We should read both episodes in relation to each other as he has directed us to do.

> [53] And they led Jesus to the high priest; and all the chief priests and the elders and the scribes were assembled. [54] And Peter had followed him at a distance, right into the courtyard of the high priest; and he was sitting with the guards, and warming himself at the fire.
> [55] Now the chief priests and the whole council sought testimony against Jesus to put him to death; but they found none. [56] For many bore false witness against him, and their witness did not agree. [57] And some stood up and bore false witness against him, saying, [58] "We heard him say, 'I will destroy this temple that is made with hands, and in three days I will build another, not made with hands.'" [59] Yet not even so did their testimony agree. [60] And the high priest stood up in the midst and asked

Jesus, "Have you no answer to make? What is it that these men testify against you?" ⁶¹But he was silent and made no answer. Again the high priest asked him, "Are you the Christ, the Son of the Blessed?" ⁶²And Jesus said, "I am; and you will see the Son of man sitting at the right hand of Power, and coming with the clouds of heaven." ⁶³And the high priest tore his mantle, and said, "Why do we still need witnesses? ⁶⁴You have heard this blasphemy. What is your decision?" And they all condemned him as deserving death. ⁶⁵And some began to spit on him, and to cover his face, and to strike him, saying to him, "Prophesy!" And the guards received him with blows.

⁶⁶And as Peter was below in the courtyard, one of the maids of the high priest came; ⁶⁷and seeing Peter warming himself, she looked at him, and said, "You also were with the Nazarene, Jesus." ⁶⁸But he denied it, saying, "I neither know nor understand what you mean." And he went out into the gateway. ⁶⁹And the maid saw him, and began again to say to the bystanders, "This man is one of them." ⁷⁰But again he denied it. And after a little whle again the bystanders said to Peter, "Certainly you are one of them; for you are a Galilean." ⁷¹But he began to invoke a curse on himself and to swear, 'I do not know this man of whom you speak." ⁷²And immediately the cock crowed a second time. And Peter remembered how Jesus had said to him, "Before the cock crows twice, you will deny me three times." And he broke down and wept.

Peter Followed Him. 14:53-54.

The opening verse (53) makes two affirmations: the leading away of Jesus and the assembling of priests, elders and scribes. Mark has built on the tradition that Jesus was brought before the Jewish high priest (cf. Lk 22:54; Jn 18:13). Peter is introduced—he had followed Jesus "at a distance." It will soon emerge how very far behind he is on the way of discipleship. Jesus' testimony is framed by Peter's denial. He is faithful unto death, while Peter proves unfaithful. At Caesarea Philippi Peter showed that he could not accept the notion of suffering messiahship (8:31-33). Now he will disassociate himself from the suffering Messiah. But first the trial of Jesus gets underway.

Are You the Christ, the Son of the Blessed? 14:55-65.

The opening remark (v.55) harks back to 3:6; 11:18; 12:12 and 14:1—Jesus had long been tried and condemned. All that remains is how to make away with him. His enemies needed evidence. And the witnesses were there. Jesus is the suffering Just One surrounded by false witnesses. The influence of the psalms is manifest: "for false witnesses have risen against me, and they breathe out violence" (Ps 27:12); "malicious witnesses rise up; they ask me of things that I know not" (Ps 35:11). Mark stresses their lack of agreement. The repetition of the lack of agreement (v.56b, "and their witness did not agree," v.59, "Yet not even so did their testimony agree") is the frame for a Marcan insertion: the temple saying, v.58. He thus signals the special importance of the saying.

It would seem that the falseness of the suborned witnesses lies in their malicious purpose. Because, in fact, the saying does square with the marked anti-Jerusalem bias we have seen running through the gospel. Besides, the cursing of the fig tree episode does present Jesus as "destroying the temple": "the fig tree which you cursed has withered" (11:21). He did claim to have brought the temple to an end: that is the point of the mocking repetition of the charge as he hung on the cross (15:29). Ironically, the taunt was true, symbolically demonstrated by the rending of the temple veil (15:38). The temple had lost its meaning for Christians. And this is because Jesus has built another temple "not made with hands"—the community. This was his purpose in calling and forming disciples. John offers a different explanation: Jesus spoke of the temple of his body (Jn 2:21). It suits Mark's purpose, however, that the testimony of these ill-intentioned witnesses cannot be the decisive factor in Jesus' trial. That must be the formal messianic claim of Jesus himself (v.62).

When pressed by the high priest to respond to the charge, Jesus maintains a rigid silence (vv.60-61a). The silence of Jesus, carefully emphasized ("but he was silent and made no answer") is dramatic preparation for the solemn confession of v.62. The high priest is forced to take direct action; his question and Jesus' answer form the heart of this passage. Thoroughly Marcan, these verses are the culmination of his christology. The titles "Christ" and "Son of God" stand in the heading of the gospel (1:). The high priest now ironically bestows them on Jesus (Son of the Blessed is the equivalent of Son of God). When Jesus was acknowledged as Christ at Caesarea Philippi he enjoined silence (8:30). But now Jesus himself, positively and publicly, acknowledges that he is the Christ, and that he is indeed the Son of God. But he does so on his own terms, in terms of "Son of Man." With his firm "I am" he makes, for the first and only time, an explicit messianic claim—the messianic secret has been formally disclosed. In his reply he quotes Ps 110:1 and Dan 7:13: as enthroned and coming Son of Man his true identity will be revealed. When he returns in glory as the victorious Son of Man, then he will be fully known. "You will see"—these verses are a Marcan composition and the evangelist is addressing his readers directly out of the narrative. That is why he has taken pains to attract attention to the declaration. Addressed to the high priest "you will see" makes little sense, but addressed to the first readers of the gospel it makes very good sense. They could "see," that is, "know" Jesus as ascended and enthroned at the right hand of God. Furthermore, they "will see" his parousia. Throughout the gospel Mark had directed the attention of his readers to the coming of Jesus as Son of Man. It is to be expected that this last Son of Man saying will point to the parousia. It looks ahead to 16:7, to the encounter with the glorious Son of Man in the "Galilee" of a Jewish-Gentile Christian world. It is not accidental that Mark has no appearance stories. For him Jesus is with God and will appear again only at the parousia.

Jesus' confession provokes the death-sentence and that is how it had to be because he cannot be known for who he is until he has died and risen from the dead (cf. 9:9). In terms of the trial narrative, his claim was self-incriminating. The Sanhedrin can now achieve its stated purpose (v.55). The rending of garments had become, in the case of the high priest, a carefully regulated formal judicial gesture. Only Mark (followed by Matthew) specifies a charge of blasphemy. It reflects the situation of the early church: Jewish authorities had begun to consider the messianic claims accredited to Jesus as blasphemous. And Christians would have suffered for their confession of him (cf. 13:9-11).

The mocking episode (v.65) appears to be a separate element of tradition introduced by Mark at this point. The "some" implies members of the Sanhedrin. That Mark intends the implication is evident when we note that he has them explicitly mock Jesus on the cross (15:31). Historically unlikely, it is fitting in Mark's narrative. The leaders had sought his death from 3:6 on and now triumph has its hour. The irony of this scene is that Jesus is being mocked as a prophet just as his prediction of Peter's denial is being fulfilled.

I Do Not Know This Man 14:66-72.

With v.66 we return to Peter. In the setting and form of the denial, Mark is on traditional grounds. However, "Nazarene" is his title for Jesus (cf. 1:24; 10:47; 14:57; 16:1), indicative of his interest in Galilee. At the initial stage Peter is being evasive, pretending not to understand what the maid was saying (v.68). On the basis of this first (traditional) denial Mark has built the other two, so producing his familiar triple pattern. Now Peter has to come out to deny that he is "one of them," a disciple of Jesus (v.70). Finally, he is forced to disassociate himself from Jesus, calling down the wrath of God upon himself if what he says is not true (v.71). The progression is patent: evasion, denial of discipleship, denial, under oath, that he has ever known Jesus at all. The cockcrow—Mark alone mentions that the cock crowed a second time—causes Peter to remember Jesus' prediction of his denials and his own vehement protestations (14:30-31). "He broke down"—an approximate translation of an enigmatic verb, but the general idea is clear enough: Peter is utterly shattered. The denial story brings the disciple-misunderstanding theme to a head. Peter has publicly disassociated himself from Jesus. The sheep have been effectively scattered and the stricken shepherd is wholly on his own (14:27). As they see themselves in disciples who could betray and deny and forsake, Mark's readers are not likely to feel complacent. Mark insists on the loneliness of Jesus during his passion: up to the moment of death he is alone, more and more alone. His intention is not only to waken us to the poignancy of this painful solitude. He wants us to perceive in that starkness the truth that Christ alone saves.

TRIAL BEFORE PILATE.
15:1-15 (Lk 23:1-25; Mt 27:11-26; Jn 18:28-19:16).

15 And as soon as it was morning the chief priests, with the elders and scribes, and the whole council held a consultation; and they bound Jesus and led him away and delivered him to Pilate. [2]And Pilate asked him, "Are you the King of the Jews?" And he answered him, "You have said so." [3]And the chief priests accused him of many things. [4]And Pilate again asked him, "Have you no answer to make? See how many charges they bring against you." [5]But Jesus made no further answer, to that Pilate wondered.

[6]Now at the feast he used to release for them one prisoner whom they asked. [7]And among the rebels in prison, who had committed murder in the insurrection, there was a man called Barabbas. [8]And the crowd came up and began to ask Pilate to do as he was wont to do for them. [9]And he answered them, "Do you want me to release for you the King of the Jews?" [10]For he perceived that it was out of envy that the chief priests had delivered him up. [11]But the chief priests stirred up the crowd to have him release for them Barabbas instead. [12]And Pilate again said to them, "Then what shall I do with the man

whom you call the King of the Jews?" [13]And they cried out again, "Crucify him." [14]And Pilate said to them, "Why, what evil has he done?" But they shouted all the more, "Crucify him." [15]So Pilate, wishing to satisfy the crowd, released for them Barabbas; and having scourged Jesus, he delivered him to be crucified.

Mark picks up the thread of the story which had been interrupted by the account of Peter's denial. This second meeting of the Sanhedrin serves to introduce the trial scene which follows. Jesus is "delivered over" to Pilate: the recurrence of this expression throughout the passion narrative is a reminder that all of this is happening "according to the definite plan and foreknowledge of God" (Acts 2:23). It is enough to name Pilate—all Christians know who he is. By the high priest Jesus had been asked, in Jewish terms, if he were the Messiah, the Son of the Blessed. The Roman uses a title that has meaning for him: King of the Jews. In his eyes the title was political and, if Jesus really claimed it, was equivalent to high treason: political authority was Rome's prerogative. Pilate's question falls into a pattern wherein a title is bestowed which is true of Jesus but not in the sense understood by those who bestow it (3:11; 8:29; 14:61; 15:2). That is why Jesus' response ("You have said so") remains obscure. In fact he does accept the designation, but knows that he is King of a kind not imagined by Pilate. John has a splendid commentary on this exchange (Jn 18:33-37). For Mark the title is certainly important, and he has highlighted it by means of his insertion-technique— "And Pilate asked him" (15:2), "And Pilate again asked him" (15:4). From now on, in the passion narrative, the title appears at every conceivable opportunity.

The priests hasten to press charges against him. Jesus preserves the silence that is a feature of the suffering Just One (cf. Is 53:7). Pilate's "wonder" is more than surprise, it conveys a sense of religious awe (cf. 5:20; Jn 19:8-11).

Outside of the gospels we find no trace of the Passover amnesty custom described here (v.6); it would seem to be an inference drawn from this isolated Barabbas incident. Interestingly, Luke makes no mention of the custom. Barabbas was in prison with other rebels who had killed during a political affray. The crowd came to plead for this man, and Pilate presents them with an alternative: they may have instead "the King of the Jews." He has seen through the charges made against Jesus. Mark puts the responsibility where he believed it belonged, at the door of the priests. As in all the gospels, Pilate is convinced of Jesus' innocence, but yields to pressure. It is he who is really on trial; John has developed this feature in masterly fashion. Pilate's strange appeal to the crowd as to what he is to do with this King of the Jews is very effective. The nation rejects its king and calls for his death on the cross. Pilate helplessly protests Jesus' innocence—"Why, what evil has he done?"—but they clamor for blood. Pilate yielded, "wishing to satisfy the crowd." He released a murderer and condemned an innocent man. Jesus was scourged: a terrible flogging was the normal prelude to crucifixion. Plate "delivered him" (v.15): he had played his role in a drama directed by God.

HAIL, KING OF THE JEWS.
15:16-20 (Lk 23:11; Mt 27:27-31).

> [16]And the soldiers led him away inside the palace (that is, the praetorium); and they called together the whole battalion. [17]And they clothed him in a purple cloak, and plaiting a crown of thorns they put it on him. [18]And they began to salute him, "Hail, King of the Jews!" [19]And they struck his head with a reed, and spat upon him, and they knelt down in homage to him. [20]And when they had mocked him, they stripped him of the purple cloak, and put his own clothes on him. And they led him out to crucify him.

Into the narrative of the sentencing and execution of Jesus (15:6-15 + 21-32) Mark has inserted the incident of mocking by soldiers (15:16-20), thereby highlighting the title "King of the Jews." This brutal mockery is, ironically, Jesus' enthronement. The soldiers led him inside the palace, the Roman procurator's headquarters in Jerusalem. The "whole battalion" means, most likely, those who were around at the time. But the statement does add to the mock solemnity of the situation: this "King" had his palace guards. The "purple cloak" was, very likely, one of the red-colored military cloaks; the "crown" was a rude replica hastily woven of thorns. A "purple" cloak and a "crown" of thorns furnished a mock ritual of kingly dignity. Striking and spitting seem out of place and most likely come from the other mocking scene in 14:65. Here the emphasis is on royal "homage." The irony of the situation is patent, and it admirably serves Mark's christology. Jesus is King, but only in humility (11:7-10) and suffering. Now they can lead him out to his throne: the cross.

AND THEY CRUCIFIED HIM.
15:21-32 (Lk 23:26,33-39; Mt 27:32-44; Jn 19:17-24).

> [21]And they compelled a passer-by, Simon of Cyrene, who was coming in from the country, the father of Alexander and Rufus, to carry his cross. [22]And they brought him to the place called Golgotha (which means the place of a skull). [23]And they offered him wine mingled with myrrh; but he did not take it. [24]And they crucified him, and divided his garments among them, casting lots for them, to decide what each should take. [25]And it was the third hour, when they crucified him. [26]And the inscription of the charge against him read, "The King of the Jews." [27]And with him they crucified two robbers, one on his right and one on his left. [29]And those who passed by derided him, wagging their heads, and saying, "Aha! You who would destroy the temple and build it in three days, [30]save yourself, and come down from the cross!" [31]So also the chief priests mocked him to one another with the scribes, saying, "He saved others; he cannot save himself. [32]Let the Christ, the King of Israel, come down now from the cross, that we may see and believe." Those who were crucified with him also reviled him.

The Marcan drama reaches its climax in the crucifixion scene. The evangelist had prepared for Jesus' death in 3:6; from that point on, explicitly or by allusion, he continued to harp on it. In painting this scene he has drawn upon Old Testament passages portraying the figure of the suffering Just One, who suffers but is finally vindicated. Various motifs which build up the image of the Just One, taken mainly from the psalms, surface in this passage. Mark's concern is to establish that everything took place according to the scriptures, that is, according to the will of God.

It was customary for the condemned man to carry his cross beam. Mark tells us that a certain Simon of Cyrene (a town in North Africa, but perhaps Simon now lived in Palestine) was "impressed" by the soldiers to carry the beam. Alexander and Rufus are evidently well known to Mark's community. "To carry his cross" is, literally "to *take up* his cross," a conscious echo of the phrase in 8:34; it is a lesson in discipleship. Luke correctly caught Mark's intent: they "laid on him the cross, to carry it behind Jesus" (Lk 23:26). The Christian, however, should carry his cross, not under compulsion, but willingly. Golgotha, an Aramaic name, properly *golgoltha*, means "a skull." The name may have been suggested by a skull-shaped hill; though the text speaks only of "place" and does not specify hill. It was presumably outside the city wall and close to a road (v. 29). It was Jewish custom, based on Prov 31:6-7, to provide condemned criminals with drugged wine as a means of lessening their torment. Jesus willed to suffer and die with an unclouded mind. And they crucified him. "So, in the simplest possible terms, the dread act is recorded" (Taylor). By custom, the clothes of the condemned fell to the executioners. Mark, with Ps 22:18 in mind, sees in this, too, a divine purpose.

The evangelist marks the time off in three-hourly intervals (15:25,33,34). For that matter, precise statements of time are a feature of the trial and passion narrative: 14:72; 15:1, 25,33,42; 16:1. This is to indicate that the passage of time was in accord with the will of God. Nothing at all has happened by chance or unexpectedly. The third hour is 9 a.m. It is impossible to reconcile this time reference with Jn 19:14

where Jesus was *sentenced* at 12 noon of 14 Nisan. John's purpose is to have Jesus die at the hour when the Passover lamb was slaughtered. Both evangelists are making theological statements.

Reference to the superscription (15:26) is in accordance with Roman practice; the King is now enthroned. All the gospels agree that Jesus was crucified between two criminals. Many manuscripts of Mark carry as v.28: "And the scripture was fulfilled which says, He was reckoned with the transgressors." It is a borrowing from Lk 22:37, but it does make explicit the intent of Mark who would have seen in this disturbing fact a fulfillment of Is 53:12. Two sets of taunts are now leveled at Jesus. The fact that there are passersby suggests crucifixion near a roadway. Their taunt is influenced by Lam 2:15 and Ps 22:7-8—"They wag their heads"; "He committed his cause to the Lord; let him deliver him, let him rescue him." And they "derided," literally, "blasphemed" him. They are, of course, really blaspheming God, so doing the very thing that justified Jesus' condemnation to death (14:64). Their words hark back to the temple charge in 14:58. The irony is that precisely by not saving his life (8:35), by not coming down from the cross, Jesus is bringing the temple to an end (15:38) and building the new temple.

The mocking invitation for Jesus to come down from the cross is echoed by the leaders of official Judaism. The presence of the chief priests and scribes at the crucifixion and their crude railing cannot be historical. But, in Mark's plan, it is fitting that they should be the principal scoffers. They, the implacable opponents of Jesus, had to be fitted in at this climactic moment. "He saved others"—a reference to Jesus' ministry of healing, regularly described as *sozein*, "to heal," or "to save" (e.g. 5:23,28,34). He who could save others will not save himself, for it is by losing his life that he will save himself (8:35). And not only his own life; he is giving it as a ransom for all (10:45).

Up to now, Jesus had been "King of the Jews," now he is "the Messiah, the King of Israel." Since Maccabean times "Jews" had become the gentile name for the people of

Israel, so King of the Jews is normal in dealing with Pilate; the priests, naturally, used "Israel" as a self-designation. Jewish tradition had anticipated that in the days of Messiah the true Israel would be established. Now Jesus is being ironically addressed as the King of this eschatological Israel. They are still looking for "signs" (cf. 8:11-12): if Jesus does come down from the cross they will "see" and believe. In Mark, "seeing" is primarily associated with the "seeing" of Jesus at the parousia (13:26; 14:62). But there can be no "seeing" until Jesus has died and risen. Temple saying and christological titles, prominent in 14:58 and 14:61-62 are brought together here (15:29,32); the significance of both is being worked out on the cross. The denouement comes in 15:38-39. Meanwhile, Jesus' isolation is total: even his companions in suffering deride him (v.32b).

Mark has firmly presented the crucifixion of Jesus as an enthronement. The title appears at once in Pilate's opening question: "Are you the King of the Jews?" (15:2) Jesus accepts the designation but with the implication that he understands it differently. Pilate consistently calls him King of the Jews (vv.9,12); indeed, in v.12 he is the one "whom you call" King of the Jews. The soldiers pay homage to the "King of the Jews" (15:16-19) and the official superscription "The King of the Jews" is fixed on Jesus' cross. And priests and scribes mock him as "Christ, the King of Israel" (15:32). For Mark this is a narrative of the enthronement of Christ as King; and it can be such in light of the christological profession of 14:62. Jesus' royal status is wholly paradoxical.

DEATH AND REVELATION.
15:33-39 (Lk 23:44-48; Mt 27:45-54; Jn 19:17-30).

> [33]And when the sixth hour had come, there was darkness over the whole land until the ninth hour. [34]And at the ninth hour Jesus cried with a loud voice, Eloi, Eloi, lama sabachthani?" which means, "My God, my God, why hast thou forsaken me?" And some of the bystanders hearing it said, "Behold, he is calling Elijah." [36]And one

ran and, filling a sponge full of vinegar, put it on a reed
and gave it to him to drink, saying "Wait, let us see
whether Elijah will come to take him down." [37]And Jesus
uttered a loud cry, and breathed his last. [38]And the
curtain of the temple was torn in two, from top to bottom.
[39]And when the centurion, who stood facing him, saw that
he thus breathed his last, he said, "Truly this man was
the Son of God!"

The grim drama is being played out. Crucified at the
third hour (9 a.m.), Jesus has spent three hours in agony.
Now, at the sixth hour (noon), breaks the hour of darkness,
of momentary demonic triumph—"your hour and the
power of darkness" (Lk 22:53). Jesus had begun his mission
in an encounter with Satan (1:12-13) and carried on the war
in his exorcisms. Now, helpless on the cross, he seems to
be crushed by these very powers. The close of that time of
darkness, the ninth hour (3 p.m.) marks the hour of fulfillment. Paradoxically, it seems to sound the nadir of Jesus'
defeat. This is brought out by the twofold reference to a
"loud cry." The expression (*phōnē megalē*) occurs only
four times in Mark. In 1:26 and 5:7 it is the loud cry of a
demoniac, one oppressed by an evil spirit. Jesus himself
now (15:34,37) reacts with a loud cry to the intolerable
pressure of evil. He suffers the absence of God: his cry of
dereliction is one of total desolation. The common explanation that the cry (v.34) is the opening verse of Ps 22, a psalm
which ends on a confident note, is a factually true observation but makes nonsense of Mark's intent. He has Jesus die
in total desolation, without any relieving feature at all.
It would have seemed that, up to this point, Jesus' isolation
could go no further: deserted by his disciples, taunted by his
enemies, derided by those who hung with him, suffocating
in the darkness of evil. But the worst is now: abandoned
by God. His suffering is radically lonely. But his God is
"*my* God" (v.34). Even in this, as at Gethsemane, it is "not
what I will, but what thou wilt." Here, even more than then,
the sheer humanness of Jesus is manifest. Now he knows
what it means to give his life a ransom for many. Now the

Son is wholly delivered into the hands of men. And the Father, too, in the Son, has abandoned himself to the humanity he would save—this is the deep meaning of that cry. The Father thereby holds out the gift of forgiveness to all who will recognize this vulnerable love.

The bystanders thought that Jesus called on Elijah, who was popularly believed to come to the aid of the just in tribulation. Misunderstanding hounds Jesus to the end. His cry of dereliction was one of total abandonment to the Father; they take it to be a desperate cry for help, "Vinegar" is likely the Roman soldiers' *posca*, a mixture of water, sour wine, and egg. The gesture was kindly meant (v.36), but Mark, likely with Ps 69:21 in mind, thinks of it as an addition to Jesus' misery. Again the "loud cry" is significant: it depicts Jesus' awareness of his struggle with evil. All the more so because Mark describes a sudden, violent death— "breathed his last" is not strong enough to convey his meaning (v.37). Jesus died abandoned, seemingly crushed by the forces of evil. This is perfectly in keeping with Mark's *theologia crucis*. Forthwith he can point to the victory of Jesus.

In the first place the rending of the curtain of the temple (v.38) marks a transformation at the very moment of Jesus' death. The temple has lost its significance (cf. 11:12-25; 13:2; 14:58). The privilege of Israel has come to an end; access to the divine presence is henceforth open to all. Far more important is the confession of the centurion (v.39). It is an extraordinary statement from a man who stood facing a helpless victim on a cross and watched him as he died: "Truly, this man was Son of God!" Now that Jesus has been recognized as the one who suffered and died he can be called Son of God in the proper sense. The Revised Standard translation has "a son of God" since in the Greek the noun "son" is without the definite article. But so it is in 1:1 where "Son of God"is certainly a christological title. The whole thrust of the gospel demands that the title bear its full christological sense in 15:39, all the more so because for Mark the cross is the only true sign of who Jesus really is. The centurion has looked upon the dead Jesus, and has seen the Son of God! Only one who can accept that paradox can, like him, make the true christian profession of faith. Only such a one can hope to see the Son of Man coming with the clouds of heaven (14:62).

THE FAITHFUL WOMEN.
15:40-41 (Lk 23:49; Mt 27:55-56; Jn 19:25-27).

> [40]There were also women looking on from afar, among whom were Mary Magdalene, and Mary the mother of James the younger and of Joses, and Salome, [41]who, when he was in Galilee, followed him, and ministered to him; and also many other women who came up with him to Jerusalem.

The disciples had fled but some women from Galilee had not quite lost heart, even if they looked on "from afar." Their presence here is not only that they may see where Jesus is buried (15:47) and hear the tidings of his resurrection (16:6). Because they are said to have followed him "when he was in Galilee" we are reminded of his assurance that after the resurrection he will go before the disciples into Galilee (14:28). They will be bidden to assure the disciples that "they will see" him in Galilee. The introduction of these women, immediately after the death of Jesus points the reader to resurrection—and to the parousia.

They had "followed him." This is the only place in the gospels where the discipleship of women is mentioned. And it is not by chance that they, and "many other women" (v.41), are natives of Galilee. It is because they had continued to follow him, if even "from afar" that the last message is entrusted to them. They alone, of all others, had followed to the cross. Luke is the evangelist who gets the credit for alerting us to Jesus' solicitude for womankind. But Mark had beforehand made his telling contribution. The chosen male disciples have abandoned Jesus (14:50). These women disciples have stood steadfast and have not been ashamed of Jesus (8:38).

THE BURIAL.
15:42-47 (Lk 23:50-56; Mt 27:57-61;Jn 19:38-42).

> ⁴²And when evening had come, since it was the day of Preparation, that is, the day before the sabbath, ⁴³Joseph of Arimathea, a respected member of the council, who was also himself looking for the kingdom of God, took courage and went to Pilate, and asked for the body of Jesus. ⁴⁴And Pilate wondered if he were already dead; and summoning the centurion, he asked him whether he was already dead. ⁴⁵And when he learned from the centurion that he was dead, he granted the body to Joseph. ⁴⁶And he bought a linen shroud, and taking him down, wrapped him in the linen shroud, and laid him in a tomb which had been hewn out of the rock; and he rolled a stone against the door of the tomb. ⁴⁷Mary Magdalene and Mary the mother of Joses saw where he was laid.

The story of Jesus' burial was important because it established that Jesus had really died and because it assured that the women who found the empty tomb had seen that the body had previously been laid in it. Mark sticks to his three-hour scheme even though "evening" (6 p.m.) would mean that the sabbath had begun. The "day of preparation" (v.42)—here is where we learn that Jesus died on a Friday. Joseph of Arimathea is otherwise unknown. There is no suggestion in Mark that Joseph is a disciple; he has become one in Mt 27:57. The disciples had fled; it was left to another to perform the funeral rites. Joseph lived in expectation of a fulfillment of Israel's messianic hopes. As such, he was one concerned to fulfill the law; in this case that the body of one hanged should not be left overnight on the tree (Dt 21:23). It was Roman practice to let the bodies of crucified remain on the cross; so Joseph "screwed up his courage" and approached Pilate. The latter's surprise is understandable; it was unusual for a crucified man to die so quickly.

Joseph was duly granted "the *corpse*" of Jesus; Mark starkly insists on the reality of Jesus' death. Only Mark mentions the buying of the shroud, which, if this were the Passover, seems most unlikely. Again, according to Mark, the body of Jesus was not anointed (16:1; cf. 14:8); Jn 19:39-40 insists on the anointing. The only witnesses of the burial are women, a preparation for the final passage (16:1-8). But it also makes Mark's point that women disciples continue to play a role when the twelve have fled.

THE WOMEN AT THE TOMB.
16:1-8 (Lk 24:1-10; Mt 28:1-8; Jn 20:1-2).

> **16** And when the sabbath was past, Mary Magdalene, and Mary the mother of James, and Salome, bought spices, so that they might go and anoint him. ²And very early on the first day of the week they went to the tomb when the sun had risen. ³And they were saying to one another, "Who will roll away the stone for us from the door of the tomb?' ⁴And looking up, they saw that the stone was rolled back; for it was very large. ⁵And entering the tomb, they saw a young man sitting on the right side, dressed in a white robe; and they were amazed. ⁶And he said to them, "Do not be amazed; you seek Jesus of Nazareth, who was crucified. He has risen, he is not here; see the place where they laid him. ⁷But go, tell his disciples and Peter that he is going before you to Galilee; there you will see him, as he told you." ⁸And they went out and fled from the tomb; for trembling and astonishment had come upon them; and they said nothing to any one, for they were afraid.

Mark relates that the three women named in 15:40, intending to anoint the body of Jesus, bought spices when the sabbath had ended (after 6 p.m.). The motive adduced here—anointing of a corpse a day and two nights after death—is surprising. It may be that the Johannine tradition could make it seem less surprising: the substantial mixture of myrrh and aloes provided by Nicodemus (Jn 19:39-40) were meant to preserve the body until it could be properly anointed. On the other hand, Mt 28:1 states that the women came simply to visit the tomb. At any rate, according to our evangelist, these women arrived at the tomb on the (Sunday) morning "very early . . . when the sun had risen"—very much Mark's style. To their surprise they found the stone rolled away. Mark makes no attempt to explain how or by whom the deed was done; but by observing, "it was very large," he points to a portentous happening.

The "young man," dressed in white, is an angel; in his presence the women were filled with something like shuddering awe. Their awe and his words of assurance are stock features of such angelic visitations. They had come seeking Jesus; they had seen where his body had been laid (15:47). Again they look upon the spot but he is no longer there—he has risen! The "young man" plays the role of *angelus interpres*, of interpreting angel, a feature of apocalyptic. They were faced with the riddle of an empty tomb; he explains why the tomb is empty. It is a neat literary way of presenting, as briefly as possible, the fact of the empty tomb and the real reason of its emptiness. It is not unlikely, however, that Mark has given to this "young man" his own visage. There is a link between this *neaniskos* and the one in 14:51-52. The evangelist intimates that, for his readers, he is this *angelus interpres*, the rightful herald of cross and of resurrection.

The women had sought Jesus *of Nazareth*: an important title for Mark. He has used it from the beginning (1:9,24) and stresses it again at the end (14:67; 16:6), a reminder that Jesus is the man of Galilee. And he is "the crucified one"—practically a title too. Yet, "he is not here": Mark draws attention to the absence of Jesus. This was the experience of his community as they awaited the parousia.

The women were given a message, the echo of a promise made by Jesus on the way to Gethsemane (14:28), a message for the disciples, and especially for Peter (that is the force of the Greek). Jesus is going before them into Galilee; they will see him there. Galilee is a symbol as much as a place. Mark has been at pains to show the wider "Galilee" as the place of the breakdown of the barrier between Jew and Gentile, as the locale of the Gentile mission. There the disciples had been first assembled (1:16-20) and there they will now "see": they will encounter the Risen Christ. And there, too, they will "see" the Son of Man at his coming (13:26-27; 14:62). Meanwhile, life goes on in the darkness of faith for Jesus is not yet fully revealed. The cross still casts its shadow and life is real and earnest (13:9-13). But the consummation is sure and will be as fully a reality as the former ministry in Galilee.

The men disciples of Jesus had abandoned him and fled for their lives (14:50). The women disciples did not lose heart: they followed him as far as women might, looking on the crucifixion-scene "from afar" (15:40). Mark names three of the group — the impression is of a relatively large group. All of these women are firmly cast as disciples. They were Galileans who had "followed" Jesus and had "come up with him" to Jerusalem — again discipleship. It is because they had continued to follow him, if even "from afar," that the final message is entrusted to them. They alone, of all others, had followed to the cross. The chosen men disciples had abandoned Jesus. These women disciples have stood steadfast and have not been ashamed of Jesus (8:38).

But have not the women, too, failed at the end? They were given a message: "Go, tell his disciples and Peter that he is going before you to Galilee" (16:7). But what kind of messengers did they turn out to be? — "they said nothing to anyone, for they were afraid" (v. 8). Relevant here is 10:32. There Jesus is presented as going up to Jerusalem, striding ahead of his disciples who were "filled with awe . . . and were afraid." But their fear did not paralyse them from following Jesus. So with the women who had come to the tomb to honor one who was dead. They find themselves faced with the awesome truth of the Living One. They are in the grip of trembling and "ecstasy." "They therefore leave in "fear," gripped by the same wondrous awe that had stunned biblical witnesses from Moses to Paul. The fearful and resplendent presence of the living God is now seen as never before in the crucified Messiah's victory over death." (Donald Senior, C.P., *The Passion of Jesus in the Gospel of Mark*, vol. 2, *The Passion Series* [M. Glazier: Wilmington, DE,] 1984, p. 137). The women had not failed: Mark's gospel is the proof of it! Obviously, Peter and the other men and women *had* been told. And is it not thought-provoking that so much scholarly concern has focused on the "problem" of the "failure" of the women. Much less interest, let it be said, has attached to the disturbing fact that it is women who were "apostles to the apostles."

There is no doubt that Mark has left us with a sense of incompleteness. While this is certainly so in respect to the ending of his gospel, it is not so in regard to his Christology. Christ is Son of God, the suffering, risen one who is to come. He is the one who had triumphed on the cross and sits at the right hand of God (14:62). All that remains is for him to come to gather his elect (13:27). If there is incompleteness it is on the part of the community. And therein is realism. For the risen Lord continues to be hidden. It is not enough to *go* to Galilee; it is only when they will *see* him that he will be fully known. The words—and they said nothing to anyone—draw a veil of mystery over the risen Lord; they are a variant of the messianic secret. The Lord must remain hidden—until he comes. And we do not know the day or the hour of his coming It is a time of trembling and astonishment and fear. It is not for nothing that Mark has set the betrayal in the context of the eucharist, the sleeping at Gethsemane, the denial at the trial—all as warnings to his readers. In this time before the coming of the Son of Man, the reader must watch and pray that he or she may not enter into temptation.

THE ENDINGS OF THE
MARCAN GOSPEL.

If, today, we are prepared to accept that Mark did intend to end his gospel at 16:8, this was not always so. Even early Christians had been disconcerted by this abrupt closure of the gospel. Attempts were made to round off Mark's work. The manuscript tradition has preserved three different endings.

1. THE LONGER ENDING.
16:9-20.

Though rather widely attested, the fact remains that in the older Greek manuscripts of Mark and in important manuscripts of early translations, this passage does not appear. Eusebius and Jerome assert that it was wanting in almost all Greek manuscripts known to them. The vocabulary and style of the passage show that it was not written by Mark; it is based on a knowledge of the traditions found in the other gospels. It may well be a composition of the second century. Nonetheless, by Roman Catholics the passage is regarded as canonical (part of Scripture).

9Now when he rose early on the first day of the week, he appeared first to Mary Magdalene, from whom he had cast out seven demons. [10]She went and told those who had been with him, as they mourned and wept. [11]But when they heard that he was alive and had been seen by her, they would not believe it.

[12]After this he appeared in another form to two of them, as they were walking into the country. [13]And they went back and told the rest, but they did not believe them.

[14]Afterward he appeared to the eleven themselves as they sat at table; and he upbraided them for their unbelief and hardness of heart, because they had not believed those who saw him after he had risen. [15]And he said to them, "Go into all the world and preach the gospel to the whole creation. [16]He who believes and is baptized will be saved; but he who does not believe will be condemned. [17]And these signs will accompany those who believe: in my name they will cast out demons; they will speak in new tongues; [18]they will pick up serpents, and if they drink any deadly thing, it will not hurt them; they will lay their hands on the sick, and they will recover."

[19]So then the Lord Jesus, after he had spoken to them, was taken up into heaven, and sat down at the right hand of God. [20]And they went forth and preached everywhere, while the Lord worked with them and confirmed the message by the signs that attended it.

No serious attempt has been made to knit this ending closely with the Marcan text. Thus, v.9 looks back, not to 16:8 but to 16:2; Mary Magdalene is introduced as though she had not been named in 15:40; 16:1. The four main sections are loosely linked.

The Appearance to Mary Magdalene. 16:9-11.
These verses owe much to Jn 20:11-18 and Lk 24:10-11. The description of Mary as she "from whom he had cast out seven devils" comes from Lk 8:2.

The Appearance to Two Travelers. 16:12-13.
No more than an echo of the Emmaus narrative, Lk 24:13-35.

The Appearance to the Eleven. 16:14-18.

Cf. Lk 24:36-49; Jn 20:19-23; Mt 28:18-20. The reproach (v. 14) is severe, more so than in 8:14-21. The writer stresses, for his day, the vital importance of the resurrection of Jesus, its basic place in christian faith. The commission to preach the gospel (vv. 15-16) may be based on Mt 28:18-19, or may offer a parallel version of a saying which emerged in a gentile church. The signs of vv. 17-18 are those recorded in the synoptics and Acts. Cf. Mk 3:15; Acts 2:3-4; 10:46; 19: 6; Lk 10:19; Acts 28:3-4; Mk 6:13. The only new feature is the drinking of deadly poison without harm.

Ascension and Apostolic Mission. 16:19-20.

Cf. Lk 24:50-53; Acts 1:4-14. The ascension of the "Lord Jesus"— a title frequent in Acts but found nowhere else in the gospels—is described in words borrowed from the story of Elijah (2 Kgs 2:11) and from Ps 110:1. Verse 20 obviously presupposes a period of missionary activity. The Lord Jesus himself cooperates with his ministers in their preaching of the gospel.

2. THE SHORTER ENDING.

A few manuscripts of Mark carry another ending, known as the Shorter Ending which is inserted after Mk 16:8 instead of (or sometimes combined with) Mk 16:9-20. Though it is quite un-Marcan in style it was obviously composed to link up neatly with 16:8. It runs as follows:

> But they reported briefly to Peter and those with him all that they had been told. And after this, Jesus himself sent out by means of them, from east to west, the sacred and imperishable proclamation of eternal salvation.

3. THE FREER LOGION.

Rather than an ending proper, this is a gloss added to Mk 16:14 in the 5th century Codex W of the gospels. It runs:

> And they replied, saying, This age of lawlessness and unbelief is under Satan, who by means of evil spirits does

not permit the true power of God to be apprehended; therefore reveal thy righteousness now. They were speaking to Christ, and Christ said to them in reply: The limit of the years of the authority of Satan has been fulfilled, but other terrible things draw near, even for the sinners on whose behalf I was delivered up to death, that they might turn to the truth and sin no more, in order that they may inherit the spiritual and incorruptible glory of righteousness which is in heaven.

FOR FURTHER READING.

1. General Reading.

D.E. Nineham, *Saint Mark*. The Pelican Gospel Commentaries. (London & Baltimore: Penguin Books, 1963).

This is the best of the Pelican Gospel Commentaries. It is scholarly, readable and readily accessible.

E. Schweizer, *The Good News According to Mark* (Richmond, Va./London: John Knox Press/S.P.C.K., 1970).

Brings out the evangelist's aim and shows a marked pastoral concern.

Paul J. Achtemeier, *Mark*. Proclamation Commentaries (Philadelphia: Fortress Press, 1975).

For its size (pp. 117) the most helpful introduction to the thought of Mark.

S. Freyne, in Freyne-Wansbrough, *Mark and Matthew* (London: Sheed & Ward, 1971).

A commentary designed to promote discussion—stimulating. A bonus is a helpful commentary on Matthew in the same volume.

W.L. Lane, *Commentary on the Gospel of Mark*. The New International Commentary on the New Testament. (Grand Rapids, Michigan: Eerdmans, 1974).

> Staunchly conservative. Offers helpful insights throughout. Nudges one to think out more seriously one's reasons for other options.

A.E. Rawlinson, *The Gospel according to St. Mark* (London: Methuen, 1925).

> A salutary reminder that scholars of an earlier generation can continue to help us.

E. Martin, *Mark: Evangelist and Theologian* (Exeter/Grand Rapids: Paternoster/Zondervan, 1973).

> A study of Mark as a theological document, with special emphasis on Christology. A judicious survey of recent scholarly work on Mark.

D. McGann, *The Journeying Self*. The Gospel of Mark through a Jungian Perspective (New York: Paulist 1985).

> A stimulating and challenging approach to Mark; an application of the gospel to the inner human journey of the person.

2. More specialised works.

V. Taylor, *The Gospel According to St. Mark* (London: Macmillan, 1966).

> The best modern commentary on the Greek text of Mark. Splendid on form-criticism. Written before the advent of redaction-criticism.

H.C. Kee, *Community of the New Age: Studies in Mark's Gospel*. (Philadelphia/London: Westminster/SCM, 1977).

> Mark wrote for *his* community. This book seeks to determine the social and cultural factors which influenced that community, as a key to understanding why Mark wrote as he did. Suggestive even where one has to disagree.

W. Kelber, *The Kingdom in Mark: A New Place and a New Time*. (Philadelphia: Fortress Press, 1974).

> A persuasive case for the composition of Mark's gospel sometime after 70 A.D. One does not need to endorse all the views of the author.

J.R. Donahue, *Are You the Christ? The Trial Narrative in the Gospel of Mark*. SBL Dissertation Series 10. (Missoula, Mont.: Society of Biblical Literature, 1973).

> A careful study of the trial narrative in Mark 14. A strong argument for the view that it is Mark's arrangement, and is closely related to the rest of the gospel.

W.H. Kelber (ed.), *The Passion in Mark* (Philadelphia: Fortress, 1976).

> A redaction critical study of the Marcan passion narrative. Especially helpful are the essays of N. Perrin, J.R. Donahue and W. Kelber.

M. Boucher, *The Mysterious Parable: A Literary Study*. The Catholic Biblical Quarterly Monograph Series 6. (Washington, D.C.: CBA, 1977).

> Throws helpful light on the vexed question of parable and allegory. A balanced study of the parables in Mark.

M. -E. Boismard in Benoit-Boismard, *Synopse des Quatres Evangiles en Francais* (Paris: Cerf, 1972).

> A brilliant study of the synoptic traditions. An always stimulating, if often personal, contribution to the literary criticism of the gospels.

D. Senior, *The Passion of Jesus in the Gospel of Mark*. Wilmington, Delaware: Michael Glazier, Inc., 1984).